Whalen, Thomas J.
A higher purpose

A HIGHER PURPOSE

A Higher Purpose

PROFILES IN PRESIDENTIAL COURAGE

Thomas J. Whalen

IVAN R. DEE

Chicago 2007

www.ivanrdee.com

Political cartoons used in the text are reproduced with the kind permission of the following: page 19, Library of Congress; page 45, source unknown; page 67, *Harper's Weekly*; page 94, Collection of the New-York Historical Society; page 117, source unknown; page 141, Franklin D. Roosevelt Presidential Library; page 172, Jim Berryman, © 1951 by the *Washington Post*; page 198, © The Herb Block Foundation; page 222, Auth, © 1974 by the *Philadelphia Inquirer*, reprinted by permission of Universal Press Syndicate, all rights reserved.

Library of Congress Cataloging-in-Publication Data:
Whalen, Thomas J.
   A higher purpose : profiles in presidential courage / Thomas J. Whalen.
   p. cm.
   Includes index.
   ISBN-13: 978-1-56663-630-8 (cloth : alk. paper)
   ISBN-10: 1-56663-630-2 (cloth : alk. paper)
   1. Presidents—United States—Biography. 2. Courage—United States—Case studies. 3. United States—Politics and government—Decision making—Case studies.
   I. Title. E176.1.W54 2007
   973.09'9—dc22
                                                        2006039539

In loving memory of Joseph D. Spinale, 1922–2006

Acknowledgments

IN WRITING THIS BOOK I have several special people to thank. First and foremost is Joseph D. Spinale, my stepfather who passed away shortly before I completed the manuscript. Joe was as amiable and warmhearted a person as one can find in life. He always had a kind word and a smile to give. I greatly miss him. My mother, MaryAnne Whalen Spinale, is a ball of energy and enthusiasm who has always supported me. She has my everlasting love and gratitude.

Dan Hammond and Christopher Callely once again proved they are true friends in always being there for me and offering thoughtful commentary on my work. Elizabeth Crowley lent me her keen editorial insight and love of history to sharpen my focus. Old coach and history teacher Fred Hammond provided welcome inspiration. So did the Boston College institution, Thomas H. O'Connor. Steve Blumenkrantz and Don Clemenzi lent great moral support, as did Joseph King, Mike Feloney, Mary Hammond, Wayne Ferrari, Greg Morose, Robert Gormley, Bob Connors, and Scott Ferrara.

Ivan Dee did a splendid job in getting this book ready for publication. I greatly value his contributions. Among my many supportive friends and colleagues at Boston University, I especially wish to thank Linda Wells, Jay Corrin, Christopher Fahy, Andy Andres, June Grasso, Bill Tichin, Michael Kort, Robert Wexelblatt, Ben Varat, Barbara Storella, Shelly Hawks, Ed Rafferty, Susan Lee, Polly Rizova, Kathleen Martin, John Mackey, Naomi-Lomba-Gomes, John McGrath, Stephanie Kermes, Sally Epstein, Matt Dursin, Diane Payne, and Tracey Nickerson.

Finally, I thank my students, who over the years have kept me intellectually on my toes and appreciative of what a rewarding job I have.

T. J. W.

Peabody, Massachusetts
March 2007

Contents

Preface

IN OUR CURRENT POLITICAL SYSTEM, the American presidency and courage are rarely spoken of in the same sentence. With a few notable exceptions, recent occupants of the Oval Office have appeared all too willing to sacrifice principle for the sake of political expediency. Extreme partisanship, special-interest money, and an unhealthy obsession with opinion polls have discouraged modern presidents from taking unpopular stands. Instead of leading, they increasingly find themselves being led. As a result, our democracy has been diminished by our chief executives' timidity. Forgotten is the axiomatic wisdom of Andrew Jackson, who said, "One man of courage makes a majority."

The following pages seek to prove the inherent truth behind Jackson's words. By concentrating on nine historic decisions made by commanders-in-chief over the past two centuries, I intend to show that political courage and the institution of the presidency need not be regarded as mutually exclusive. Presidents ranging from Jackson to Chester A. Arthur to Gerald Ford have shown a consistent capacity to place their political lives on the line for a higher purpose. Sometimes it has worked to their political advantage; in other cases—Ford, for example—it has not. Yet the central point to remember is that they all took the risk.

As suggested by the subtitle of this book, direct inspiration has been taken from the Pulitzer Prize–winning work of the late John F. Kennedy, who served in the White House from 1961 to 1963. Kennedy chose to define political courage in Hemingwayesque terms, as "grace under pressure." In other words, the "pressures" lawmakers face coupled with "the grace with which they endured them—the risks to their careers, the unpopularity of their courses, the defamation of their characters, and sometimes, but sadly only sometimes, the vindication of their reputations and their principles."

All of the presidents examined here share this important quality. They were not content to sit idly on the political sidelines while the great events of their day passed them by. Rather, they all believed in stepping forward into what Theodore Roosevelt called the "arena" of public life and taking bold, decisive action. "It is not the critic who counts: not the man who points out how the strong man stumbles or where the doer of deeds could have done better," Roosevelt said. "The credit belongs to the man who is actually in the arena, whose face is marred by dust and sweat and blood, who strives valiantly, who errs and comes up short again and again, because there is no effort without error or shortcoming, but who knows the great enthusiasms, the great devotions, who spends himself for a worthy cause; who, at the best, knows, in the end, the triumph of high achievement, and who, at the worst, if he fails, at least he fails while daring greatly, so that his place shall never be with those cold and timid souls who knew neither victory nor defeat."

Nonetheless courage should not be confused with personal recklessness. In the wake of the terrorist attacks on the World Trade Center and Pentagon on September 11, 2001, President George W. Bush decided to launch a preemptive military strike against Iraq. In justifying this action, Bush told the American public that the Iraqi regime under the leadership of Saddam Hussein had direct ties to the Al-Qaeda terrorists responsible for 9-11 and that it illegally possessed weapons of mass destruction. "The people of the United States and our friends and allies will not live at the mercy of an outlaw regime that threatens the peace with weapons of mass murder," the president said. "We will meet that threat now, with our Army, Air Force, Navy, Coast Guard and Marines, so that we do not have to meet it later with armies of firefighters and police and doctors on the streets of our cities." Yet it was soon revealed that there were no weapons of mass destruction in Iraq and that the alleged terrorist link between Iraq and Al-Qaeda did not exist. These embarrassing revelations notwithstanding, Bush continued to claim that the war and the increasingly chaotic U.S. occupation that followed were warranted.

Is this courage? The reader may decide in light of the other instances of presidential decision-making explored in these pages.

Since antiquity, courage has been broadly categorized as either physical or moral. Great physical strength may overcome seemingly insurmountable obstacles, as in battle. Moral courage is more complicated. It relies on the individual mind for its potency. As the writer Joseph H. Odell once observed, "The highest courage is not to be found in the instinctive acts of men who risk their lives to save a friend or slay a foe; the physical fearlessness of a moment or an hour is not to be compared with immolation of months or years for the sake of wisdom or art."

For our purposes, courage will be defined along these moral lines, as that special quality of valor exhibited by certain presidents in times of crisis, placing conscience over expediency, regardless of personal or political costs. For courage does not shrink from adversity; it embraces it. As the author and educator Stephen Mansfield points out, courage "is unquestionably a kind of strength that allows men to perform extraordinary feats in the face of overwhelming opposition. It cannot be taught, though it can be inspired, and it normally springs from something like faith or resolve, a commitment larger than oneself."

Franklin Delano Roosevelt demonstrated such deep-seated resolve when he agreed to send a fleet of aging naval destroyers to aid Great Britain in her fight for survival against Nazi Germany during the fateful summer of 1940. Knowing that such a politically controversial move could cost him an unprecedented third term in the presidency, a goal he desperately wished to achieve, Roosevelt went ahead and did it anyway. "The Presidency," he said, "is not merely an administrative office. That's the least of it. It is more than an engineering job, efficient or inefficient. It is pre-eminently a place of moral leadership."

Abraham Lincoln reached a similar conclusion in 1862 when he issued the Emancipation Proclamation. This landmark measure ordered the freeing of the slaves but did not effectuate it immediately. Yet it antagonized Lincoln's enemies in the South and many of his supporters in the North. "The dogmas of the quiet past," he explained, "are inadequate to the stormy present. The occasion is piled high with difficulty, and we must rise—with the occasion. As our case is new, so we must think anew, and act anew. We must disenthrall ourselves, and then we shall save our country. . . . In giving freedom to the slave, we assure freedom to the free—honorable alike in what we give, and what we preserve. We shall nobly save, or meanly lose, the last best, hope of earth. Other means may succeed; this could not fail. The way is plain, peaceful, generous, just—a way which, if followed, the world will forever applaud, and God must forever bless."

Sometimes, however, considerable time passes before such conviction sets in. Take, for example, the case of Chester A. Arthur. A devout spoilsman his entire political career, he entered the White House in 1881 upon the tragic death of President James A. Garfield, who had died from gunshot wounds inflicted by a mentally disturbed office seeker. The incident served to impress upon Arthur the moral bankruptcy of the spoils system he had so loyally served for decades. To make amends, he spurred efforts to eliminate corruption in the federal bureaucracy and signed groundbreaking civil service reform legislation. But in doing so he alienated the very people who had helped placed him in a position to reach the presidency, political supporters like the unscrupulous Roscoe Conkling of New York. It cost Arthur a second term. The late U.S. Senator Robert F. Kennedy undoubtedly had leaders like Arthur in mind when he said that few "are willing to brave the disapproval of their fellows, the censure of their colleagues, the wrath of their society. Moral courage is a rarer commodity than bravery in battle or great intelligence."

Just the same, it should be noted that acting courageously does not always guarantee a "right" or morally favorable outcome. Certainly Grover Cleveland's staunch opposition to the annexation of Hawaii in 1893 did not prevent that island kingdom from being absorbed by the United States a few years later. Nevertheless his determination to stick by his principles in embarking on such an unpopular course ranks as a brave political act. "The hallmark of courage . . . is the capacity to stand on one's convictions—not obstinately or defiantly (these are gestures of defensiveness, not courage) nor as a gesture of retaliation, but simply because these are what one believes," the psychologist Rollo May observed.

In telling the story of these courageous presidents, I am not presumptuous enough to believe that this will be the final word on the subject. Surely some of my selections are bound to generate head-scratching and controversy. Yet, as the late *Boston Globe* columnist Ray Fitzgerald once suggested, that's the "fun of any list, isn't it?—to start an argument, promote discussion, bring out differences of opinion?"

It is in this spirit that I hope readers will gain a greater appreciation and respect for the institution that has become the "vital center" of our democracy.

A HIGHER PURPOSE

CHAPTER ONE

Slaying a Hydra of Corruption

ANDREW JACKSON AND THE BANK WAR

It was fast approaching midnight on July 8, 1832, when Martin Van Buren arrived at the White House. The former New York governor turned presidential adviser had been sent for by Andrew Jackson to discuss an issue of utmost urgency, one that threatened to destroy the president's domestic program of innovative political and economic reform, if not his entire administration.

Congress had just approved the renewal of the charter for the Bank of the United States. Jackson was apprehensive. Over the years the quasi-public bank, under the skilled leadership of its president, Nicholas Biddle, had acquired an inordinate amount of influence in the halls of Congress; many senators and congressmen were said to be working for it rather than for their constituents. The bank had increasingly geared its lending policies to the needs of the very wealthiest in American society and operated with virtually no system of governmental or private oversight. It was a kingdom unto itself. From Jackson's perspective, this "hydra of corruption" needed to be chopped down to size. Yet to do so with strong executive action placed his presidency at great risk. Biddle and his bank had the money, resources, and political connections to make the bank's detractors pay, and in a presidential election year, that could mean defeat at the polls.

Nonetheless if anyone was up to such a challenge, Van Buren believed, it was Jackson. "In the course of my public life," he wrote, "I have not met with another man who came up to Gen. Jackson's standard as well in respect to the strength of his belief in the certainty that a public servant honestly laboring for the welfare of his Country would receive the good-will and support of the people as long as they remained confident of his integrity as in his constant readiness to stake his political reputation upon that faith regardless of consequences merely personal to himself."

Jackson didn't disappoint him this time either. Taking firm hold of Van Buren's hand upon greeting him, the president calmly revealed his plans for Biddle and the BUS: "The bank, Mr. Van Buren, is trying to kill me, *but I will kill it!*"

Such indomitable resolve was forged early in Jackson's life. The son of poor Scotch-Irish parents who had immigrated to America in the latter half of the eighteenth century, young Andrew had an arduous upbringing. His father died shortly before he was born on March 15, 1767, leaving his mother, Elizabeth Hutchinson, to raise him and his two older brothers by herself in the Waxhaw region of what is now South Carolina. An indifferent student, Jackson seemed to enjoy practical jokes on his friends and cussing a blue streak more than devoting serious thought to his studies. He also had the unfortunate habit of angering quickly, a trait that would stay with him into adulthood. "By G-d," he once warned a group of his peers who saw him collapse from the recoil of a gun blast, "if one of you laughs, I'll kill him!" "He thrived on conflict," noted one of his more discerning biographers, "yet even when victorious never allowed himself to feel triumphant. He continually needed to prove himself. In short, he was a violent and unpredictable youngster—a most difficult and lively companion."

The American Revolution did not improve Jackson's disposition. A volunteer in the Continental Army at thirteen, he served as a mounted orderly "for which I was well fitted," he later said, "being a good rider and knowing all the roads." In 1780 he and his brother Robert were taken prisoner by the British after trying to elude a company of enemy dragoons at his cousin's home. Ordered by a British officer to clean the man's boots, Jackson impetuously refused, claiming he "expected such treatment as a prisoner of war had a right to look for." Enraged at this response, the officer slashed at Jackson with his saber, cutting the boy's head and left hand. Marched by foot to a military prison in Camden, South Carolina, Andrew and Robert Jackson suffered through the severest of deprivations, including near starvation.

To make matters worse, the brothers contracted smallpox, the horrific disease that at the time killed millions of people throughout the world. Luckily for Andrew, he was nursed back to health by his mother after he and Robert were released in a prisoner exchange. Robert was less fortunate: his weakened body could not fight the disease, and he expired. Jackson had already lost his brother Hugh, who had collapsed and died from heat exhaustion during the 1779 Battle of Stono Ferry. The loss of Robert left him inconsolable; according to one account, he became "a raving maniac." Yet this suffering was but a prelude to an even greater sorrow. In 1781 his revered mother died of cholera, leaving Jackson the only surviving member of his immediate family. "I felt utterly alone," he later recalled.

In the wake of this string of losses, Jackson drifted for a time before finally deciding on the law. But his law studies too often took a backseat to his pursuit of personal pleasure. "We all knew that he was wild . . . that he gambled some and was by no means a Christian young man," recalled Nancy Jarret, a young female acquaintance from this period. "When he was calm he talked slowly and with good selected language. But . . . animated . . . he would talk fast with a very marked North-Irish brogue." Older women were even less approving. "Why, when he was here," recalled one dowager, "he was such a rake that my husband would not let him in the house. It is true he might have taken him out to the stables to weigh horses for a race, and might drink a glass of whiskey with him there."

In 1787 Jackson gained admission to the North Carolina bar and was able to parlay a personal friendship with a local judge into a job as prosecutor for the Western District of the state, which was soon to become Tennessee. He excelled in his new public role and began a highly profitable private law practice on the side. His image as an irresponsible young wastrel melted away as he became a highly respected pillar of the community. He was named a delegate to Tennessee's constitutional convention and from 1796 to 1797 represented the new state as its first congressman. He won election to the U.S. Senate in 1797 but resigned his office after only a few months to tend to pressing personal financial issues back home. Creditors had been breathing down his neck over unpaid notes he had endorsed for a Philadelphia merchant who had gone bankrupt. But Jackson's fortunes eventually recovered, and he established himself as a highly successful land speculator. The huge estate he acquired for himself consisted of several hundred fertile acres outside of Nashville. He called it the Hermitage.

While making his mark as an up-and-coming attorney and politician, Jackson courted and eventually married Rachel Donelson Robards, the beautiful and fun-loving daughter of a local boardinghouse owner. Unbeknownst to either Jackson or his bride at the time, however, their marriage was not legally valid. Rachel's divorce from her first husband had not been completed when she exchanged vows with Jackson. Red-faced and not a little mortified, the two hastily staged a second wedding ceremony in 1794 to become husband and wife officially. The incident would later come to haunt Jackson as future political opponents claimed he had engaged in illicit relations with a married woman.

This embarrassing episode aside, Jackson's marriage to Rachel became a source of great joy and happiness in his life. His love is evident in the letter he addressed to "My Dearest Heart" in 1796: "With what pleasing hopes I view the future period when I shall be restored to your arms there to spend My Days in Domestic Sweetness with you the Dear Companion of my life, never to be separated from you again during Transitory and fluctuating life."

Given this strong devotion to his wife, Jackson bristled at real or perceived slights to her character. In 1806, when a fellow lawyer named Charles Dickinson was overheard uttering disparaging remarks about Rachel at a local watering hole, Jackson promptly challenged him to a pistol duel. Accepting the challenge, Dickinson met Jackson on the field of honor at Harrison's Mills, Kentucky. Dickinson managed to get off the first salvo, a bullet that pierced the future chief executive's midsection. Betraying no sign of pain, Jackson steadied himself and returned fire, landing a fatal shot through Dickinson's abdomen. "Oh, I believe that he pinked me," Jackson said as he exited the scene with a friend. In fact Dickinson's volley had seriously wounded Jackson, landing so close to his heart that it could not be safely removed by surgery. The bullet remained in Jackson's chest, a painful reminder of his bloody encounter with Dickinson that he would carry in him for the rest of his life. "But I should have hit him," Jackson explained afterward, "if he had shot me through the brain."

In 1802 Jackson was elected major general of Tennessee's militia. He pined for a chance at military glory. That opportunity arrived with the outbreak of the War of 1812. Jackson commanded a small but determined band of volunteers and regular soldiers that on January 8, 1815, squared off against a vastly superior British invasion force in New Orleans. "I will smash them, so help me God!" Jackson reportedly exclaimed on the eve of battle. He was as good as his word. His troops were able to catch the British by surprise in a thick fog and inflict enormous casualties. Observed one amazed British officer, "Of all the sights I ever witnessed, that which met me there was most humiliating. Within the small compass of a few hundred yards were gathered nearly a thousand bodies, all of them arrayed in British uniforms. Not a single American was among them; all were English, and they were thrown by dozens into shallow holes, scarcely deep enough to furnish them with a slight covering of earth. An American officer stood by smoking a cigar, and apparently counting the slain with a look of savage exultation, and repeating over and over to each individual that approached him, that their loss amounted to only eight men killed and fourteen men wounded."

The victory lifted Jackson to the status of a national icon. "Rarely," wrote his biographer James C. Curtis, "have the American people lavished praise so freely. Or with such enthusiasm." Following a string of humiliating defeats delivered by the British, New Orleans easily represented the most impressive American victory of the war. "Suddenly American citizens had cause to celebrate," Curtis concluded. And Jackson was at the center of the celebration. "Our beloved Jackson deserves immortality," gushed one newspaper editor. "He was always in the hottest and thickest of the fight; and although his health is much impaired he still sticks to his post."

Jackson was not a well man. He had already experienced a bout of dysentery and was still dealing with the painful after-effects of an 1813 pistol fight with a former aide-de-camp, Thomas Hart Benton. Jackson had stumbled his way into the confrontation after learning that Benton had criticized him for acting as a second to an acquaintance in an earlier duel. While both men emerged from the fight alive, Jackson was shot in the left shoulder and very nearly lost that arm. Waving aside expert medical advice that his limb be amputated, Jackson succinctly conveyed his opinion on the matter. "I'll keep my arm!" he announced. Abiding by his wishes, his attending physicians held back, and the arm was saved. Ironically, the two combatants later reconciled and became tight political friends after Benton became a U.S. senator from Missouri.

More controversy awaited Jackson in 1818 when he chased raiding Seminole Indians into Spanish Florida. The Seminoles had launched a number of deadly attacks against American settlers along the Georgia border, and President James Monroe had ordered Jackson to stop them. He did that and much more. Leading his troops directly into Florida, the insurgents' base of operations, Jackson burned down several Seminole villages and deposed the ruling Spanish colonial government for its inability to prevent the attacks. For added measure he summarily executed two British subjects, Robert Armbrister and Alexander Arbuthnot, for their alleged role in "giving aid and comfort to America's enemies."

While this bold action succeeded in preventing further territorial encroachments into Georgia, it created a minor international incident when Great Britain loudly protested the murder of its two subjects. Even in Washington, members of Monroe's administration believed that Jackson's heavy-handedness warranted an official court-martial. Jackson, however, remained steadfast in his belief that he had faithfully carried out his duty.

"In all things I have consulted public good and the safety and security of our southern frontier," he avowed. "I have established peace and safety, and hope the government will never yield it."

For his part, President Monroe publicly defended Jackson's actions, going so far as to place Florida under his military leadership after Spain had formally departed the region with the completion of the Adams-Onis Treaty in 1819. But after serving only four months in this new post, Jackson cordially asked Monroe to relieve him. "I have determined to take a little respite from the laborious duties with which I have been surrounded and leave the charge of the Floridas to the Secretaries appointed for the same," he explained. Returning to Tennessee, Jackson was besieged by various political well-wishers and cognoscenti urging him to announce his candidacy for the presidency. But his initial reaction to these entreaties was one of studied incredulity. "Do they think that I am such a damned fool as to think myself fit for President of the United States?" he scoffed. "No, sir; I know what I am fit for. I can command a body of men in a rough way; but I am not fit to be President."

His modesty notwithstanding, there was one political office that Jackson did feel eminently qualified for: United States senator. The Tennessee legislature elected him a second time to that august position in 1823, and Jackson handled its attendant responsibilities with his trademark energy and flair. He also refused to waver in offering his opinion on a number of highly controversial topics, like the protective tariff. I "am in favor of a judicious examination and revision of it," he wrote, "and so far as the Tariff before us embraces the design of fostering, protecting, and preserving within ourselves the means of national defense and independence, particularly in a state of war, I would advocate and support it. The experience of the late war ought to teach us a lesson; and one never to be forgotten. If our liberty and republican form of government, procured for us by our revolutionary fathers, are worth the blood and treasure at which they were obtained, it is surely our duty to protect and defend them."

While Jackson knew this stance would not be well received by many Americans, especially Southern plantation owners who had come to rely on foreign trade, he nevertheless supported higher tariffs. As he once explained, "I cannot be intimidated from doing that which my judgment and conscience tells me is right by any earthly power."

In 1824 Jackson gave in to popular calls to run for president, despite his own very mixed feelings on the subject. "I have long since prepared my heart to say with heart-felt submission, 'May the Lord's will be done!'" he revealed to a friend. "If it is intended by Providence that I should fill the presidential chair, I will submit to it with all humility, and endeavor to labor four years with an eye single to the public good, imploring the guidance of Providence in all things. But be assured, it will be an event that I never wished, nor expected."

Opposing him in the general election were three prominent and highly respected political figures: John Quincy Adams of Massachusetts, William H. Crawford of Georgia, and Henry Clay of Kentucky. Like Jackson, all three claimed membership in the dominant Republican party. But as the party was badly divided over a series of sectional issues involving slavery, the protective tariff, and internal improvements, and as there was no clear consensus on a presidential nominee, it was left to individual state legislatures, and in Crawford's case the congressional caucus, to present their own candidates. While Jackson had the enthusiastic endorsement of the Tennessee legislature, he also had the advantage of being a certifiable national hero because of his well-publicized exploits in New Orleans and Florida. Still, though he won some 42 percent of the popular vote and the plurality among the four candidates, Jackson failed to capture a majority of the electoral vote on election day. He led the field with ninety-nine electoral votes, most of them from the South and breakaway Northern states like Pennsylvania, Illinois, and Indiana.

Under the Twelfth Amendment to the Constitution, the election was thrown into the House of Representatives, where Adams won by securing the votes of thirteen states as opposed to just seven for Jackson. Yet the stench of what quickly became known as a "corrupt bargain" hung over the proceedings. Concerned that a Jackson administration would represent "the greatest misfortune" ever to afflict the nation, Clay had persuasively urged his congressional friends to support Adams. Shortly thereafter, Clay was tapped to become Adams's secretary of state. Whether Clay's prestigious new position was connected to his political wheeling and dealing on Adams's behalf is impossible to determine. No conclusive documentation has yet proven that such a quid pro quo arrangement had existed.

What is certain, however, is that Jackson and his bitterly disappointed supporters believed there was one. "So you see," Jackson confided afterward, "the Judas of the West [Clay] has closed the contract and will receive the thirty pieces of silver—his end will be the same." To even the score, Jackson stepped down from his Senate seat and began building a formidable political organization that would gain him the presidency four years later. For by 1828 Adams was winding down one of the most spectacularly unsuccessful administrations in the nation's fifty-two-year history. A woefully incompetent administrator lacking any semblance of a common touch, the sour Adams, son of the former president and founding father John Adams, was denounced throughout the Union as "a monarchist" who was "hostile to the aspirations of the majority of the American people." Facing such a weakened political foe, Jackson had little difficulty defeating him in the general election, carrying the majority of electoral votes in fifteen states, including New York, Pennsylvania, Ohio, Kentucky, North Carolina, Tennessee, South Carolina, and Virginia.

But his political victory was marred by personal tragedy. In late December 1828 Rachel Jackson succumbed to a fatal heart attack. Devastated by the loss, Jackson held his political opponents personally responsible. During the presidential contest, Adams's supporters had resurrected old charges about Rachel's "adultery," going so far as to suggest that she was morally unfit to become First Lady. Believing the slanders had proven too much for Rachel's delicate constitution to bear, Jackson was beside himself in anger and grief. "May God Almighty forgive her murderers," he thundered, "as I know she forgave them. I never can."

On March 4, 1829, Jackson was sworn in as president amidst one of the most spirited inauguration ceremonies Washington, D.C., had ever witnessed. Ordinary people from all walks of life clogged the streets to attend the political gala. "It was grand it was sublime!" wrote one amazed observer. "Thousands and thousands of people, without distinction of rank, collected in an immense mass around the Capitol, silent, orderly, and tranquil." Many of the well-wishers let their exuberance and possibly some alcohol get the better of them during a public reception at the White House afterward, when they broke china and celebrated with fistfights. For hardened traditionalists like Supreme Court Justice Joseph Story, the rollicking proceedings confirmed long-standing fears about the kind of political constituency Jackson represented. "I never saw such a mixture," Story sniffed. "The reign of King 'Mob' seemed triumphant. I was glad to escape from the scene as soon as possible."

What Story dismissed as anarchy, others soon took to calling "Jacksonian Democracy," a political movement with Jeffersonian esteem for the agrarian life and a regard for the common man as honest, hardworking, moral, and self-reliant. The movement owed its existence to changes taking place within the American political system. "Well before Jackson's election, most states had lifted most restrictions on the suffrage of white male citizens or taxpayers," concludes the historian Edward Pessen in his study of the era. "Jackson was the beneficiary rather than the initiator of these reforms."

Since the "Common Man" was now able freely to express himself at the ballot box, he sought out candidates who best typified the rising social, political, and economic aspirations of his rank. Jackson easily fit the bill. With his unadorned personal manner, demonstrated grit, and fiercely independent spirit, "Old Hickory" conveyed a sense of shared identity with the laboring classes. He was truly the "People's President." Indeed, he came to feel, according to Martin Van Buren, that "to labor for the good of the masses was a special mission assigned to him by his Creator, and no man was ever better disposed to work in his vocation in season and out of season."

This beneficent attitude goes a long way in explaining why Jackson was so vehemently opposed to the Bank of the United States. Established in 1791, the bank had been the brainchild of the country's first secretary of the treasury, the brilliant if erratic Alexander Hamilton. Hamilton wanted a centralized bank that not only would act as a repository for federal funds but would help further the long-term economic growth and development of the young nation. Expansion would be accomplished, Hamilton maintained, through prudent financial management practices and the establishment of a stable system of currency circulation. For the most part, the BUS handled this charge with great efficiency and success, especially after it was rechartered by Congress in 1816. Yet over time many people, including Jackson, believed the bank had exceeded its initial mandate by catering to the wealthiest segments of society with sweetheart loan and credit extension deals and by becoming too enmeshed in national politics. The institution undeniably wielded enormous power. It was "a financial colossus," acknowledges the historian Robert Remini, "entrenched in the nation's economy, possessing the means of draining specie from state banks at will and regulating the currency according to its own estimate of the nation's needs."

The individual most responsible for this state of affairs was Nicholas Biddle, a Philadelphia native who took the reins of the bank in 1819. Brilliant, proud, impatient, and not a little vain, Biddle saw to it that the BUS "was subject to no regulatory check except what was imposed by the laws of business and the profit-minded demands of the stockholders." It was this lack of accountability that most disturbed Jackson. He felt such "powers and privileges" were "unauthorized by the Constitution" and "dangerous to the liberties of the people." Nor did it help matters that the president believed several unconfirmed reports from around the country that Biddle had secretly earmarked bank funds to be used against the candidate from Tennessee in the 1828 election. Now Jackson was looking for political payback.

To curb such "corrupting influence," in the first two years of his administration Jackson repeatedly asked Congress to modify the "principles and structure" of the bank so as "to obviate constitutional and other objections." While Congress flatly rejected this request, an increasingly agitated Biddle was far from mollified. He feared Jackson could build sufficient political support for his views to jeopardize the bank's scheduled congressional recharter in 1836. To head off such a likelihood, Biddle gave serious thought to having the BUS petition for early charter renewal in 1832. All the while he publicly denied any suggestion that he or his bank was playing politics. "For myself, I do not care a straw for him [Jackson] or his rivals," Biddle claimed. "I covet neither his man servant—nor even his maid servant, his ox nor any of his asses."

Nonetheless it took all the persuasive powers of Biddle's close political ally Henry Clay to convince him that his best course of action lay in going forward with the early recharter. If reelected, Clay argued, Jackson would enjoy few or no political restraints. He would not have to worry, for example, over the inherent political danger of vetoing the bank's recharter, for he would not again be standing for reelection. By taking him on early, the political stakes would be too high for Jackson to risk a veto. Clay was not without his own political agenda: the Kentucky lawmaker was desperately searching for an attention-grabbing issue like the BUS to challenge Jackson in the 1832 presidential election.

Biddle revealed his intentions in January 1832. "We have determined on applying to the present Congress for a renewal of the charter," he declared. "To this course I have made up my mind after great reflection and with the clearest convictions of its propriety." No less a luminary than Daniel Webster of Massachusetts went out of his way to praise Biddle. "I cannot but think you have done exactly right," the distinguished lawyer and political leader said. "Whatever may be the result, it seems to me the path of duty is plain. In my opinion, a failure of this session, if there should be one, will not at all diminish the chances of success next session." Of course, Webster was no mere unbiased observer. Over the years he had performed several legal duties for the BUS and had been handsomely compensated. He later reminded Biddle of this fact when the Bank War began to heat up. "Since I have arrived [in Washington]," he wrote, "I have had an application to be concerned, professionally, against the Bank, which I have declined, of course, although I believe my retainer has not been renewed, or *refreshed* as usual. If it be wished that my relation to the Bank should be continued, it may be well to send me the usual retainers."

Regardless of his true motivation, Webster spearheaded a drive in the Senate to see the bank recharter bill gain speedy passage. But standing in his way was former Jackson nemesis Thomas Hart Benton. Like the president, the Missouri senator believed the BUS had become a haven for corruption that sapped the financial and moral vigor of "honest folks" who earned their daily bread from the sweat of their own labor. "When the renewed charter is brought in for us to vote upon," he announced, "I shall consider myself as voting upon a bill for the establishment of lords and commons in this America, and for the eventual establishment of a King, for when the lords and commons are established, the King will come of himself!"

Despite such hyperbole, the bank recharter bill had little difficulty moving through the House and Senate, for Biddle had skillfully lobbied several of its members with financial and other inducements. All that remained, then, was Jackson's presidential signature for the measure to become law. Unsurprisingly, the "Hero of New Orleans" was in no mood to accommodate either Biddle or his bank. "I will prove to them that I never flinch," he vowed, "that they were mistaken when they expect to act upon me by such considerations."

In his veto message of July 10, Jackson made plain that he felt the bank recharter bill was inconsistent with established constitutional principles. "The bank is professedly established as an agent of the executive branch of the Government," he claimed, "and its constitutionality is maintained on that ground. Neither upon the propriety of present action nor upon the provisions of this act was the Executive consulted. . . . There is nothing in its legitimate functions which makes it necessary or proper."

As for the issue of economic fairness, Jackson contended that the BUS had become a bloated monopoly that served the interests of a few at the expense of the many. "It is to be regretted that the rich and powerful too often bend the acts of government to their selfish purposes," he declared. "Distinctions in society will always exist under every just government. Equality of talents, of education, or of wealth cannot be produced by human institutions. In the full enjoyment of the gifts of Heaven and the fruits of superior industry, economy, and virtue, every man is equally entitled to protection by law; but when the laws undertake to add to these natural and just advantages artificial distinctions, to grant titles, gratuities, and exclusive privileges, humble members of society—the farmers, mechanics, and laborers—who have neither the time nor the means of securing like favors to themselves, have a right to complain of the injustice of their Government."

Word of Jackson's veto sowed anger and discontent in many quarters. "It is a mixture of the Demagogue and the Despot, of depravity, desperation and feelings of malice and vengeance properly smothered," exclaimed one Kentucky newspaper. "It is the type of the detested hypocrite, who, cornered at all points, still cannot abandon entirely his habitual artifice, but at length, finding himself stripped naked, in a tone of defiance says: 'I am a villain; now do your worst and so will I.'" In Philadelphia a group of outraged citizens formed a committee decrying the president's action. "Resolved," the committee declared, "that we have read with astonishment, indignation, and alarm, the message of the President of the United States, accompanying his return of the bill for rechartering the Bank of the United States. With astonishment, that the highest officer of the government, should wantonly trifle with the best interest of the country, and reject the expressed wishes of a majority of the People; with indignation at the injustice which distinguishes every line of that discreditable document; and with alarm at the unconstitutional and disorganizing doctrines which have for the first time prevailed in the proceedings of our government."

Imperial Presidency: Jackson is ostracized by political opponents for his bank veto.

Nor did the veto find favor in the pages of the Washington-based *Daily National Intelligencer.* "It shows an entire misapprehension, equally of the duties of the Executive and the rights of the two Houses of Congress," the paper fumed. "The present Constitution was not established to take all the Federal powers *from* Congress, and give them to the President. The office of President was created, that he who fills it may execute the laws, not make them. In effect, does not the Message claim for the President the right to establish a Bank! . . . The Message claims for the President power to prescribe time, manner, and place, of action, of all of which it is the undoubted right of Congress, co-ordinately with him, to judge, and which no President heretofore has ever pretended the right to dictate. This assumption of authority was reserved for the present day, and for him who, his flatterers have told him, was 'BORN *to command.*' In the course which the President has taken on this occasion, he has been, in our opinion, unwisely and unrighteously counseled."

In Congress, Daniel Webster used the occasion to lecture Jackson on his constitutional duties. "Mr. President," the Massachusetts lawmaker inveighed, "we have arrived at a new epoch. We are entering on experiments with the government and the Constitution, hitherto untried, and of fearful and appalling effect. This message calls us to the contemplation of a future which resembles the past. Its principles are at war with all that public opinion has sustained, and all which the experience of government has sanctioned. It denies first principles; it contradicts truths, heretofore received as indisputable. It denies to the judiciary the interpretation of law, and claims to divide with Congress the power of originating statutes. It extends the grasp of executive pretension over every power of the government. But this is not all. It presents the chief magistrate of the Union in the attitude of arguing away the powers of that government over which he has been chosen to preside."

If this were not enough, Webster continued, Jackson had recklessly misused his powers of office to "inflame" the poorer classes against the rich. The president's action "appeals to every passion which may betray men into a mistaken view of their own interests, and to every passion which may lead them to disobey the impulses of their understanding. . . . If the sentiments of the message shall receive general approbation, the Constitution will have perished even earlier than the moment which its enemies originally allowed for the termination of its existence. It will not have survived to its fiftieth year."

Basking in the middle of this political imbroglio was Biddle. "As to the presidential veto message," he confessed, "I am delighted with it. It has all the fury of the unchained panther, biting the bars of his cage. It is really a manifesto of anarchy, such as Marat and Robespierre might have issued to the mob [during the French Revolution]; and my hope is that it will contribute to relieve the country from the domination of these miserable people."

Alas, Biddle did not get his wish. While a significant portion of the electorate opposed Jackson's action against the BUS, a far greater number approved. The results on election day 1832 confirmed this. Jackson scored a landslide victory, securing electoral majorities in 16 states, including the key political battlegrounds of New York, New Jersey, Ohio, Pennsylvania, Tennessee, and Virginia. His chief challenger, Henry Clay, carried only six states and lagged far behind the president in the popular vote, 687,502 (55 percent) to 530,189 (42 percent). "Who but General Jackson would have had the courage to veto the bill rechartering the Bank of the United States," praised one supporter, "and who but General Jackson could have withstood the overwhelming influence of that corrupt Aristocracy?" Jackson himself had expressed no doubt about the final outcome. "Isaac," he informed a friend before the election, "it'll be a walk.

If our fellows didn't raise a finger from now on the thing would be just as well as done. In fact, Isaac, it is done now."

Yet the Bank War was far from over. Fearful that Biddle would try to circumvent his veto by some unscrupulous political maneuver, Jackson decided on a preemptive attack. He removed all federal deposits from the BUS and had them transferred to select state repositories, thus depriving the institution of its main source of financial succor. He laid out his reasoning for the move in a carefully worded statement to his Cabinet on September 18, 1833. "Should the bank be suffered longer to use the public moneys in the accomplishment of its purposes, with the proofs of its faithlessness and corruption before our eyes, the patriotic among our citizens will despair of success in struggling against its power, and we shall be responsible for entailing it upon our country forever," he explained.

From Jackson's perspective, nothing less than the cause of individual freedom was at stake. "The divine right of kings and the prerogative authority of rulers have fallen before the intelligence of the age," he insisted. "Standing armies and military chieftains can no longer uphold tyranny against the resistance of public opinion. The mass of the people have more to fear from combinations of the wealthy and professional classes— from an aristocracy which through the influence of riches and talents, insidiously employed, sometimes succeeds in preventing political institutions, however well adjusted, from securing the freedom of the citizen."

Annoyed but not necessarily surprised by the action, Biddle demonstrated he knew how to counterpunch. He ordered significant reductions in the number of loans the BUS granted, prompting a national financial panic as state banks "were unable to satisfy the many demands placed upon them by the [credit] squeeze." "This worthy President thinks that because he has scalped Indians and imprisoned Judges, he is to have his way with the Bank," Biddle sneered. "He is mistaken."

But Jackson was not easily cowed. Sensing victory, he stood his ground, even when members of his own party counseled him to moderate his course. "There is no real distress," he wrote a political ally during this period. "It is only with those who live by borrowing, trade on loans, and gamblers in stocks. It would be a godsend to society if all such were put down. . . ." Nor did Jackson soften his tone when a Northern business delegation enjoined him to reconsider his action. "What do you come to me for, then?" he asked sardonically. "Go to Nicolas Biddle. We have no money here, gentlemen. Biddle has all the money. He has millions of specie in his vaults, at this moment, lying idle, and yet you come to me to save you from breaking. I tell you, gentlemen, it's all politics."

Politics too was behind Henry Clay's effort to have the Senate adopt a resolution of censure against Jackson in February 1834. Still smarting from his 1832 presidential defeat, Clay made common cause with other vocal anti-Jackson elements, including outraged Biddle supporters, to form a new political party called the Whigs. Dedicated to limiting Jackson's supposed autocratic tendencies—detractors now took to calling him "King Andrew I"—congressional Whigs under Clay's leadership were able to secure the requisite number of votes for the censure's passage. The decree condemned Jackson for displaying what Clay called a "spirit of defiance to the Constitution and all law" and marked the first and only time in American history that a sitting president received such a formal reprimand.

As was to be expected, Jackson did not take kindly to the censure. He issued an official rebuttal on April 17, claiming the Senate resolution represented an illegal and unwarranted attempt to curtail his powers as commander-in-chief—"unauthorized by the Constitution, contrary to its spirit and to several of its express provisions, subversive of that distribution of the powers of government which it has ordained and established, destructive of the checks and safeguards by which those powers were intended

on the one hand to be controlled and on the other to be protected, and calculated by their immediate and collateral effects,
by their character and tendency, to concentrate in the hands of a
body not directly amenable to the people a degree of influence
and power dangerous to their liberties and fatal to the Constitution of their choice."

Jackson's agitated state was brief, for the nation's economy
quickly rebounded from the financial panic that Biddle had created. As Jackson's biographer H. W. Brands observed, "The liq-
uidity crisis eased as the federal deposits flowed into the state
banks and from the state banks into the economy." In the
process, the tide of public opinion turned undeniably against
Biddle, now viewed as an unprincipled political operator who
had risked the nation's prosperity to preserve the power of his
bank. Even old allies like Governor George Wolf of Pennsylvania abandoned him out of fear such an association would cause
serious political damage.

Wolf, a former staunch supporter of the BUS, publicly denounced Biddle and his agents for "bringing indiscriminate ruin
on an unoffending community." Taking his lead, the Upper
House of the Pennsylvania Legislature adopted legislation endorsing Jackson's policy of disfranchising the BUS. "It was to
have been hoped," an appreciative Jackson wrote Wolf, "that
our past experience had sufficiently demonstrated the futility of
all attempts, however formidable in their character or source, to
control the popular will: but there are unfortunately too many
amongst us who are not only destitute of knowledge of the people, but who seem wholly incapable of acquiring it."

The final blow for Biddle came on April 4, 1834. The
House of Representatives overwhelmingly approved a series of
resolutions declaring that "the bank of the United States ought
not to be rechartered" and that "the public deposites ought not
to be restored." Put simply, Congress pulled the plug on the

BUS. "I have obtained a glorious triumph," rejoiced Jackson. Supporters of Biddle were understandably less celebratory. "The history of this day should be blotted from the annals of the Republic," complained one denizen. "The Chief Magistrate of the United States seized the public Treasure, in violation of the law of the land; and the Representatives of the People have confirmed the deed!!!"

Biddle never recovered politically. He spent the remainder of his days castigating himself over the defeat. "Biddle broods with smiling face and stifled groans over the wreck of splendid blasted expectations and ruined hopes," John Quincy Adams noted in 1840 after dining with the former bank director. "A fair mind, a brilliant genius, a generous temper, an honest heart, waylaid and led astray by prosperity, suffering the penalty of scarcely voluntary error—'tis piteous to behold."

Jackson experienced a far more graceful public exit, retiring from the presidency as one of the most popular and influential chief executives in history. He died at his beloved Hermitage on June 8, 1848, still an active force on the national political scene at age seventy-eight. Wrote William Cullen Bryant of the *New York Evening Post*, "Faults he had, undoubtedly; such faults as often belong to an ardent, generous, sincere nature—the weeds that grow in rich soil. Notwithstanding this, he was precisely the man for the period in which he well and nobly discharged the duties demanded of him by the times." Indeed, the times demanded a more populist brand of political leadership, one that sought to champion the cause of ordinary Americans who lacked the economic clout or social pedigree to advocate for themselves.

"I . . . believe," Jackson once said, "that just laws can make no distinction of privilege between the rich and poor, and that when men of high standing attempt to trample upon the rights of the weak, they are the fittest objects for example and punishment. In general, the great can protect themselves, but the poor and humble require the arm and shield of the law."

Jackson certainly practiced what he preached when it came to the Bank War. In neutralizing Biddle and the BUS, he showed that no individual or financial agency, however powerful, had license to subvert the underlying democratic institutions of the Republic. "The severe lessons of experience will, I doubt not, be sufficient to prevent Congress from again chartering such a monopoly," he said in his Farewell Address of 1837. "But you must remember, my fellow citizens, that eternal vigilance by the people is the price of liberty; and that you must pay the price if you wish to secure the blessing."

It was a price Jackson had never hesitated to pay.

CHAPTER TWO

Ending a Monstrous Injustice

ABRAHAM LINCOLN AND THE
EMANCIPATION PROCLAMATION

As the second tumultuous summer of the Civil War raged on, Major Thomas T. Eckert, the head of the War Department's telegraph office, found himself increasingly preoccupied with the quirky behavior of Abraham Lincoln. In June 1862 the sixteenth President of the United States, a frequent visitor to Eckert's Washington, D.C., office, had approached him about borrowing some paper, "as he wanted to write something special." After receiving the foolscap, Lincoln sat down at a desk to begin writing. "I do not recall whether the sheets were loose or had been made into a pad," Eckert later said. "There must have been at least a quire. He would look out of the window a while and then put his pen to paper, but he did not write much at once. He would study between times and when he had made up his mind he would put down a line or two, and then sit quiet for a few minutes. After a time, he would resume his writing, only to stop again at intervals to make some remark to me or to one of the cipher operators as a fresh dispatch from the front was handed to him."

Most of the news Lincoln received during this period was discouraging. In the struggle to preserve the Union, large federal armies had repeatedly failed in their attempts to bring rebellious Southern states into submission. As military defeat piled upon military defeat, from the Shenandoah Valley to the Seven Days to Second Bull Run, Lincoln did his best to maintain an optimistic façade. But it wasn't easy. "In the present civil war," he ruminated, "it is quite possible that God's purpose is something different from the purpose of either party—and yet the human instrumentalities, working just as they do, are of the best adaptation to effect His purpose. I am almost ready to say this is probably true—that God wills this contest, and wills that it shall not end yet. By His mere quiet power, on the minds of the now contestants, He could have either *saved* or *destroyed* the Union without a human contest. Yet the contest began. And having begun He could give the final victory to either side any day. Yet the contest proceeds."

Despite all this prepossessing fatalism, Lincoln continued to concentrate his thoughts on the "mysterious document" he had been laboring over so exhaustively in the telegraph office. "Sometimes he would not write more than a line or two, and once I observed that he had put question marks on the margin of what he had written," Eckert recalled. "He would read over each day all the matter he had previously written and revise it, studying carefully each sentence." At the end of each visit, Lincoln would have the young officer "take charge of what he had written and not allow anyone to see it."

Complying fully with these instructions, Eckert would lock the material in his desk at night before handing it back to Lincoln the following day, a routine that would be repeated "nearly every day for several weeks." While naturally curious about the secret contents in his care, Eckert did not press his commander-in-chief for details. He was just happy that Lincoln had chosen his office as a favored hideaway, a place where the president could toil "more quietly and command his thoughts better than at the White House, where he was frequently interrupted." Lincoln eventually revealed the particulars of his work. He told Eckert that "he had been writing an order giving freedom to the slaves in the South, for the purposes of hastening the end of the war."

The story of how Lincoln became the "Great Emancipator" is a curious amalgam of high ideals, hardheaded pragmatism, and old-fashioned grit. It begins on Sinking Spring Farm near Hodgenville, Kentucky, where Lincoln was born on February 12, 1809, in a rustic one-room log cabin with a dirt floor and a single window. His father, Thomas Lincoln, had built the dwelling with his own hands, exhibiting the kind of rugged self-reliance that young Abe would emulate his entire life. When the land on Sinking Spring proved "a barren waste," Thomas decided in 1811 to uproot his family to another "more fertile" farm ten miles north.

"It didn't seem no time till Abe was runnin' around [there] in buckskin moccasins and breeches, a tow-linen shirt an' coon-skin cap," recalled family cousin Dennis Hanks. "That's the way we all dressed then. We couldn't keep sheep fur the wolves, an' pore folks didn't have sca'cely any flax except what they could get tradin' skins. We wasn't much better off'n the Indians, except 't we tuk an interest in religion an' polytiks. We et game and fish an' wild berries an' lye hominy, an' kep' a cow. Sometimes we had corn enough to pay fur grindin' meal an' sometimes we didn't, or thar wasn't no mill nigh enough. When it got so we could keep chickens, an' have salt pork an' corn dodgers an' gyarden sass an' molasses, an' have jeans pants an' cowhide boots to w'ar, we felt as if we was gittin' along in the world."

This charmingly simple existence was not destined to last, as a number of unsettled legal claims against Thomas Lincoln's property compelled the brawny Kentuckian to pull up stakes yet again in 1816 and move his family to a new homestead in southern Indiana. Here tragedy entered the future chief executive's life as his "sainted mother," Nancy Hanks, succumbed to "milk sickness," a fatal malady whose origins could be traced to the poisonous snakeroot plant. Victims usually suffered through disorienting fits of fever, dizziness, and extreme nausea before finally giving way. "Abe was som'ers 'round nine years old, but he never got over the mizable way his mother died," Dennis Hanks said.

Wallowing in the "bitterest agony," Lincoln experienced some measure of emotional reprieve a year later when his father married the widow Sarah Bush Johnston. A woman of "great energy" and "remarkable good sense," Sarah showered love and affection on her stepson, which he "warmly returned." "He was the best boy I ever saw," she later said. "I never gave him a cross word in all my life . . . his mind and mine, what little I had, seemed to run together, move in the same channel." With her encouragement, Lincoln briefly attended a local school, his only brush with formalized education and its emphasis on *"readin', writin' and cipherin,'* to the Rule of Three." "He was always at school early and attended his studies," remembered a classmate. "He was always at the head of his class, and passed us rapidly in his studies. He lost no time at home, and when he was not at work was at his books. He kept up his studies on Sunday, and carried his books with him so that he might read when he rested from labor."

In addition to his superior performance in the classroom, Lincoln also showed ability as a public speaker. "When father and mother would go to church," his stepsister Matilda Johnston recalled, "Abe would take down the Bible, read a verse, give out a hymn, and we would sing. Abe was about 15 years old. He preached, and we would do the crying. Sometimes he would join in the chorus of tears. One day my brother, John Johnston, caught a land terrapin, brought it to the place where Abe was preaching, threw it against the tree, and crushed the shell. It suffered much—quivered all over. Abe then preached against cruelty to animals, contending that an ant's life was as sweet to it as ours to us."

Surviving on the frontier was a serious business, and Lincoln devoted most of his early youth to helping his father scratch out a living on the family farm, cutting down trees, clearing the land, and cultivating crops. So adept did he become at wielding an ax that his father hired him out to neighbors to perform a variety of chores, such as splitting rails. "My how he could chop!" admired one acquaintance. "His ax would flash and bite into a sugar tree or a sycamore, and down it would come. If you heard him felling trees in a clearing, you would say there were three men at work, the way the trees fell."

At nineteen, impatient to see the wider world, Lincoln accepted an offer from a local ferry operator to transport farm produce down the Mississippi River on a flatboat. "I was a hired hand merely, and I and the son of the owner, without other assistance made the trip," Lincoln later reminisced. "The nature of part of the cargo-load, as it was called, made it necessary for us to linger and trade along the sugar coast; and one night we were attacked by seven negroes with intent to kill and rob us. We were hurt some in the melee, but succeeded in driving the negroes from the boat, and then 'cut cable,' 'weighed anchor,' and left." For his troubles Lincoln received twenty-four dollars, which he "dutifully" deposited in the hands of his father upon returning to Indiana. A year earlier he had earned his first dollar by hauling luggage for a pair of weary travelers, a seemingly innocuous event that became, in his words, "a most important incident in my life." "I could scarcely credit that I, the poor boy, had earned a dollar in less than a day: that by honest work I had earned a dollar. I was a more hopeful and thoughtful boy from that time."

In 1830, after helping his parents move to Illinois, Lincoln signed on for another trip down the Mississippi under the employ of "a brisk and venturesome businessman" named Denton Offutt. "Offutt bought 30 odd large fat live hogs," Lincoln recalled, "but found difficulty in driving them from where [he] purchased them to the boat, and thereupon conceived the whim that he could sew up their eyes and drive them where he pleased. No sooner thought of than decided, he put his hands, including [mine], at the job, which was completed." With no other surprises forthcoming, Lincoln spent the rest of the journey getting acquainted with Offutt. He "conceived a liking for [me] and believing he could turn [me] to account, he contracted with [me] to act as clerk for him . . . in charge of a store and mill at New-Salem, then in Sangamon, now in Menard County."

Eager to strike out on his own and leave behind the banality of everyday farm life, Lincoln poured his considerable energies into managing Offutt's store. "He was among the best clerks I ever saw," said one observer; "he was attentive to his business—was kind and considerate to his customers and friends and always treated them with great tenderness—kindness and honesty." Capitalizing on this popularity, Lincoln tested the waters of local politics in 1832 by announcing his candidacy for a seat in the state legislature. Running on a platform that called for increased aid for education and usury laws to curb the high interest rates being charged by banks, he experienced a bittersweet showing at the polls. He easily carried his home precinct of New Salem yet fared poorly in surrounding communities, finishing eighth in a field of thirteen candidates. "Every man is said to have his peculiar ambition," he had informed voters during the campaign.

"Whether it be true or not, I can say for one, that I have no other so great as that of being truly esteemed of my fellow-men, by rendering myself worthy of their esteem."

Shaking off the defeat, Lincoln ran again for the state legislature in 1834 and won, the first of four consecutive terms he would serve as a representative of Sangamon County. Professing a desire to become the "DeWitt Clinton of Illinois," Lincoln impressed his legislative colleagues with his strong work ethic, engaging personality, and firm grasp of parliamentary procedure. "The techniques of politics—appeal, persuasion, compromise, maneuver—became thoroughly familiar to him," notes his biographer Benjamin Thomas. He "learned the ways and nature of politicians. He found how best to use his personal attributes and discovered that moral convictions must sometimes be temporarily subordinated if a man is to work effectively in politics."

In terms of political loyalties, Lincoln was a devout Whig, a believer in strong central government and an "American System" of internal improvements and high protective tariffs to promote private industry and commerce. He also faulted those of his generation who relied more on their hearts than their heads in attempting to solve the great problems of the day. "Reason, cold, calculating, unimpassioned reason, must furnish all the materials for our future support and defence," he declared. "Let those materials be moulded into general intelligence, sound morality and, in particular, a reverence for the Constitution and the laws; that we improved to the last; that we remained free to the last."

But politics and philosophy were not Lincoln's only concerns during this period. In 1842, after a long and tempestuous courtship, he married Mary Todd, a vivacious banker's daughter who suffered from severe migraine headaches and a volatile temper. "Nothing new here, except my marrying, which to me is a matter of profound wonder," he cavalierly wrote a friend five days after the wedding. Despite the impudent tone of the letter, Lincoln deeply loved his oftentimes difficult spouse. Their union would produce three sons who survived beyond infancy.

In between serving in the state legislature and courting Mary Todd, Lincoln also worked to become a practicing attorney. After several years of private study, he gained admission to the Illinois bar in 1836 and quickly established himself as "one of the premier lawyers in the state" by specializing in corporate and railroad cases. In this capacity he became reasonably secure financially, earning enough money to maintain an upper-middle-class lifestyle for himself and his family. "If you are resolutely determined to make a lawyer of yourself," he once advised an aspiring young law student, "the thing is half done already. . . . Get the books and read and study them till you understand them in them their principal features; and that is the main thing. . . . Always bear in mind that your own resolution to succeed is more important than any other one thing."

In 1846 Lincoln sought higher public office by running as a candidate for the U.S. House of Representatives. Winning by a comfortable margin, he came face to face with the issue that was destined to define his life and career. Slavery had existed since the founding of America, but not until the early decades of the nineteenth century did the institution threaten to tear the country apart along sectional lines. Owing to their region's economic dependence on slave labor, white Southerners embraced the enslavement of blacks as a God-given right they were willing to defend with their lives. "The African must be a slave," maintained Senator James Henry Hammond of South Carolina, "or there's an end of all things, and soon." Many Northerners, meanwhile, grew increasingly apprehensive about this mindset, viewing slavery as an outdated, barbarous practice that retarded the moral, spiritual, intellectual, and economic development of the nation. In 1833 some outspoken activists calling themselves abolitionists took the provocative step of forming the American Anti-Slavery Society, an organization dedicated to the wholesale elimination of involuntary servitude. "I am in earnest—I will not equivocate—I will not excuse—I will not retreat a single inch—and I will be heard," avowed its founding member William Lloyd Garrison, who had won recognition in abolitionist circles with his Boston-based anti-slavery journal *The Liberator*.

While not an abolitionist per se, Lincoln was nonetheless a staunch opponent of slavery, which he likened to "a monstrous injustice." In his mind, support for the institution flew in the face of all established logic and reason:

"If A. can prove, however conclusively, that he may, of right, enslave B.—why may not B. snatch the same argument, and prove equally, that he may enslave A.?—

"You say A. is white, and B. is black. It is *color* then; the lighter, having the right to enslave the darker? Take care. By this rule, you are to be slave to the first man you meet with a fairer skin than your own.

"You do not mean *color* exactly?—You mean the whites are *intellectually* the superiors of the blacks, and therefore have the right to enslave them? Take care again. By this rule, you are to be slave to the first man you meet with an intellect superior to your own.

"But, say you, it is a question of *interest*; and, if you can make it your *interest*, you have the right to enslave another. Very well. And if he can make it his interest, he has the right to enslave you."

As much as Lincoln personally abhorred slavery, he conceded that the issue was primarily a state matter, and that the federal government had little constitutional authority to "interfere" with the institution where it already existed. While the passage of time and changing historic circumstances would cause Lincoln to alter this opinion significantly, he was always resolute in his determination to prevent the spread of slavery into the Western territories. For he believed that if such a development were allowed to proceed unchecked, slavery would eventually overrun the remaining free states like a "cancer." "As I would not be a slave, so I would not be a master," Lincoln said. "This expresses my idea of democracy. Whatever differs from this, to the extent of the difference, is not democracy."

Lincoln revisited these themes in 1858 when he challenged incumbent Democrat Stephen A. Douglas for the U.S. Senate. Lincoln ran as a Republican, a new political party that had supplanted the Whigs as the Democrats' main challenger. Unlike their predecessors, however, Republicans were unequivocally opposed to slavery and its extension beyond Southern borders. Lincoln did his best to remind voters of this fact. "This government was instituted to secure the blessings of freedom," he maintained during one of his historic debates with Douglas during the campaign. "Slavery is an unqualified evil to the Negro, to the white man, to the soil, and to the State." His eloquence notwithstanding, Lincoln could surmount neither Douglas's popularity nor the process by which senators were then elected by their state legislatures. Illinois Republicans had not secured enough seats in the legislature to put Lincoln over the top, and he lost, 54 to 46. Typically, Lincoln found humor in his narrow defeat. "I feel like the boy who stumped his toe," he said afterward. "I am too big to cry and too badly hurt to laugh."

While the loss definitely stung, Lincoln by no means gave up politically. "The fight must go on," he insisted. "The cause of civil liberty must not be surrendered at the end of one or even one hundred defeats." Because of his standout performance against the diminutive Douglas and his growing stature as one of the country's leading anti-slavery spokesmen, the party faithful tapped him as the Republican nominee for the presidency in 1860. His main challenger once again figured to be the "Little Giant." Indeed, Douglas did win the Democratic nomination, but not before Southern delegates, suspicious of a Northerner leading the party ticket, split away to nominate their own candidate, former vice president John C. Breckinridge of Kentucky. Facing a divided Democratic opposition, Lincoln waltzed to victory in the general election, winning the majority of electoral votes in every Northern state except New Jersey.

But he had little time to bask in his triumph. On December 20 a convention called by the South Carolina legislature voted unanimously to leave the Union. In listing its reasons for secession, the convention cited Lincoln's elevation to the presidency as a leading cause. "A geographical line has been drawn across the Union, and all the States north of that line have united in the election of a man to the high office of President of the United States whose opinions and purposes are hostile to Slavery," the convention asserted. "We, therefore, the people of South Carolina . . . have solemnly declared that the Union heretofore existing between this State and the other States of North America is dissolved, and that the State of South Carolina has resumed her position among the nations of the world, as a separate and independent state, with full power to levy war, conclude peace, contract alliances, establish commerce, and to do all other acts and things which independent States may of right do."

Following South Carolina's example, the remaining Southern states also left the Union, forming along with the Palmetto State a new national government called the Confederate States of America. Led by the Mississippi plantation owner and former U.S. secretary of war Jefferson Davis, the Confederacy formally went to war against the federal government on April 12, 1861, when it bombarded Fort Sumter in Charleston Harbor. "All the pent-up hatred of the past months and years is voiced in the thunder of these cannon, and the people seem almost beside themselves in the exultation of a freedom they deem already won," noted one eyewitness. The federal garrison easily fell, leaving Lincoln with the daunting task of raising a "Grand Army of the Republic" to suppress the rebellion. This the new president accomplished with remarkable speed and skill, but military victories came too few and far between in the perilous months ahead as the Union appeared teetering on the brink of disaster. "The bottom is out of the tub," a dejected Lincoln said.

As battlefield losses mounted, Lincoln came under increasing pressure from abolitionists and their supporters to act on emancipation, the proposed freeing of all slaves from captivity. "Teach the rebels and traitors that the price they are to pay for the attempt to abolish this Government must be the abolition of slavery," exclaimed former slave turned social activist Frederick Douglass. "Let the war cry be down with treason, and down with slavery, the cause of treason!" But Lincoln held back. He feared taking such prohibitive action would cause loyal slave-holding "border states," including Maryland, Kentucky, Delaware, and Missouri, to defect to the Confederacy, thus dooming any prospects for a Union victory. "I want to have God on my side," he explained, "but I must have Kentucky."

Advocates of emancipation were not so easily deterred. Largely due to their political clout, the Republican Congress passed two major legislative initiatives in 1862 that abolished slavery in the District of Columbia and forbade Union military commanders from returning runaway slaves to their former masters. Lincoln officially signed off on both measures but again stopped short of endorsing full and immediate emancipation. Instead he supported a voluntary scheme that called on slaveowners to be financially compensated by the federal government for agreeing to release their chattel from bondage gradually. "While it is true that the adoption of the proposed resolution would be merely initiatory, and not within itself a practical measure," he conceded, "it is recommended in the hope that it would soon lead to important practical results."

Unimpressed, Horace Greeley, the pro-emancipation editor of the highly influential *New York Daily Tribune*, publicly wrung his hands over what he felt were Lincoln's halfhearted efforts to meet "this Crisis in the Nation's destiny." In a letter addressed to the president, published on the front page of the *Tribune* on August 20, 1862, Greeley claimed to be speaking on behalf of "those who triumphed in your election" but who were now "sorely disappointed and deeply pained by the policy you seem to be pursuing with regard to the slaves of Rebels." "On the face of this wide earth, Mr. President," Greeley declared, "there is not one disinterested, determined, intelligent champion of the Union cause who does not feel that all attempts to put down the Rebellion and at the same time uphold its inciting cause are preposterous and futile—that the Rebellion, if crushed out tomorrow, would be renewed within a year if Slavery were left in full vigor . . . and that every hour of deference to Slavery is an hour of added and deepened peril to the Union." Put another way, Lincoln needed to stamp out slavery right away, wherever it existed, if the Union were to stand any chance of winning the war.

Whether it was the patronizing tone of Greeley's letter or just the personal need to explain himself, an obviously agitated Lincoln wasted little time in responding. "My paramount object in this struggle is to save the Union and is not either to save or destroy slavery," he pointedly wrote to Greeley. "If I could save the Union without freeing any slave I would do it, and if I could save it by freeing all the slaves I would do it; and if I could save it by freeing some and leaving others alone I would also do that.

What I do about slavery, and the colored race, I do because I believe it helps to save the union; and what I forbear I forbear because I do not believe it would help to save the Union. I shall
do less whenever I shall believe what I am doing hurts the cause,
and I shall do more whenever I shall believe doing more will
help the cause."

Yet even as he wrote these lines, Lincoln's views on emancipation had already undergone a momentous shift. After much
deliberation on the "military necessity" of the issue, he had
come to realize that if slavery were to be truly eradicated, he
needed first to attack "the peculiar institution" at its roots. This
meant going after the individual slaveholders of the South who
were supporting the armies of the Confederacy with the man-
ual labor their bondsmen provided. As Secretary of War Edwin
M. Stanton wrote, "The slaves, if not armed and disciplined,
were in the service of those who were, not only as field laborers and producers, but thousands of them were in attendance
upon the armies of the field, employed as waiters and teamsters;
and the fortifications and intrenchments were constructed by
them."

The best way to neutralize this advantage, Lincoln decided,
was to press forward with a presidential proclamation outlawing
slavery in rebel-controlled areas. Insofar as this bold move ran
the risk of alienating loyal slaveowners in key border states,
even though they would not be specifically mentioned in the
decree, Lincoln concluded it was a gamble worth taking. "The
slaves [are] undeniably an element of strength to those who had
their service and we must decide whether that element should
be with us or against us," he said. "We must free the slaves or
be ourselves subdued." As to the specific legality of such an act,
Lincoln also did not mince words. He believed, as the historian
James McPherson has pointed out, that the federal government's solemn obligation to uphold the Union trumped any

concerns over the infringement of individual property rights, in this case the ownership of other human beings. "Often a limb must be amputated to save a life," he later explained.

Lincoln alerted his Cabinet to his intentions on July 22. "I said [to them]," he later recounted, "that I had resolved upon this step, and had not called them together to ask their advice, but to lay the subject-matter of a proclamation before them, suggestions as to which would be in order, after they had heard it read. . . ." Among the more cogent "suggestions" was one from Secretary of State William H. Seward, who voiced reservations about the timing of the measure. "The depression of the public mind, consequent upon our repeated reverses, is so great that I fear the effect of so important a step," he replied. "It may be viewed as the last measure of an exhausted government, a cry for help; the government stretching forth its hands to Ethiopia, instead of Ethiopia stretching forth her hands to the government." Seward suggested holding the decree until a significant "military success" was achieved by Union armies in the field. "The wisdom of the view of the Secretary of State struck me with very great force," Lincoln said. "It was an aspect of the case that, in all my thought upon the subject, I had entirely overlooked. The result was that I put the draft of the proclamation aside . . . waiting for a victory."

After several disastrous Union setbacks, the Battle of Antietam finally provided Lincoln with the military triumph he so desperately sought. In what has been described as the bloodiest single engagement of the war, an invading Confederate army under General Robert E. Lee was repulsed by a superior federal force led by George B. McClellan at Antietam Creek in Maryland on September 17, 1862. "Maryland is entirely free from the presence of the enemy, who has been driven across the Potomac," a jubilant McClellan wired back to Washington. "No fears need now be entertained for the safety of Pennsylvania."

Acting swiftly, five days later Lincoln made public what would become known as the Preliminary Emancipation Proclamation. In concise legalistic language, the document stipulated that "all persons held as slaves within any state . . . in rebellion against the United States shall be then, thenceforward, and forever free; and the executive government of the United States, including the military and naval authority thereof, will recognize and maintain the freedom of such persons and will do no act or acts to repress such persons, or any of them, in any efforts they may make for their freedom." The proclamation was "preliminary" only in the sense that if any of the rebellious Southern states chose to rejoin the Union by January 1, 1863— admittedly an unlikely prospect—the terms of the decree would not apply to them. Otherwise emancipation would take place with the formalized issuance of a second and final presidential order.

"We shout for joy that we live to record this righteous decree," exulted Frederick Douglass upon learning of Lincoln's history-making announcement. The *New York Herald* acclaimed it as "THE PROCLAMATION OF FREEDOM." "By a single blow [Lincoln] has palsied the right arm of rebellion," the paper said. "Slavery is the root of the rebellion; he digs it up by the roots. Property in slaves, the appalling events of the last two years show, is dangerous to the existence of the nation; he destroys such property. The Rebels are dependent for their daily subsistence upon their slaves; he makes those slaves freemen. As slaves they are the mere subjects of Rebels, to toil for them, to be used by them as beasts of burden; as freemen they are the loyal allies of a free Government, asking only in return the protection which such a Government gives to the humblest citizen. By a word the President transforms a State sunk in the semi-barbarism of a medieval age to the light and civilization of the Nineteenth Christian Century."

Among abolitionists, not everyone came away with the same degree of enthusiasm. As William Lloyd Garrison confided to his daughter, "The President's Proclamation is certainly matter for great rejoicing, as far as it goes for the liberation of those in bondage; but it leaves slavery, as a system or practice, still to exist in all the so-called loyal Slave States, under the old constitutional guaranties, even to slave-hunting in the Free States, in accordance with the wicked Fugitive Slave Law. . . . What was wanted, what is still needed, is a proclamation, distinctly announcing the total abolition of slavery." Still, a former critic like Ralph Waldo Emerson, who had earlier taken Lincoln to task for dragging his feet on emancipation, could not but be impressed. "Forget all, that we thought shortcomings, every mistake, every delay," the celebrated New England poet and lecturer opined. "In the extreme embarrassments of his part, call these endurance, wisdom, magnanimity, illuminated, as they now are, by this dazzling success."

Below the Mason-Dixon Line, Lincoln's action was greeted with predictable howls of outrage. Jefferson Davis labeled the proclamation "the most execrable measure recorded in the history of guilty man." Robert E. Lee saw it in conjunction with Lincoln's decision to suspend habeas corpus around the same time as yet another example of "The Military Government of the United States" trampling on the "civil liberty" of its citizens. "I have strong hopes that the conservative portion of [the Northern populace], unless dead of feelings of liberty, will rise and depose of the party now in power," wrote the "Grey Fox." The *Richmond Daily Whig* sustained the invective by claiming the proclamation represented "the last resort of a defeated, perplexed and desperate government." "It is a good sign for the South," the paper reasoned. "It shows, not only the extent to which the Northern government is willing to go in its crusade against the South; not only that it is willing to attempt the overthrow of Southern Institutions and Southern society, and the total subversion of that system of industry on which depends so much of the prosperity of the civilized world; but it shows that the Lincoln government has become convinced that the South cannot be subdued so long as the North pays even only an ostensible regard to the laws and usages of war, the claims of property and the rights of humanity." The *Charleston Mercury* also saw a silver lining for the Confederacy, predicting that the effect of the document "upon our servile population" would be "null." "The South is not going to be frightened; and the real, unavoidable effect will be to thoroughly unite the South, Border States and all, and to make the war, or our part, one of desperation, if not extermination, against the North."

Abroad the proclamation won considerable attention, especially in Great Britain where the ruling liberal government had been toying with the idea of establishing full diplomatic relations with the Confederacy. "Where he has no power Mr. Lincoln will set the negroes free; where he retains power he will consider them as slaves," sniffed the *London Times*. "This is more like a Chinaman beating his own two swords together to frighten his enemy than like an earnest man pressing forward his cause." One cynical member of Parliament agreed with this assessment, claiming the document was not "worth anything more than the paper on which it was inscribed." "The emancipation proclamation," he caustically added, "even if it had been in the interest of the negro, would have been a political crime; but when we reflect that it was put forth, not in the interest of the negro or of civilization, but that it was merely a vindictive measure of spite and retaliation upon nine millions of whites struggling for their independence, it was one of the most devilish acts of fiendish malignity which the wickedness of man could ever have conceived."

Desperate Gamble: **A British view of Lincoln's
Emancipation Proclamation.**

Despite these venomous attacks, the American ambassador
to the Court of St. James reported that the pendulum of British
public opinion had swung decisively toward Lincoln's government. "I think there can be little doubt that the popular current
now sets in our favor," wrote Charles Francis Adams. Helping
him reach this conclusion was a meeting he had with a delegation of "substantial and respectable" citizens from London who
voiced strong approval for the proclamation. "They left me with
hearty shakes of the hand, that marked the existence of an active
feeling at bottom," he related. "It was not the lukewarmness and
indifference of the aristocracy, but the genuine English hearti-
ness of good-will." Such popular enthusiasm for emancipation,
which essentially ended any serious talk of British diplomatic

recognition for the South, prompted the great liberal political philosopher John Stuart Mill to ponder what a Union loss might mean to long-term prospects for individual liberty. "The triumph of the Confederacy," he wrote, "would be a victory of the powers of evil, which would give courage to the enemies of progress and damp the spirits of friends all over the civilized world. [This war] is destined to be a turning point, for good or evil, of the course of human affairs."

In the United States, Lincoln was reaching a turning point of his own with respect to the reception for his decree. "It is known to some that while I hope something from the proclamation, my expectations are not as sanguine as are those of some friends," he wrote Vice President Hannibal Hamlin on September 28. "The time for its effect southward has not come; but northward the effect should be instantaneous. It is six days old, and while commendation in newspapers and by distinguished individuals is all that a vain man could wish, the stocks have declined, and troops come forward more slowly than ever. This, looked soberly in the face, is not very satisfactory. We have fewer troops in the field at the end of six days than we had at the beginning—attrition among the old outnumbering the addition of the new. The North responds to the proclamation sufficiently in breath; but breath alone kills no rebels."

Of particular concern to Lincoln was the impact the proclamation was having on the morale of his troops. Some disquieting signs indicated that a number of Union soldiers were anything but pleased. Just a few months earlier, one volunteer had boldly proclaimed to his fiancée that he was not fighting for "the emancipation of the African race." "I want nothing to do with the negro," he wrote. "I want them as far from me as is possible to conceive. . . . When President Lincoln declares the slaves emancipated I will declare myself no longer an American citizen."

In early October, Lincoln decided to pay a personal visit to the Army of the Potomac at its encampment in Maryland. Expecting the worst, he was pleasantly surprised to find no "symptoms of dissatisfaction" nor any "allusion to the proclamation" among the rank and file of the soldiery. "I heard only words of praise," observed Union General John McClearnand, who accompanied Lincoln on the trip. Indeed, the commander-in-chief received an affectionately warm welcome from his troops, leaving the usually loquacious Lincoln at a loss for words. "In my present position," he told the men, "it is hardly proper for me to make speeches. Every word is so closely noted that it will not do to make a matured one just now. If I were as I have been most of my life, I might perhaps talk amusing to you for half-an-hour, and it wouldn't hurt anybody; but as it is, I can only return my sincere thanks for the compliment paid our cause and our common country."

Lincoln was not as sentimental regarding his commanding general. George McClellan had let it be known that "the Presidt's late proclamation" filled him with great consternation, to the point that he was entertaining thoughts of resigning his military commission and lodging a formal protest with Lincoln. "I cannot make up my mind to fight for such an accursed doctrine as that of a servile insurrection," he said. Talked out of taking such a provocative stand by New York Democrat William Aspinwall, who advised him to "submit to the Presdt's proclamation" and to perform his "duty" as a soldier, McClellan had reluctantly agreed to disseminate the full text of the historic decree to his troops via a general field order.

Fully aware of McClellan's barely contained disdain for the proclamation, Lincoln swallowed hard and let the matter slide for the time being. He did not wish to jeopardize any chance for a decisive Union victory by raising so divisive an issue in the immediate aftermath of Antietam. Yet with McClellan's characteristic timidity in pursuing Lee's retreating army into Virginia, Lincoln's patience with his egocentric field commander finally ran out. "I have just read your despatch about sore-tongued and fatigued horses," he sarcastically wrote McClellan on October 25. "Will you pardon me for asking what the horses of your army have done since the Battle of Antietam that fatigues anything?"

McClellan was soon relieved of his command, but not even the borderline insubordination of the "Little Napoleon" could have prevented the inexorable advance of liberty. For as 1862 gave way to 1863, Lincoln issued the Final Emancipation Proclamation, which officially freed all the slaves living under rebel rule. He also declared that any blacks "of suitable condition" desiring to join the Union army or navy could now do so with the federal government's blessing. Tens of thousands of African Americans responded enthusiastically to this call to arms. "The day dawns—the morning star is bright upon the horizon!" wrote Frederick Douglass. "The iron gate of our prison stands half open. One gallant rush from the North will fling it wide open, while four millions of our brothers and sisters shall march out into Liberty! The chance is now given you to end in a day the bondage of centuries, and to rise in one bound from social degradation to the plane of common equality with all other varieties of men."

All told, more than 180,000 blacks, many of them former slaves, donned the blue Union uniform during the war, distinguishing themselves in such engagements as the Battle of Fort Wagner, South Carolina. During this famous 1863 assault, nearly half of the all-black Fifty-fourth Massachusetts Infantry regiment sacrificed their lives in an unsuccessful attempt to capture a key enemy fortification near the mouth of Charleston harbor. "It is not too much to say that if this Massachusetts 54th had faltered when its trial came, two hundred thousand troops for whom it was a pioneer would never put in the field," reported the *New York Tribune*. "But it did not falter. It made Fort Wagner such a name for the colored race as Bunker Hill has been for ninety years to the white Yankees."

Despite the conspicuous valor displayed by African-American soldiers in combat, many in the North remained skeptical about the employment of "colored troops." The Copperheads, an anti-war faction of the Democratic party, had helped sow these seeds of doubt by comparing Southern blacks to "semi-savages" unworthy of freedom. In some quarters there were calls for Lincoln to retract the "wicked, atrocious, and revolting" Emancipation Proclamation altogether. But Lincoln remained steadfast in his determination to end slavery. "You say you will not fight to free Negroes," he wrote one critic. "Some of them seem willing to fight for you. . . . [When this war is won] there will be some black men who can remember that, with silent tongue and clenched teeth and steady eye and well-poised bayonet, they have helped mankind on to this great consummation; while, I fear, there will be some white ones, unable to forget that with malignant heart and deceitful speech, they strove to hinder it."

By 1864 the "great consummation" Lincoln spoke of had yet to arrive, and this fact filled him with tremendous anxiety. With a presidential election looming that fall, Lincoln feared that "lack of progress" on the battlefield along with continual carping over his emancipation policies would doom his candidacy. On August 23 he shared his concerns with his Cabinet. "This morning as for some days past," he expounded, "it seems exceedingly probable that this administration will not be re-elected. Then it will be my duty to so cooperate with the President-elect as to save the Union between the election and the inauguration; as he will have secured his election on such ground that he cannot possibly save it afterward."

Lincoln had good reason to worry. His Democratic opponent was none other than George McClellan, the popular ex-general whom he had sacked two years earlier. Seeking political revenge, McClellan portrayed himself as the "savior of his country," battling the "ignorance, incompetency, and corruption of Mr. Lincoln's administration." But with Union armies achieving major victories in Georgia and northern Virginia in September, McClellan's attack wore thin and his electoral fortunes plummeted accordingly. Lincoln was able to record an easy victory on election day, capturing twenty-two of twenty-five Northern states and 54 percent of the popular vote. "It has long been a grave question whether any government, not too strong for the liberties of its people, can be strong enough to maintain its existence in great emergencies," he said afterward. "On this point the present rebellion brought our republic to a severe test, and a presidential election, occurring in regular course during the rebellion, added not a little to the strain. . . . [But the tide of events] has demonstrated that a people's government can sustain a national election in the midst of a great civil war."

Buoyed by the overwhelming extent of his victory and the now certain collapse of the Confederacy, Lincoln sought to articulate his vision for a post–Civil War America. That opportunity came during his Second Inaugural Address on March 4, 1865, widely regarded as one of the finest speeches ever delivered by a president. "With malice toward none," he declared movingly, "with charity for all; with firmness in the right as God gives us to see the right, let us strive on to finish the work we are in; to bind up the nation's wounds; to care for him who shall have borne the battle, and for his widow, and his orphan—to do all which may achieve and cherish a just, and a lasting peace, among ourselves, and with all nations."

Two months before striking this high note on national reconciliation, Lincoln had pressured Congress into adopting a constitutional amendment abolishing slavery throughout the entire Union, including loyal border states that had been exempted under the Emancipation Proclamation. While both the House and Senate approved by wide margins what would eventually become the Thirteenth Amendment, Lincoln did not live long enough to see it ratified by the necessary two-thirds of the states to become "the supreme law of the land." An assassin by the name of John Wilkes Booth, a noted stage actor and Confederate sympathizer, shot Lincoln in his presidential box while he and his wife were watching a play at Washington's Ford's Theater on Good Friday, April 14. The President died from his wounds the next day.

Lincoln's death plunged the country into sorrow. "We cannot realize our President is dead," wrote one stunned member of the Army of the Potomac. Perhaps nowhere was the sense of loss more profound than within the African-American community. As Secretary of the Navy Gideon Welles observed, "On the Avenue in front of the White House were several hundred colored people, mostly women and children, weeping and wailing their loss. This crowd did not appear to diminish through the whole of that cold, wet day; they seemed not to know what was to be their fate since their great benefactor was dead, and their hopeless grief affected me more than almost anything else, though strong and brave men wept when I met them."

That this level of mourning was so intense should not be surprising. Although he had struggled mightily with the issue of emancipation throughout his entire presidency, Lincoln in the end came down on the side of freedom and the indescribable right to human dignity. "If my name ever goes into history, it will be for this act," he had reportedly said upon signing the Final Emancipation Proclamation on New Year's Day, 1863.

It would be hard for posterity to argue with him.

CHAPTER THREE

From Gentleman Boss to Reformer

THE POLITICAL REDEMPTION OF
CHESTER A. ARTHUR

Chester A. Arthur was at his New York City home on the night of September 19, 1881, when word arrived that President James A. Garfield had died. The vice president did not take the news well. He "is sitting alone in his room sobbing like a child, with his head on his desk and his face buried in his hands," Arthur's doorkeeper told journalists at the scene. Arthur officially became president at 2:15 A.M. the following morning when he was administered the oath of office by New York Supreme Court Justice John Brady.

The two and a half months leading up to this historic moment had not been easy for Arthur. On Saturday morning, July 2, Garfield had been shot twice in the back by a deranged office seeker named Charles J. Guiteau while the president waited to board a train at the Baltimore & Potomac station in Washington, D.C. "I did it . . . and Arthur will be President," exclaimed Guiteau after he was taken into custody. In the weeks that followed, it seemed that Garfield would pull through, but infection settled in and in early September he took a fatal turn for the worse. In the interim, forebodings were raised throughout the land as the moral character and leadership qualifications of Garfield's second in command came into question.

"When Chester A. Arthur was elected Vice President of the United States," the *New York Times* editorialized, "no thought was further from the minds of the people who voted for him than that circumstances should ever elevate him to the highest position in the Nation. When JAMES A. GARFIELD was yesterday reported as lying at the point of death, new bitterness was added to the poignancy of public grief by the thought that CHESTER A. ARTHUR would be his successor. . . . Gen. Arthur has held for [several] months an office which acquires importance only in view of such an emergency as the crime of GUITEAU was intended to create. Such dignity as beseems even the formal responsibilities of that office he has but indifferently maintained; such reticence and self-restraint as belong to its possibilities and its estimation in the eyes of thoughtful men he has entirely disregarded. Active politicians, uncompromising partisans, have held before now the office of Vice-President of the United States, but no holder of that office has ever made it so plainly subordinate to his self-interest as a politician and his narrowness as a partisan."

The *Times* was not far from the truth. As a longtime spoilsman and devout member of the Stalwarts, a powerful conservative group within the Republican party opposing civil service reform, Arthur had acted in a decidedly partisan manner as vice president. He spent most of his time trying to secure federal jobs for his Stalwart friends and thought nothing of undermining Garfield politically—the president had been sympathetic to the Half-Breeds, a rival liberal faction of the party seeking reform of the civil service. "It is out of this mess of filth that Mr. Arthur will go to the Presidential chair in case of the President's death," wrote the reformer E. L. Godkin of *The Nation*.

Yet Arthur had a surprise in store for his critics when he entered the White House. Instead of confirming their worst fears about him, he shocked them all by becoming a champion for clean government and civil service reform. As he pledged to a grieving nation on September 22, "All the noble aspirations of my lamented predecessor which found expression in his life, the measures devised and suggested during his brief Administration to correct abuses, to enforce economy, to advance prosperity, and to promote the general welfare . . . will be garnered from the hearts of the people; and it will be my earnest endeavor to profit, and to see that the nation shall profit, by his example and experience."

But in charting this bold course Arthur was also sealing his own fate politically. His fellow Stalwarts did not appreciate his efforts on behalf of reform. Three years later they would, in fact, dump him from the Republican ticket. Still, in Arthur's mind, this unceremonious end to his political career was worth it. Like the biblical Paul on the road to Damascus, he had come to realize from hard experience that sacrifice was the price one paid for personal redemption.

Life began for Arthur in the small rural farming community of North Fairfield, Vermont, on October 5, 1829. The son of a Baptist minister, Arthur moved around frequently as a child because his father was unable to secure a permanent parish in either Vermont or neighboring upstate New York. This itinerant lifestyle did not seem to affect young Chester, or "Chet" as his friends called him. He excelled in his studies and at age fifteen was accepted for admission to Union College in Schenectady, New York. Taking a curriculum that emphasized the Greek and Roman classics, he graduated in 1848 with Phi Beta Kappa honors.

He also displayed an irreverent wit, as evidenced by this tongue-in-cheek account of the Old Testament: "Moses being the only man that survived the distruction [sic] of earth's inhabitants by water, after living some length of time in the open air, set his son Nebuchadnezzar to build Solomon's temple. In the course of which happened the confusion of languages, and this was the cause why the temple was left unfinished. About this period Alexander the Great after a siege of some months, took the tower of Babel by storm, and put all the inhabitants to the sword. But soon after he was attacked with vertigo, and fell into the bulrushes, where he was found by Pharaoh's daughter, and taken care of."

After college Arthur taught school for a time before journeying to New York City to begin a legal career. He passed the state bar in 1854 but struggled to establish himself as an attorney. "His abilities lay not in court but in office work, which calls for caution, resourcefulness, and skill in personal consultation," noted his biographer George Frederick Howe. "To build up a clientele required an extensive acquaintance, and Arthur was a recent arrival in the city without family connections to aid him. Moreover, a reputation for wise counsel had to be acquired, and he was young and unknown. It was an uphill fight as he had no money, but there were ways by which he could advance his reputation."

One such way was to become active in politics. Arthur joined the Whig party and received a crash course on how "machine politics" worked. "The Whig Party was . . . under the absolute rule, in this State, of Mr. Thurlow Weed," he later recalled. "The Whig Convention did nothing but give voice to his previously expressed wishes. His programmes extended to the smallest details, and were carried out to the letter. . . . Political leaders then had organized gangs of ruffians at their command and could compel obedience at caucuses. The tactics were simple and effective. If their opponents were as superior in numbers as in respectability, it was customary to station 'heelers' in the lines of voters, and these fellows would at a signal break up the lines. On one occasion these ruffians were provided with awls, which they prodded into the flesh of the majority, thus dispersing them. Ballot boxes were stuffed almost openly."

Arthur also learned that the business of politics did not necessarily end with electoral success. After all, as the popular saying of the day went, "To the victor goes the spoils." In simplest terms this meant that the winning party or parties were expected to award government jobs to those loyal adherents who had helped them achieve victory at the polls. This "spoils system" had been in place since the dawn of the Republic, and the impressionable Arthur saw no reason at this early juncture of his career to question the morally suspect logic behind it. "I was always to be counted . . . on to stand by the friends who for so long acted together," he said.

While politics consumed most of his life, Arthur did find time for romance, in 1859 winning the hand of Ellen "Nell" Lewis Herndon. The daughter of a naval officer, Nell had first met Arthur three years earlier in New York City during a visit to a relative, and fell in love at once. "I know you are thinking of me now," Arthur wrote Nell during this period. "I feel the pulses of your love answering to mine. If I were with you now, you would go & sing for me 'Robin Adair' then you would come & sit by me—you would put your arms around my neck and press your soft sweet lips over my eyes. I can feel them now." The marriage would produce three children, William Lewis Herndon, Chester Alan Jr., and Ellen Herndon.

When the Whigs disbanded after the 1852 presidential election, Arthur joined Thurlow Weed in helping organize the fledgling Republican party of New York. This political affiliation paid major dividends once the Civil War began in 1861. In recognition of these earlier party-building efforts, Republican governor Edwin D. Morgan appointed Arthur quartermaster general of New York. His chief responsibility was to equip and arm the state's troops for battle. "Arthur's duties were such that for several months he was able to sleep only three hours a night," recounts his biographer Thomas Reeves. "He was, by all accounts, congenial, efficient, and honest. His legal talents were employed at one point when he helped draft a new state militia law and advocated it before state legislative committees. His position required him to have a sophisticated knowledge of military law."

So outstanding was his performance that General S. V. Talcott, Arthur's immediate successor, singled him out for high praise. "I found," Talcott wrote, "on entering on the discharge of my duties, a well organized system of labor and accountability, for which the State is chiefly indebted to my predecessor, General Chester A. Arthur, who by his practical good sense and unremitting exertion, at a period when everything was in confusion, reduced the operations of this department to a matured plan, by which large amounts of money were saved to the government, and great economy of time secured in carrying out the details of the same."

Arthur also seemed pleased by his efforts, boasting of his accomplishments in this 1862 report: "Through the single office and clothing depot of this Department in the city of New York, from August 1 to December 1, the space of four months, there were completely clothed, uniformed, and equipped, supplied with camp and garrison equipage, and transported from the State to the seat of war, sixty-eight regiments of infantry, two battalions of cavalry, and four battalions and ten batteries of artillery."

Arthur stepped down from active duty in 1863 to return to private law practice. His primary motivation for this move was apparently financial. After two years of faithfully serving his country, Arthur believed he needed to devote his attention to providing for his family. This he did spectacularly well in the years ahead as his law firm, Arthur & Gardiner, thrived. Arthur himself, clothed in impeccably tailored suits, dining at the finest downtown establishments, and socializing in the most exclusive New York circles, seemed a representative figure of the "Gilded Age," a term coined by the novelist Mark Twain to describe American culture in the tumultuous decades following the Civil War. Gaudy materialism, personal excess, and unrestrained greed became the celebrated norms of the era. "The American thought of himself as a restless, pushing, energetic, ingenious person, always awake and trying to get ahead of his neighbors," wrote Henry Adams of this period. Arthur fit right in.

But financial prosperity could not inoculate him from personal tragedy. On July 8, 1863, his two-year-old son William died. "I have sad, sad news to tell you," he wrote a family member. "We have lost our darling boy. He died yesterday morning at Englewood, N.J., where we were staying for a few weeks—from convulsions, brought on by some affection of the brain. It came upon us so unexpectedly and suddenly. Nell is broken hearted. I fear much for her health. You know how her heart was wrapped up in her dear boy."

Arthur's deep sorrow did not prevent him from continuing his involvement in politics. In the 1860s and 1870s he became closely linked to the Stalwart wing of the Republican party. Called the Stalwarts because of their intense loyalty to President Ulysses S. Grant and the conservative policies of his administration, including its staunch opposition to civil service reform, this powerful political faction was led by U.S. Senator Roscoe Conkling of New York. Stubborn, fiery, calculating, and petty, Conkling was a man of exceptional ability who did not suffer fools gladly. "Civility he clearly did not consider one of the cardinal virtues," wrote his biographer David M. Jordan. "In his eyes, disloyalty was a mortal sin, but he was so extremely sensitive to slights that he marked off as traitors any of his followers who chose not to accompany him in his self-immolation. He loved a fight more than anything, and he generally rejected conciliation or compromise."

Challenging Conkling and the Stalwarts for supremacy of the Republican party was a group that became known as the Half-Breeds. This liberal faction earned its political moniker by being only lukewarm in its support of Grant. They decried the well-documented graft and corruption of the Grant years and favored civil service reform. Their leader was former Speaker of the House of Representatives James G. Blaine of Maine, a commanding and charismatic figure whose soaring rhetoric was matched only by his driving personal ambition. "He had a breezy, buoyant manner that was most engaging," the journalist William C. Hudson confirmed. "Ostensibly frank in his intercourse with all whom he came in contact, a subsequent examination of what had been said would yet show that discretion had governed every remark. . . . He was approachable, and once said to a friend who criticized him for throwing himself open to the approach of newspapermen: 'Oh, I'm one of them myself, and I like the breed of dogs. Besides, it's a better thing to have the boys who write about you dip their pens in the ink of friendship than in that of gall.'"

With Conkling's and the Stalwarts' strong backing, in 1871 Arthur was chosen by President Ulysses S. Grant to be collector of the New York Customhouse. Covering a jurisdiction that included the coastal regions of New York State and most of New Jersey, the customhouse was a political hack's dream come true. "Seventy-five percent of the nation's customs receipts came through the sprawling New York port," note the presidential historians Philip Kunhardt, Jr., Philip Kunhardt III, and Peter

Kunhardt, "creating countless ways to siphon off money—from fixed scales and rigged measurements to out-and-out bribery. Though Arthur was never personally charged with bribery or payoffs, he tolerated the crookedness of others. And when this was pointed out to him by a friend, the portly spoilsman bridled. 'You are one of those goody-goody fellows,' he blurted out, 'who set up a high standard of morality that other people cannot reach.'"

Appalled by the stench of corruption hanging over the customhouse, President Rutherford B. Hayes removed Arthur from his post in 1878. Crestfallen, Arthur, who was now sporting the nickname of "Gentleman Boss" for his spoilsman ways, reluctantly went back to being a private attorney, albeit a well-compensated one. But just as his public life suffered a major setback, his personal life experienced an even worse blow. In January 1880 his beloved wife Nell came down with pneumonia and was dead within days. The loss proved devastating to Arthur, who sank into a deep personal despair.

Luckily, politics intervened to distract him from further thoughts of debilitating grief. For 1880 was a presidential election year, and Arthur was tapped by Conkling to be a Stalwart delegate at the Republican National Convention held in Chicago that summer. Entering the convention, former chief executive Ulysses S. Grant appeared certain to win his party's nomination for the presidency. But Blaine and the Half-Breeds had no intention of seeing the Civil War hero become the GOP's standard-bearer once again. Through deft political maneuvering and no small amount of intrigue, they were able to deadlock the convention and deprive Grant of an opportunity for an unprecedented third term in the White House.

Emerging from this political clamor was Congressman James A. Garfield, a dark-horse candidate from Ohio who captured the Republican nomination on the thirty-sixth ballot. A sympathizer to the Half-Breed political cause, though by no means a Half-Breed himself, Garfield was a political moderate whom party leaders sized up as an acceptable compromise candidate. "Garfield's nomination at Chicago was the best that was possible," Rutherford B. Hayes explained afterward. "He is the ideal candidate because he is the ideal self-made man." Garfield had risen from an impoverished childhood to become a major general in the Union army during the Civil War. During the convention he had impressed delegates with an impassioned call for party unity. "We want the vote of every Republican—of every Grant Republican, and every anti-Grant Republican, in America—of every Blaine man and every anti-Blaine man."

All that remained, then, was the selection of a running mate. After much deliberation it was decided within Garfield's inner circle that Arthur would be the best available choice to balance the ticket. He was a Stalwart from a must-win electoral state in the East, who despite his controversial tenure at the New York Customhouse was "almost universally liked within the Grand Old Party." But no one had thought it prudent to run Arthur's name by Conkling first. Still in a snit over Grant's nomination defeat, Conkling was not in a receptive mood when Arthur approached him in the convention hall about being offered the vice presidency. "Well sir, you should drop it as you would a red hot shoe from the forge," Conkling advised. Arthur, however, thought differently. "The office of the Vice President is a greater honor than I ever dreamed of attaining," he replied. He added, "Senator Conkling, I shall accept the nomination and I shall carry with me the majority of the [New York] delegation." According to William C. Hudson, an eyewitness to the exchange, Conkling then broke off the meeting in a fit of anger. "For another moment," Hudson wrote, "Arthur looked after him regretfully and then the man who in a year's time was to be seated in the White House as President turned and walked out of the room. In a later session that day Arthur was nominated."

In the general election that followed against Democratic nominee Winfield S. Hancock of Pennsylvania, Arthur had a major hand in securing victory for the Republican ticket. He tirelessly raised enormous amounts of cash, handpicked stump speakers, edited speeches, smoothed out organizational snags, and buttonholed many wavering Stalwarts into supporting Garfield. "He has worked for weeks with such application as few men are capable of standing, and has seen several men about him laid up with fatigue while he has been compelled to keep right on," the *New York Times* lauded.

Arthur's performance as vice president drew considerably less praise. Having reconciled with Conkling since their earlier spat at the Republican convention, Arthur now worked closely with the New York power broker to promote Stalwart interests within the Garfield administration. Together they applied political pressure on the president to place Stalwarts in a number of top federal jobs. But Garfield was no pushover. A strong believer in civil service reform, he put his foot down when it came to the collectorship of the New York Customhouse. He named William H. Robertson, a former congressman and Blaine supporter, to that important post. Outraged at this selection, Arthur, at Conkling's urging, did his best to derail Robertson's appointment by helping launch a public petition drive against his candidacy. He lobbied Garfield in person to reconsider his choice, claiming Robertson's selection would plunge the New York Republican party into internecine political warfare. Garfield demurred. "Of course I deprecate war," he pointedly wrote a friend. "But if it is brought to my door the bringer will find me home." Robertson remained.

For his exertions against Robertson, Arthur was portrayed in the press as Conkling's political errand boy. Lambasted one newspaper, "The great Republican party of the union did not elevate him to the high position he now holds in order that he might condescend to foment jealousies and to grease the New York machine, nor to play the boss at the back of Lord Roscoe, but to deport himself in a gentlemanly and respectable manner."

Then came Garfield's fateful rendezvous with Guiteau at the Baltimore & Potomac station. With the president's death, many Washington insiders predicted that Arthur would continue his cozy personal relationship with Conkling and the Stalwarts. Rutherford B. Hayes became so disillusioned he felt compelled to record in his diary that the "death of the president at this time would be a national calamity whose consequences we can not now confidently conjecture. Arthur for President! Conkling the power behind the throne, superior to the throne!" Fortunately for Hayes and the rest of the country, none of these alarmist fears was realized.

From the very beginning of his administration, Arthur went out of his way to demonstrate he was his own man, no longer under the thrall of the corrupt spoils system that gave him his start in politics and of which Conkling was a part. As one old political friend ruefully noted, "We regard Arthur as our leader, and when he became President, knowing as he did the thankless tasks we have to do here, we expected that we would be appreciated— not to say rewarded. We thought he would throw in our direction enough of the patronage to make our work less onerous. On the contrary, he has done less for us than Garfield, or even Hayes." New York Stalwart leader John O'Brien lamented, "He isn't 'Chet' Arthur anymore; he's the President."

This point was driven home when Arthur met privately with Conkling on October 8, 1881, at the Washington residence of Senator John Percival Jones of Nevada. "Instead of a happy reunion of master and pupil," the historian Kenneth D. Ackerman recounts, "Arthur and Conkling had had a terrible fight. Conkling, seeing his old protégé Arthur finally in power, apparently had confronted him behind closed doors that afternoon with one single direct demand: William H. Robertson, the new Collector of the New York Custom House recently rammed down Conkling's throat by that man Garfield in the White House, must be fired. Garfield was dead now, Arthur was president, and the insult must be undone."

Only Arthur didn't see it that way. He maintained he was "morally bound to continue the policy of [Garfield]." Moreover he believed any removal of Robertson would not only "reignite the Stalwart and Half-Breed wars with a vengeance," it would also "divide the country and sabotage his own fragile reputation in one stroke—all just to settle Roscoe Conkling's old grudge." Arthur held his ground and curtly informed Conkling that under no circumstances would he ask Robertson to step down. Displeased by this answer, Conkling left the meeting in a pique, complaining of Arthur's lack of loyalty. Publicly, however, Conkling played down his rift with Arthur, claiming he had just dropped by for an overdue chat with his longtime friend and political ally. "I have not seen him since he became President until today," Conkling pointedly told a journalist from the *Washington Post*. "We had a conversation on various subjects. I do not know when I shall see him again, but it seems that the gentlemen of the press are exercised over it. I assure you that you have no reason to be, and I wish you a very good evening."

Still, by his very actions Arthur had managed to convey a larger message. He was no longer to be considered "Lord Roscoe's puppet," and his disinclination to cashier Robertson had more to do with high ideals than selfish political considerations. As Arthur's biographer Zachary Karabell observes, "The assassination of Garfield had placed the issue of civil service reform at the center of the national agenda, and one of the tenets of reform was that naked favoritism should not dictate appointments." Arthur appeared to have intuitively grasped this new reality immediately. "For the Vice-Presidency I was indebted to Mr. Conkling," he confessed to a friend, "but for the presidency of the United States my debt is to the Almighty."

Another factor undoubtedly accounting for Arthur's change of attitude was personal guilt. He had become president only through the auspices of a mentally disturbed office seeker, a self-professed Stalwart, it turned out, who believed Garfield's murder and Arthur's subsequent ascension would "unite the Republican Party and save the Republic." Now Arthur seemed intent on righting a terrible wrong and atoning for any complicity, however circuitous or unintentional, he may have had in bringing on this tragic event. "Men may die, but the fabrics of our free institutions remain unshaken," he said. "No higher or more assuring proof could exist of the strength and permanence of popular government than the fact that though the chosen of the people be struck down his constitutional successor is peacefully installed without shock or strain except the sorrow which mourns the bereavement."

Arthur went on to make civil service reform and the elimination of corruption and waste in the federal government the highest priorities of his new administration. In these concerns his first bold move was his veto of the Rivers and Harbors Bill on August 1, 1882. A measure that earmarked a then whopping $19 million in federal funds for internal improvements, the bill represented pork-barrel legislation at its worst. Lawmakers then as now generally regarded such bills as "delicious sources of patronage and influence." The vast bulk of the proposed spending package was reportedly being funneled into local public works projects of questionable utility or purpose. Unwilling to see this "scandalous misappropriation of public money" for the supposed "advancement of local jobbery" become law, Arthur sent it back to Congress with a stern yet well-reasoned rebuke. "My principal objection to the bill is that it contains appropriations for purposes not for the common defense or general welfare, and which do not promote commerce among the States," he wrote. "These provisions, on the contrary, are entirely for the benefit of the particular localities in which it is proposed to make the improvements. I regard such appropriation of the public money as beyond the powers given by the Constitution to Congress and the President."

Arthur also made known his concerns about setting a bad fiscal precedent. "Appropriations of this nature, to be devoted purely to local objects, tend to an increase in number and in amount," he explained. "As the citizens of one State find that money, to raise which they in common with the whole country are taxed, is to be expended for local improvements in another State, they demand similar benefits for themselves, and it is not unnatural that they should seek to indemnify themselves for such use of the public funds by securing appropriations for similar improvements in their own neighborhood. Thus as the bill becomes more objectionable it secures more support. . . . The extravagant expenditure of public money is an evil not to be measured by the value of that money to the people who are taxed for it. They sustain a greater injury in the demoralizing effect produced upon those who are intrusted with official duty through all the ramifications of government."

While Congress quickly passed the Rivers and Harbors Bill over Arthur's veto, the president's action drew widespread public approval. Telegrams poured into the White House praising Arthur for his stand against "public extravagance." Lincoln's former secretary of war, a still spry Simon Cameron, raved, "It was the act of a great statesman and all men say so." The *New York Times*, which had earlier expressed doubts about Arthur's suitability for high office, now revised its opinion. "President Arthur has had the sagacity and the courage to do exactly the right thing

A Good Shot: **Reformer Arthur takes aim at government waste.**

with the River and Harbor Appropriation Bill," the paper said. "It ought not to require a great amount of sagacity and courage to do the right thing in such a case. So far as sound principle and the public demand were concerned his course was perfectly clear, but he was subject to so much pressure from those with whom he desired to be in accord and who presumed to have great political influence that it doubtless required considerable resolution and firmness, as well as clearness of vision, to take the right stand. But the president has proved equal to the emergency, and has not only put his veto upon the great scheme of plunder, but has given reasons for his action that are unanswerable."

Equally unanswerable was the stench of graft and corruption associated with the Star Route affair. A major scandal inherited from the Garfield administration, it involved the fraudulent awarding of mail route contracts to favored private operators in the Southwest. These operators would then proceed to grossly overcharge the federal government for their services. "In one well-publicized example," relates Garfield's biographer Ira Rutkow, "a single route cost the government $50,000 a year for speeded-up service—the original contract called for an expenditure of approximately $1,000—even though no letter or newspaper had been delivered for a period of a month and a half."

To the dismay of Garfield and later Arthur, federal investigators quickly discovered that "such widespread fraud could occur only with the consent of highly placed officials within the Post Office and other areas of the government." At the center of the scandal was Stephen W. Dorsey, a former GOP senator from Arkansas who had used his Washington connections to acquire contracts for postal routes in Dakota, Montana, and New Mexico. All told, it was believed that Dorsey and his fellow co-conspirators had helped defraud taxpayers of millions of dollars.

To his credit, Arthur ordered his attorney general, Benjamin H. Brewster of Pennsylvania, to bring aggressive action against the offenders, despite the fact that some, like Dorsey, were old and trusted political allies. "I want this work to be done as you are doing it, in the spirit in which you are doing it; I want it to be done earnestly and thoroughly," Arthur told Brewster. "I desire that these people shall be prosecuted with the utmost vigor of the law. I will give you all the help I can." Alas, not much came of these prosecutions, as government attorneys repeatedly failed to convince juries that criminal malfeasance had occurred. "A great part of the evidence must have been beyond their comprehension," theorized the *New York Times* after one acquittal.

While his pressing of the Star Route postal fraud cases bore little fruit, Arthur's efforts on behalf of civil service reform proved far more successful. He played a vital if underappreciated role in transforming the way job applicants designated for civil service were awarded positions in the federal government. Henceforward such candidates would be required to pass through an openly competitive examination process. But in order to achieve this landmark change, Arthur had first to overcome his well-deserved reputation as a spoilsman. As the historian George Frederick Howe pointed out, "His record as a machine politician, one who had been removed from office after an investigation and despite the protection of his 'boss,' sinister rumors charging his participation in political corruption, his electioneering at Albany after his election to the Vice Presidency, and finally, the fact that he was thought to have shown not the slightest favorable interest in reform—all augured ill."

Arthur was able to surmount these popular doubts by becoming a thoughtful and persistent advocate for civil service reform. He outlined his rationale for seeking change in his second annual message to Congress in December 1882: "The civil list now comprises about 1,000,000 persons, far the larger part of whom must, under the terms of the Constitution, be selected by the President either directly or through his own appointees.

"In the early years of the administration of the Government the personal direction of appointments to the civil service may not have been an irksome task for the Executive, but now that the burden has increased fully a hundredfold it has become greater than he ought to bear, and it necessarily diverts his time and attention from the proper discharge of other duties no less delicate and responsible, and which in the very nature of things can not be delegated to other hands.

"In the judgment of not a few who have given study and reflection to this matter, the nation has outgrown the provisions which the Constitution has established for filling the minor offices in the public service.

"But whatever may be thought of the wisdom or expediency of changing the fundamental law in this regard, it is certain that much relief may be afforded not only to the President and to the heads of the Departments, but to Senators and Representatives in Congress, by discreet legislation. They would be protected in a great measure by the bill now pending before the Senate, or by any other which should embody its important features, from the pressure of personal importunity and from the labor of examining conflicting claims and pretensions of candidates.

"I trust that before the close of the present session some decisive action may be taken for the correction of the evils which inhere in the present methods of appointment, and I assure you of my hearty cooperation in any measures which are likely to conduce to that end."

As for the "appropriate term and tenure" of federal appointees, Arthur argued that "the one should be definite and the other stable, and that neither should be regulated by zeal in the service of party or fidelity to the fortunes of an individual." He continued: "It matters little to the people at large what competent person is at the head of this department or of that bureau if they feel assured that the removal of one and the accession of another will not involve the retirement of honest and faithful subordinates whose duties are purely administrative and have no legitimate connection with the triumph of any political principles or the success of any political party or faction."

Reaction to Arthur's speech was overwhelmingly positive. "No portion of the President's Message will receive more attention or, on the whole, will receive more commendation than that which is devoted to the question of Civil Service Reform," praised the *New York Daily Tribune*. "His progress [on this front] is perceptible not so much in any particular suggestion which he now makes and approves of as in the tone that pervades all that he has to offer on the subject . . . he speaks out like a man in earnest who has seriously at heart what falls from his lips. . . . The President now declares himself at one with the best sentiment of the country in his attitude on Civil Service Reform."

The *Chicago Tribune* echoed these sentiments: "In his message to Congress President Arthur gives the order 'Right about face' to the Stalwart army. His recommendations on the subject of a reform of the civil service by law are so hearty as to leave no doubt of his earnest desire that the tenure of office of the vast army of subordinate Government employees should be made stable—dependent upon faithful service and good behavior."

Swayed by Arthur's reasoning and mindful of the ever-growing public support for some sort of civil service reform in the wake of Garfield's assassination, the Republican-controlled Congress chose to act. It passed the Pendleton Act of 1883, which gave Arthur the power "to appoint a small, bipartisan commission to aid him in making and executing rules and regulations covering appointments to the Federal Civil service." The "necessary prelude" to any position in the federal government would be the taking of a competitive test. While the Pendleton Act covered only a tenth of the existing federal workforce, it left the door open for future chief executives to increase the size and scope of its coverage, which many did in the twentieth century. Arthur enthusiastically signed the measure into law on January 16. Noted Thomas C. Reeves, "The irony of ex-Collector Arthur, the 'Gentleman Boss,' affixing his signature to the nation's first civil service reform legislation was not entirely overlooked."

Arthur carried out his duties pertaining to the administration of the new law with commendable skill and efficiency. "Our functions cannot be successfully discharged without the constant, firm, and friendly support of the President," the Civil Service Commission's first annual report lauded. "That support has never failed. The Commission has never asked advice or an exercise of authority on the part of the President which has been refused. . . . As to that of the President, it can express its unhesitating belief, that neither discrimination on the ground of political or religious opinions, nor favoritism of any sort has been allowed to defeat, delay, or in any wise impair or improve the chances or opportunities of any person under the civil service act."

For his part, Arthur too voiced satisfaction with the overall results. "On the 29th of February last," he declared in his final message to Congress on December 1, "I transmitted to the Congress the first annual report of the Civil Service Commission, together with communications from the heads of the several Executive Departments of the Government respecting the practical workings of the law under which the Commission had been acting. The good results therein foreshadowed have been more than realized.

"The system has fully answered the expectations of its friends in securing competent and faithful servants and in protecting the appointing officers of the Government from the pressure of personal importunity and from the labor of examining the claims and pretensions of rival candidates for public employment."

Yet in performing his due diligence on this matter of vital national importance, Arthur delivered a fatal blow to his own chances at being renominated. He had become "virtually a man without a party." "Arthur had fallen into a trap that is usually fatal to politicians: he had lost his base," confirms Zachary Karabell. "Having spent his entire political career as part of one faction, he had earned the near-permanent distrust of competing factions and of the opposing Democrats." Put another way, Arthur had alienated too many party chieftains to carry the 1884 GOP nominating convention. That honor went instead to James Blaine, who after having earlier resigned from Arthur's Cabinet as secretary of state, had skillfully mended enough fences with Stalwarts in the party to take the nomination easily.

Arthur was not without his share of political admirers. "I was a delegate at the Chicago convention in 1880, but at that time I was one to whom the nomination of Mr. Arthur was not acceptable," confessed Delaware resident Christian Bebiger to the *Chicago Daily News*. "But since being called to fill the position of the lamented Garfield there is no man who could have filled the situation with more honor and credit to himself and the republican party and all thinking people must honor him for his official career in the executive chair." Wrote Samuel Clemens, who went by the pen name Mark Twain, "I am but one in the 55,000,000; still, in the opinion of this one-fifty-five millionth of the country's population, it would be hard indeed to better President Arthur's administration. But don't decide till you hear from the rest." Hamilton College president S. G. Brown agreed with Clemens's assessment. "The administration of President Arthur seems to me to have been conducted with remarkable prudence and wisdom, not for party ends, but for the welfare of the whole nation," Brown wrote. "The president came to his high office when the public mind was intensely excited, when every heart was oppressed with the memory of the great crime, and every eye, friendly or hostile, was watching for a sign of weakness, a failure; that under such circumstances, not only no noteworthy mistakes should have been committed, but that the administration in every department should have been so clearly marked by a policy at once firm and conciliatory in the interests of order and justice, of economy and integrity, seems clearly to indicate an intelligent, well-defined, and thoroughly patriotic purpose."

The Reverend Henry Ward Beecher claimed that he could scarcely imagine anyone doing better as president after coming to power under such difficult and trying circumstances. "In my opinion," Beecher praised, "President Arthur has proved himself felicitous in all that he has written, wise in the selection of men for office, with remarkable capacity for silence, and yet frank when he speaks." Even rival Democrats like Congressman W. E. Robinson of New York could not but express admiration. "We have had twenty-one presidents, and with all of them except six I have been personally acquainted," he wrote. "Of all of the whigs and republicans President Arthur promises to leave the most approved record. . . . Were I republican, Mr. Arthur would be my candidate for his successor."

His hopes for a second term dashed, Arthur watched from the political sidelines as Blaine went down to defeat against the Democrat Grover Cleveland in that fall's general election. By this time the ravaging effects of Bright's disease, a fatal kidney malady that Arthur had kept hidden from the public throughout his tenure in the White House, had begun taking its deadly toll. Physically weakened and frequently bedridden, Arthur survived another two years before dying at his New York City home on November 18, 1886.

In death Arthur was remembered fondly as a president who came to office under the most trying of circumstances and surpassed everyone's low expectations for him with unusually firm and decisive leadership. "Surely no more lonely and pathetic figure was ever seen assuming the powers of government," eulogized Elihu Root, a distinguished New York attorney who would go on to play high-profile roles in the McKinley and Roosevelt administrations. "He had no people behind him, for Garfield, not he, was the people's choice. He had no party behind him, for the dominant faction of his party hated his name, were enraged by his advancement, and distrusted his motives. He had not even his own faction behind him; for he already knew that the just discharge of his duties would not accord with the ardent desires of their partisanship, and that disappointment and estrangement lay before him there.

"He was alone. He was bowed down by the weight of fearful responsibility and crushed to earth by the feeling, exaggerated but not unfounded, that he took up his heavy burden, surrounded by dislike, suspicion, distrust, and condemnation as an enemy of the martyred Garfield and the beneficiary of his murder. . . . Then came the revelation to the people of America that our ever fortunate Republic had again found the man for the hour. His actions were informed and guided by absolute self-devotion to the loftiest conception of his great office. . . . His skill as a politician in the best sense, and his experience as an administrator made him a judge of men and their motives, and enabled him to shun the pitfalls which encompass the feet of an unwary Executive. His instinctive sympathy and chivalric regard for the memory and purposes of the lamented Garfield disarmed resentment. The dignified courtesy of his manners and the considerate sincerity of his speech conciliated the friendship even of his enemies. The extremists of his own party faction found that their demands for the fruits of revolution were addressed to one no longer a leader of a faction, but the President of the whole people, conscious of all his obligations and determined to execute the people's will.

"The strain of that terrible ordeal and the concentrated and unremitting effort to those burdened years exhausted the vital forces of his frame and brought him to the grave in the meridian of his days. He gave his life to his country as truly as one who dies from wounds or disease in war."

Nowhere in this heartfelt tribute was Arthur referred to as "Gentleman Boss." That appellation, like the old spoils system itself, no longer applied.

CHAPTER FOUR

A Matter of Honor

GROVER CLEVELAND AND THE
HAWAIIAN ANNEXATION CONTROVERSY

Grover Cleveland could be forgiven if he felt the urge to gloat when he took the oath of office in the east portico of the Capitol on March 4, 1893. It had been four long years since he left the White House, following a close but unsuccessful bid for a second term. He had captured the majority of the popular vote in that earlier race, but mirroring the outcome of another controversial presidential election some 112 years later, he had fallen short in the electoral college.

While the loss stung him deeply, he kept his disappointment to himself. "It is not proper to speak of it as my defeat," the staunch Democrat commented. "It was a contest between two great parties battling for the supremacy of certain well-defined principles. One party has won and the other has lost—that is all there is to it." His vivacious young wife Frances, whom he had married two years into his first term, was far less inhibited in expressing her emotions. As she was exiting the White House for what was believed to be the last time, she cheekily told a caretaker: "Now Jerry, I want you to take good care of all the furniture and ornaments in the house and not let any of them get lost or broken, for I want to find everything just as it is now, when we come back again."

Whether the effects remained the way the First Lady had wanted them is unknown. What is certain, however, is that Cleveland viewed his return to power with an unusual degree of solicitude. "Sir," he had informed a gathering of friends and political cohorts a few months before his second inaugural, "it is a solemn thing to be President of the United States. While we find in our triumph a result of popular intelligence which we have aroused, and a consequence of popular vigilance which we have stimulated, let us not for a moment forget that our accession to power will find neither this intelligence nor this vigilance dead or slumbering."

Cleveland had good reason to assume such an earnest approach. The country was experiencing a number of thorny crises when he took over from Benjamin Harrison, his Republican predecessor (or successor, depending on how you look at it). An economic downturn, widespread labor strife, and a rancorous public debate over the coinage of silver all vied for Cleveland's attention. But the one issue requiring the most immediate action had to do with the status of the Hawaiian Islands. A political revolution had taken place on the remote Pacific archipelago, and the victors, a group of wealthy American sugar planters and businessmen, were seeking immediate admission to the Union. A treaty of annexation had already been drawn up and submitted to the Senate by the Harrison administration.

What remained unresolved was Cleveland's attitude toward the new treaty, which appeared certain to earn Senate passage. Would he merely sign off on the pact as many politicos and pundits expected, or would he withhold his support because of disturbing accounts that called into question the legitimacy of the Hawaiian revolutionary government? If the new president chose the latter path, he would risk the ire of one of the most powerful political movements then emerging in the country: imperialism. Its adherents sought immediate annexation of the islands as a first step toward establishing an overseas empire for the United States. "We shall cover the oceans with our merchant marine," enthused one supporter. "We shall build a navy to the measure of our greatness. Great colonies, flying our flag and trading with us, will grow about our posts of trade. Our institutions will follow our flag on the wings of our commerce. And American law, American order, American civilization and the American flag will plant themselves on shores, hitherto bloody and benighted, but, by those agencies of God, henceforth to be made beautiful and bright."

No matter how one saw it, Cleveland had a big decision on his hands, one with the potential to influence the lives of future generations of Hawaiians and alter the course of American foreign policy. Whether he would be damaged politically for the course of action he ultimately chose was immaterial in his mind. As he once said, "It is better to be defeated standing for a high principle than to run by committing subterfuge."

Grover Cleveland entered this world on March 18, 1837, in Caldwell, New Jersey. The fifth of nine children of a Presbyterian minister and a book publisher's daughter, Cleveland had a relatively happy but uneventful childhood growing up in upstate New York. He went to school, performed chores in and around the family homestead, and, when time permitted, went fishing at a nearby lake. "He was then a lad of rather good sense," his sister recalled, "who did not yield to impulses—he considered well, and was resourceful—but as a student he did not shine. The wonderful powers of application and concentration which afterwards distinguished his mental efforts were not conspicuous in his boyhood."

Despite this mediocre showing in the classroom, young Grover had every intention of attending college. Yet his dreams of higher education had to be abandoned when his father died in 1853. Now sixteen, Cleveland had to find work to help support his mother and younger siblings. After a personally unsatisfactory stint as a teacher for the New York Institute for the Blind in New York City, he landed in Buffalo where he edited a book on cattle breeding for an uncle and studied law with a prosperous local firm, Rogers, Bowen, and Rogers.

In the law Cleveland found his true calling. Researching cases, writing legal briefs, presenting evidence before juries—all appealed to his exacting nature. He went on to pass the New York bar in 1859 and worked as an associate with Rogers, Bowen, and Rogers. "Mr. Cleveland is one of the most promising young members of the bar, is a thoroughly read lawyer, and possesses talent of a high order," praised one local publication. "He will have an opportunity of demonstrating this and 'more too,' and, our word for it, he will prove himself equal to the occasion." But the strain of establishing himself as a first-rate attorney exacted a personal toll. "I am still living alone as I have always done," he dispiritedly wrote a family member during this period, "maintaining life and energies by means of eating, drinking, and sleeping. Indeed, I am so addicted to these habits that I find it impossible to forgo them for any length of time. I must have my *provender* three times a day and eat and drink in proportion. It's lamentable, isn't it?"

In the late 1850s Cleveland began to wet his feet in local Democratic party politics. By 1862 he was well enough regarded by party loyalists to be selected as a ward supervisor. He parlayed these political connections into an appointment as an assistant district attorney for Erie County and quickly acquired a reputation as an honest and hardworking prosecutor. "He was in attendance at every one of the twelve grand juries which met during each of the three years of his term in office, and presented in full a large majority of the cases," Cleveland later recalled for his biographer E. T. Chamberlain. "Nearly all the indictments during this period were drawn by him, and perhaps more than half the cases he tried in court. On more than one occasion during these busy months he conducted four cases before a jury, won a favorable verdict in each, sat down at eight o'clock in the evening to make preparations for the next day, and did not rise from his desk until three o'clock in the morning. Eight o'clock found him back again at the office, fresh for a day's contest with some of the best criminal practitioners in the county."

In 1882 Cleveland was elected mayor of Buffalo after a group of prominent local Democrats recruited him to run. They had been impressed by his obvious integrity and established popularity among all classes in the city. Cleveland was the kind of man who moved easily from corporate boardroom to working-class saloon, appearing comfortable in both. Right from the start, he let his constituents know he intended to make the mayor's office "responsible to the masses." One way he demonstrated this attitude was his scrupulous concern for fiscal affairs. "We hold the money of the people in our hands to be used for their purposes," he declared. "It seems to me that a successful and faithful administration of the government of our city may be accomplished, by bearing in mind that we are the trustees and agents of our fellow-citizens, holding their funds in sacred trust, to be expended for their benefit; that we should at all times be prepared to render an honest account to them touching on the manner of its expenditure, and that the affairs of the city should be conducted, as far as possible, upon the same principles as a good business man manages his private concerns."

Dubbed "Mayor Veto" for the number of times he struck down city council initiatives that amounted to what he called "raids on the treasury," Cleveland governed wisely and prudently. "His life as Mayor was a continuous struggle for honesty and fidelity in office against the jobbers, spoilsmen, and partisans who had long preyed on the city," remembered one admirer. "He mastered the situation. . . . His fearless way of dealing with them is shown by his language in one of his vetoes: 'I withhold my assent, &c., because I regard it as the culmination of a most barefaced, impudent, and shameless scheme to betray the interests of the people, and to worse than squander the public money.'"

He also demonstrated a strong social conscience. When the Society for the Prevention of Cruelty to Children lobbied for a protection ordinance, he proactively put his office behind the effort. "It seems to me," he said, "that no pretext should be permitted to excuse allowing young girls to be upon the streets at improper hours, since its result must almost necessarily be their destruction." The same principle held true for preadolescent males: "The disposition of the boy (child though he be) to aid in his own support, or that of others, in an honest, decent way, ought not to be discouraged. But it does not call for his being in the street at late hours, to his infinite damage morally, mentally and physically, and to the danger of society."

Cleveland moved up to the governorship of New York in 1883 after dispatching the Republican candidate, former judge Charles J. Folger, in a landslide victory. He continued his practice of vetoing legislation he regarded as fiscally irresponsible and pushed for greater governmental accountability through civil service reform. "Public office is a public trust," he said. In his leadership style Cleveland was a complete hands-on manager, refusing to delegate responsibilities to staff members and working around the clock. Sometimes this backbreaking pace got the best of him. "I will tell you the deadliest secret in the world," he confided to a friend during this period, "that for the last few days I have the effects of long hours, steady work, and worse than all, incessant pesters about offices. I honestly think I can't stand it more than two weeks longer. My head a good deal of the time doesn't feel right, and when a man begins to talk about office I begin to feel irritable and my head begins to ache."

His aching head notwithstanding, Cleveland's solid if brief record as governor of the most prosperous state in the Union catapulted him to the Democratic presidential nomination in 1884. But standing directly in his path to the White House was the formidable James G. Blaine of Maine. The former U.S. senator turned secretary of state had easily captured the Republican nomination and looked to crown a noteworthy twenty-year career in politics by winning the presidency. But charges of personal corruption and general unscrupulousness dogged him. As Democrats were fond of chanting,

> Blaine! Blaine! James G. Blaine!
> The Continental Liar from the state of Maine.

Nor was Cleveland without his own political weaknesses. A case in point was his conspicuous absence from military service during the Civil War. Union veterans made up a sizable and influential segment of the electorate and could be counted on to feel remiss if, as the opposition alleged, Cleveland had dodged the draft. Although Cleveland had in fact chosen not to wear the blue uniform, his decision had nothing to do with personal cowardice. He simply believed he could not in good faith go off to fight while his widowed mother required his financial support. Instead he hired a substitute, a thirty-two-year-old Polish sailor, to take his place, a device that was permissible under the military draft laws of the day. Cleveland brushed aside the Republican charges as so much "political mendacity," but whether voters actually believed him was difficult to gauge.

Another cause for concern stemmed from Cleveland having allegedly sired a son out of wedlock in 1874 with a former dry-goods store employee named Maria Halpin. An attractive and charming widow, Halpin had been involved with Cleveland and several of his close Buffalo friends, all of whom were married. While it is by no means certain that Cleveland was actually the father of Halpin's child, he did take responsibility, perhaps to save one of his married friends the embarrassment of scandal. He also provided financial support to the child and later made arrangements for the boy to be adopted by another "respectable" family when Halpin proved herself mentally incapable of retaining custody. Notwithstanding the question of paternity, the opposition had a field day in accusing Cleveland of moral profligacy when details of the affair leaked during the campaign. Perhaps their most famous attack involved a popular ditty that went as follows:

> Ma! Ma! Where's my pa?
> Gone to the White House.
> Ha! Ha! Ha!

Cleveland survived both assaults on his character and edged Blaine in November, 219 electoral votes to 182. Blaine may have unintentionally provided Cleveland with his narrow margin of victory when he failed to contest the incendiary remarks of Reverend Samuel D. Burchard at a gathering of Protestant ministers in New York City on October 29. "We are Republicans, and don't propose to leave our party and identify ourselves with the party whose antecedents have been Rum, Romanism, and Rebellion," proclaimed Burchard. Interpreting this as a slur against their cultural heritage and religion, the politically active Irish Catholic community in New York rallied to Cleveland's candidacy and played a prominent role in delivering the crucial state to him on election day. Had New York gone the other way,

Blaine and not Cleveland would have marched to "Hail to the Chief" on inauguration day.

While most presidents would have chosen to play it safe politically after such a razor-thin victory, Cleveland instead took the opportunity to ruffle a few feathers. He vetoed a number of popular government pension bills he deemed exorbitant, launched an anti-corruption drive in the scandal-prone Department of the Interior, and alienated big business and labor with a call to lower tariff rates on imported goods. "The animating spirit of the Administration was administrative reform," he later said. "Not exclusive attention to any one phase of improvement in that service, but a wholesale ventilation and stirring up of all the branches of that service, the lopping off of useless limbs, the removal of the dead wood, and such a renewal of the activity by the introduction of new blood as the necessities of the service would demand."

In June 1886 the forty-nine-year-old bachelor surprised the nation when he married Frances Folsom, the comely twenty-one-year-old daughter of his late friend and former law colleague Oscar Folsom. Cleveland had known her since she was a baby and had acted as her legal guardian for several years following the death of her father. Reflecting the attitudes of the era, Cleveland wrote to his sister that he expected Frances to be "a sensible, domestic American wife, and I should be pleased not to hear her spoken of as 'The First Lady of the Land' or 'The Mistress of the White House.' I want her to be very happy and to possess all she can reasonably desire, but I should feel very much afflicted if she lets many notions in her head. But I think she is pretty level-headed. . . ."

By all accounts their marriage was a happy one and helped remove the rough social edges from Cleveland's often brusque personality. "No more brilliant and affable lady than Mrs. Cleveland has ever graced the portals of this old mansion," gushed one White House staff member. "Her very presence threw an air of beauty on the entire surroundings, whatever the occasion or the company." Their union would produce five children, three daughters and two sons.

Marital bliss aside, Cleveland could not gain the political support he needed to win reelection in 1888 against Republican presidential nominee and former Civil War hero Benjamin Harrison. In the disappointing aftermath of the general election, he blamed his support for lower tariffs as the primary reason for his loss. "Some of my friends say we ought to have gone before the country on the clean administration we have given," Cleveland remarked. "I differ with them. We were defeated, it is true, but the principles of tariff reform will surely win in the end."

Sent into temporary political retirement, Cleveland did his best to return to some semblance of a normal personal life. He joined an eminent New York City law firm and rented a fashionable brownstone home on Madison Avenue. There he spent most of his time doting on his young family and entertaining friends. But politics never remained far from his thoughts. Dismayed by the Harrison administration's handling of such key issues as federal spending, civil service reform, and public land usage, Cleveland privately fumed that it represented a complete repudiation of his earlier policies. In particular, he grew incensed at Harrison's supine attitude toward the "Billion Dollar Congress" of 1889–1890, when federal expenditures soared to unprecedented new heights under Republican leadership.

To right the nation's course as he saw it, and to exact no small measure of political revenge, Cleveland decided to reenter political life. In 1892 he once again faced off against Harrison and came away with a decisive electoral victory, carrying 23 states with an overall plurality of 300,000 votes. Typically he tried not to gloat. "We must hear, above victorious shouts," he informed a crowd of well-wishers afterward, "the call of our fellow countrymen to public duty, and we must put on a garb befitting public servants."

His new administration adopted a similarly sober approach on the question of Hawaiian annexation and the larger issue of territorial expansionism. From the early days of the Republic there had been numerous attempts to extend the continental borders of the United States. During the War of 1812, efforts to seize Canada militarily were blocked by British ground and naval forces. In the late 1840s, territories representing the present-day states of Texas, New Mexico, Arizona, Nevada, California, Wyoming, and Colorado were annexed following the defeat of Mexico in the Mexican-American War. In 1867 the United States purchased Alaska from tsarist Russia for $7.2 million. "In American eyes this continent is their patrimony," observed the Russian minister who helped broker the deal. "Their destiny (manifest as they call it) is to always expand." John L. O'Sullivan, the Democratic journalist who had coined the phrase "manifest destiny" in the 1840s, explained that it was the destiny of the United States "to overspread the continent allotted by Providence for the free development of our yearly multiplying masses."

By the close of the nineteenth century this expansionist drive took on even greater urgency when the great European powers of the day began scouring the globe for colonies to act as markets for their manufactured goods and as sources of raw materials. Indochina, for example, fell under exclusive French control while Great Britain, Germany, Belgium, Italy, Portugal, and Spain joined France in carving up all of Africa. In total, half of all non-Western people became subject to European political rule during this period.

On this side of the Atlantic, powerful voices clamored to ensure U.S. participation in the scramble for international booty.

Labeled "imperialists" by their detractors, this mostly elite group of journalists, academics, businessmen, and government officials argued that the United States needed to move quickly on overseas expansion or face the possibility of being permanently eclipsed by its European rivals. The international arena thus took on a Darwinian aspect. To Americans of the expansionist bent, it appeared that only those nations with superior arms and the will to subjugate "inferior races" would prevail in a fierce contest for global supremacy. Senator Henry Cabot Lodge of Massachusetts, a leading advocate for an enlarged U.S. role in the world, touched upon this "law of the jungle" theme when he wrote: "The tendency of modern times is toward consolidation. It is apparent in capital and labor alike, and it [is] also true in nations. Small states are of the past and have no future. The modern movement is all toward the concentration of people and territory into great nations and large dominions. The great nations are rapidly absorbing for their future expansion and their present defence all the waste places of the earth. It is a movement which makes for civilization and the advancement of race. As one of the great nations of the world, the United States must not fall out of the line of march."

Implicit in Lodge's argument was his belief in white supremacy. With other like-minded expansionists such as Theodore Roosevelt of New York, Lodge assumed that the white Anglo-Saxon race was best suited culturally, intellectually, and temperamentally to govern the world. These sentiments were reflected in the work of Reverend Josiah Strong of the Congregational Home Missionary Society. In an immensely popular 1883 book entitled *Our Country*, Strong preached that global domination was the divine right of white Anglo-Saxons, especially those living in North America. "There are no more new worlds," he explained. "The unoccupied arable lands of the earth are limited, and will be soon taken. The time is coming when the pressure of population on the means of subsistence will be felt here as it is now felt in Europe and Asia. Then will the world enter upon a new stage of history—the final competition of races, for which the Anglo-Saxon is being schooled. Long before the thousand millions are here, the mighty centrifugal tendency, inherent in this stock and strengthened in the United States, will assert itself. Then this race of unequal energy, with all the majority of numbers and the might of wealth behind it—the representative, let us hope, of the largest liberty, the purest Christianity, the highest civilization—having developed peculiarly aggressive traits calculated to impress its institutions upon mankind, will spread itself over the earth." Strong went on to predict that this "powerful race" would conquer Mexico, then march through Central and South America before finally advancing to "Africa and beyond." "And can anyone doubt that the result of this competition of races will be the 'survival of the fittest'?" he asked.

The writings of Alfred Thayer Mahan gave further impetus to the expansionists. A bookish naval officer who felt more at home in a library than at the helm of a ship, Mahan argued that sea power was the single most important factor in determining whether a country belonged in the first rank of nations. A large and efficient navy permitted a country to protect its seafaring trade and project its military power over vast distances, he claimed. But in order to maintain an effective naval force, a country needed to secure several "resting places" in the world where ships could be routinely refueled, provisioned, and repaired.

Thus the importance of colonies and overseas bases. "The protection of such stations must depend either upon direct military force . . . or upon a surrounding friendly population, such as the American colonies once were to England," Mahan wrote in his seminal 1890 book, *The Influence of Sea Power upon History,*

1660–1783. "Such friendly surroundings and backing, joined to a reasonable military provision, are the best of defense, and when combined with decided preponderance at sea, make a scattered and extensive empire, like that of England, secure; for while it is true that an unexpected attack may cause disaster in some quarter, the actual superiority of naval power prevents such disaster from being general or irremediable. History has sufficiently proved this. England's naval bases have been in all parts of the world; and her fleets have at once protected them, kept open the communications between them, and relied upon them for shelter. Colonies attached to the mother-country afford, therefore, the surest means of supporting abroad the sea power of a country."

Following this worldview, American expansionists looked to exploit the Hawaiian Islands, with their strategic location in the Pacific and their many excellent harbors. "Even if they were populated by a low race of savages, even if they were desert rocks, [they] would still be important to this country from their position," Lodge asserted. "The main thing is that those islands lie there in the heart of the Pacific, the controlling point in the commerce of that great ocean." As events would prove, securing them would be no easy matter. For while a host of American sugar planters, missionaries, and businessmen had been steadily pouring into the islands for several decades, the native inhabitants were anything but pleased with this development. They found themselves increasingly marginalized as the newcomers and their progeny gained control of Hawaii's major economic and political institutions.

Such was the power of the *haoles* (foreigners) that in 1887 the native ruler King Kalakaua was compelled to accept a constitution written in their hand and overwhelmingly slanted to their interests. For example, under the provisions of this new governing charter the king relinquished most of his authority to a legislature dominated by white males with extensive economic holdings throughout the islands. "The character of this constitution was clearly the work of American minds, and in evidence that the Republic of the West was rapidly coming into control in Hawaii in the persons of men bred to American law and American ideals of government," noted one sympathetic historian. In practical terms, the charter effectively shut native Hawaiians out of the political process.

This state of affairs remained unchallenged until Kalakaua died in 1891 and was succeeded by his sister Liliuokalani. Proud, stubborn, intelligent, and fiercely independent, Queen "Lil" let it be known that she was not happy with her kingdom under the political yoke of the *haoles*. "Although settled among us, and drawing their wealth from our resources, [the *haoles*] were alien to us in their customs and ideas respecting government, and desired above all things the extension of their power, and to carry out their plans of advancement, and to secure their own personal benefit," she declared. To rectify the situation, Liliuokalani moved to annul the 1887 constitution and replace it with one promising to restore full political sovereignty to the indigenous people of the islands. In justifying her action, she pointed to the thousands of petitions she had received from native Hawaiians urging her to adopt a new constitution. "No true Hawaiian chief would have done other than to promise a consideration of their wishes," she maintained.

Alarm and indignation soon settled into the ranks of the *haoles*. Who was this impetuous young woman to dare challenge their hegemony? Why, the very notion seemed absurd. She and her proposed new constitutional government simply could not be allowed to stand. A clandestine "Committee of Safety" was thus organized by disgruntled *haoles* to overthrow Liliuokalani. Led by the wealthy planter Sanford B. Dole, the group succeeded in carrying out its objective in January 1893, with a critical assist from John L. Stevens, the sympathetic American minister to Hawaii. As the bloodless coup began, Stevens, who had been apprised by the insurgents of their plans, unilaterally deployed 162 Marines from a nearby U.S. warship to Honolulu, the seat of government for the islands. The officially stated reason for the soldiers' presence was to protect "American lives and property." In reality, however, this naked show of force served to quell armed native resistance and further Liliuokalani's abdication of the throne. Her fall came shortly after Stevens granted formal U.S. recognition to the newly established Dole Provisional Government on January 17.

In a somber public statement, the besieged monarch painstakingly explained her reasons for stepping down:

"I, Lili'uokalani, by the grace of God and under the constitution of the Hawaiian Kingdom, Queen, do hereby solemnly protest against any and all acts done against myself and the constitutional government of the Hawaiian Kingdom by certain persons claiming to have established a Provisional Government of and for this Kingdom.

"That I yield to the superior force of the United States of America, whose Minister Plenipotentiary, His Excellency John L. Stevens, has caused United States troops to be landed at Honolulu and declared that he would support the said Provisional Government.

"Now to avoid any collision of armed forces and perhaps loss of life, I do, under this protest, and impelled by said forces, yield my authority until such time as the Government of the United States shall, upon the facts being presented to it, undo the action of its representative and reinstate me in the authority which I claim as the constitutional sovereign of the Hawaiian Islands."

Now safely ensconced in power, the Provisional Government wasted little time in seeking formal annexation to the

United States, a goal to which Dole and his fellow *haoles* had long aspired. "The Hawaiian pear is now fully ripe, and this is the golden hour for the United States to pluck it," wrote Stevens to his superiors in Washington. While Benjamin Harrison had only a month remaining in his presidency, he viewed the islands as vital to long-term U.S. interests and pressed the Senate for immediate approval of a treaty of annexation. Owing to its traditionally deliberative nature, the Senate chose to withhold ratification until after the March inauguration of Harrison's successor. Meanwhile Hawaii became a "temporary protectorate" of the United States at the official request of the Dole Provisional Government.

It seemed highly unlikely that Cleveland would oppose the treaty, given that the new president had once described the islands as "an outpost of American commerce and a stepping-stone to the growing trade of the Pacific." Outgoing Secretary of State John W. Foster had gone so far as to suggest that Cleveland and his advisers "would be favorable to the acquisition." But such a conclusion did not account for Cleveland's sense of "national honor, conscience, and love of justice."

While not opposed to annexation per se, he nevertheless became deeply troubled by reports that the actions of the Dole Provisional Government did not truly reflect the sentiments of the Hawaiian people. As a result, Cleveland felt he had only one morally responsible course of action. "For the purpose of re-examination," he informed the Senate, "I withdraw the treaty of annexation between the United States and the Provisional Government of the Hawaiian Islands now pending in the Senate, which was signed on February 14, 1893, and transmitted to the Senate on the 15th of the same month; and I therefore request that said treaty be returned to me. Grover Cleveland." He also announced that he was dispatching former congressman James H. Blount on a special fact-finding tour of

Larger Than Life: **Cleveland as commander-in-chief.**

the islands to discover the underlying truth behind the events
leading to the revolution.

This news did not sit well with staunch expansionists like
Theodore Roosevelt, who later characterized Cleveland's action
as "a colossal crime." Pro-annexation journals like the New
York *Commercial Advertiser* could not restrain their contempt.
"In ordering Old Glory pulled down at Honolulu," the paper

asserted, "President Cleveland turned back the hands on the dial of civilization. Native rule, ignorant, naked, heathen, is reestablished; and the dream of an American republic at the crossroads of the Pacific . . . and the fulfillment of which the more enlightened of our 65,000,000 people awaited with glad anticipation—has been shattered by Grover Cleveland, the Buffalo lilliputian! . . . He has declared that . . . American property interests may no longer have the abiding protection that such men as Dole and Armstrong and Bishop declare is essential; that the Hawaiian islands shall be tossed a prize into the arena of international strife, for which the Japanese, the English, and heaven knows who else may scramble and quarrel."

Nor did Blount's findings comfort the supporters of annexation. After a concerted investigation in which several individuals on both sides of the revolt were interviewed, the special commissioner concluded that a "shameful" conspiracy between Minister Stevens and the *haoles* had been chiefly responsible for the overthrow of Liliuokalani's government. "Mr. Stevens consulted freely with the leaders of the revolutionary movement from the evening of the 14th," Blount wrote. "These disclosed to him all their plans. They feared arrest and punishment. He promised them protection. They needed the troops on shore to overawe the Queen's supporters and government. . . . But for this no request to land troops would have been made. Had the troops not been landed, no measures would have been taken.

"The American Minister and the revolutionary leaders had determined on a new addition to the United States and had agreed on the part each was to act to the very end."

Once again the pro-annexation response was predictable, if not downright hostile. "Whoever reads with care the report made by this special agent, just published," contended one newspaper sympathetic to the expansionist cause, "cannot fail to be struck by the fact that it is saturated with the evidences of preconceived judgment of facts and rank determination to make out a case against the Administration of President Harrison and the action of Minister Stevens. . . . There is hardly the pretence of anything like judicial impartiality in the entire document; hardly a word that does not disclose a hostile motive and a fixed determination to make the facts fit a theory already adopted to aid in carrying out a deliberate and carefully arranged design. So full of the spirit of this mission and the animus of his employers was this special agent that he did not attempt even to veil his purpose in the ordinary decencies of diplomatic language and official intercourse. To smirch the character of the American Minister he did not hesitate. . . . To impeach the honor of the Harrison Administration he availed himself of all means and every opportunity, supplementing open accusation with base insinuation, and acting on all occasions the part of a paid pettifogging attorney."

Nevertheless Cleveland had personally heard and seen enough. With his worst suspicions now confirmed by Blount's report, he proceeded to reveal publicly his misgivings over the Hawaiian situation in a special message to Congress on December 18, 1893. "I believe that a candid and thorough examination of the facts will force the conviction that the provisional government owes its existence to an armed invasion by the United States," Cleveland stated. "Fair-minded people with the evidence before them will hardly claim that the Hawaiian Government was overthrown by the people of the islands or that the provisional government had ever existed with their consent. I do not understand that any member of this government claims that the people would uphold it by their suffrages if they were allowed to vote on the question."

He continued: "By an act of war, committed with the participation of a diplomatic representative of the United States and without authority of Congress, the Government of a feeble but friendly and confiding people has been overthrown. A substantial wrong has thus been done which a due regard for our national character as well as the rights of the injured people requires we should endeavor to repair. The provisional government has not assumed a republican or other constitutional form, but has remained a mere executive council or oligarchy, set up without the assent of the people. It has not sought to find a permanent basis of popular support and has given no evidence of an intention to do so. Indeed, the representatives of that government assert that the people of Hawaii are unfit for popular government and frankly avow that they can be best ruled by arbitrary or despotic power.

"The law of nations is founded upon reason and justice, and the rules of conduct governing individual relations between citizens or subjects of a civilized state are equally applicable as between enlightened nations. . . . A man of true honor protects the unwritten word which binds his conscience more scrupulously, if possible, than he does the bond a breach of which subjects him to legal liabilities; and the United States in aiming to maintain itself as one of the most enlightened of nations would do its citizens gross injustice if it applied to its international relations any other than a high standard of honor and morality. On that ground the United States can not properly be put in the position of countenancing a wrong after its commission any more than in that of consenting to it in advance. On that ground it can not allow itself to refuse to redress an injury inflicted through an abuse of power by officers clothed with its authority and wearing its uniform; and on the same ground, if a feeble but friendly state is in danger of being robbed of its independence and its sovereignty by a misuse of the name and power of the United States, the United States can not fail to vindicate its honor and its sense of justice by an earnest effort to make all possible reparation."

There would be no resubmission of the earlier treaty of annexation to the Senate. Hawaii would remain an independent
state. As for the reinstatement of Liliuokalani's government,
Cleveland thought it constitutionally prudent to let Congress
sort things out, as that body possessed "the extended powers
and wide discretion" to accomplish the task. But Congress was
not up to the challenge. Swayed by domestic political concerns
that it contravened popular American tradition "to put mon-
archs back on their thrones," Democrats joined with Republicans in quashing attempts to restore Liliuokalani to power.
They also succeeded in passing the Turpie resolution, which essentially bestowed official diplomatic recognition upon the existing Dole government.

"Quite lately a government has been established in Hawaii
which is in full force and operation in all parts of the Islands,"
Cleveland wrote. "It is maintaining its authority and discharg-
ing all ordinary governmental functions. Upon general principles and not losing sight of the special circumstances surrounding this case, the new government is clearly entitled to our
recognition without regard to any of the incidents which accompanied or preceded its inauguration."

Acknowledging political realities, Cleveland reluctantly acceded: "This recognition and the attitude of the Congress concerning Hawaiian affairs of course lead to an absolute denial of
the least present or future aid or encouragement on my part to
an effort to restore any government heretofore existing in the
Hawaiian Islands."

The annexation of Hawaii would reappear as a major foreign policy issue under Cleveland's successor, Republican
William McKinley of Ohio. A committed expansionist, McKinley believed in extending American power to the farthest
reaches of the Pacific. "We need Hawaii," he claimed, "just as
much and a good deal more than we did California. It is mani-

fest destiny." It came then as no great shock when McKinley in 1897 successfully negotiated a second treaty of annexation with the island's ruling white minority government. Liliuokalani was understandably furious. "I declare such a treaty," the deposed monarch asserted, "to be an act of wrong toward the native and part-native people of Hawaii, an invasion of the rights of the ruling chiefs, in violation of international rights both toward my people and toward friendly nations with whom they have made treaties, the perpetuation of the fraud whereby the constitutional government was overthrown, and, finally, an act of gross injustice to me."

Her strong skepticism was shared by Cleveland. Now permanently retired in Princeton, New Jersey (he did not seek a third term in 1896), the ex-president could not stomach what he considered to be "a perversion of our national mission" by McKinley. "Did you ever see such a preposterous thing as the Hawaiian business?" he wrote his former attorney general. "The papers I read are most strongly opposed to it and there ought to be soberness and decency enough in the Senate to save us from launching upon the dangerous policy which is foreshadowed by the pending treaty; but I am prepared for almost anything."

While the second treaty fell short of winning a necessary two-thirds vote for ratification in the Senate, the islands ultimately became American property on August 12, 1898, when a joint congressional resolution calling for annexation was enthusiastically signed by McKinley. This legislative maneuver required just a simple majority of the House and Senate, something McKinley and his partisan supporters had little difficulty in securing. "Hawaii is ours," Cleveland sadly noted. "As I look back upon the first steps in this miserable business and as I contemplate the means used to complete the outrage, I am ashamed of the whole affair."

Cleveland had every right to be chagrined. Through violence, greed, treachery, and obfuscation, the Hawaiian Islands had been ignominiously stripped of their independence and forced into the expansionist embrace of the United States. But in vigorously opposing its annexation, Cleveland had demonstrated exceptional mettle and a highly developed sense of ethics. As his biographer Alyn Brodsky observed, "At a time when small nations were becoming the prey of great ones, and the United States had fallen victim to the stigma of colonialism, [Cleveland] insisted that the country he had once again been called upon to lead must fulfill the noblest commitment to morality and altruism."

In thus appealing to the "better angels" of his countrymen's nature, Cleveland fulfilled a lifetime creed. "I have tried so hard to be right," he said shortly before succumbing to a fatal heart attack on June 24, 1908. His bold-spirited stance against the annexation of Hawaii provided eloquent testimony to that effort.

CHAPTER FIVE

Taking On the Trusts

THEODORE ROOSEVELT AND THE NORTHERN SECURITIES CASE

John Pierpont Morgan did not like surprises. The legendary financier had always made a point of staying on top of things, whether economic, political, or personal. This diligent attitude was reflected in his philosophy of life. "Keep your mouth shut and your eyes and ears open," he told anyone willing to listen. But in Theodore Roosevelt he had at last met his match. No one could predict the seemingly impulsive actions of the twenty-sixth president of the United States, whom one Wall Street insider had likened to a "bucking bronco."

On the night of February 18, 1902, Morgan learned this fact the hard way as he was dining with a group of business colleagues in New York City. Informed that Roosevelt had ordered the Justice Department to prosecute his recently organized Northern Securities Company as an illegal railroad combination under the provisions of the Sherman Anti-Trust Act, the normally unflappable Morgan became agitated. "Shocked" might be a better word. He was arguably the most influential

business tycoon in the country, a towering figure whose decisions had a major bearing on the success or failure of the American economy, and he was now being publicly called out like a
common criminal. Couldn't the president have discreetly fore-
warned him that his actions were in violation of federal law? After all, hadn't he contributed generously to Roosevelt's successful gubernatorial campaign in New York just four years earlier?
Certainly, in Morgan's patrician worldview, this was not how
gentlemen of substance behaved.

"Pierpont is furious," the celebrated political curmudgeon
and author Henry Adams disclosed, "because Theodore, suddenly, without warning, at a critical moment of the market
when very large amounts of money were involved and borrowed
on collateral, had hit him an awful blow square in the face." One
of Morgan's principal business partners in the Northern Securities venture was more caustic in his disdain. "It seems hard,"
James J. Hill said, "that we should be compelled to fight for our
lives against the political adventurers who have never done anything but pose and draw a salary."

But Roosevelt was no ordinary political adventurer. A man
of strong personal convictions, he sincerely believed that Morgan and his associates had transgressed the law by merging the
Great Northern, Northern Pacific, and Chicago, Burlington &
Quincy railroads into one large holding company that would
"take control of practically the entire railway system in the
Northwest—possibly as the first step toward controlling the entire railway system of the country." From Roosevelt's perspective, this "trust" simply could not be allowed to stand. It would
render the federal government and the nation "practically help-
less" before the concentrated economic might of the "House of
Morgan."

"The absolutely vital question [of this period] was whether
the Government had power to control [corporations] at all,"

Roosevelt later wrote in his autobiography. "This question had not yet been decided in favor of the United States Government. It was useless to discuss methods of controlling big business by the National Government until it was definitely settled that the National Government had the power to control it."

There were enormous risks, however. No chief executive had ever directly challenged an economic titan like Morgan. If sufficiently aroused, Morgan could wreak untold havoc upon the marketplace, bringing on a "Roosevelt Depression" and political ruination for the former Rough Rider. In pressing the Northern Securities case, Roosevelt was fearlessly declaring his willingness to hazard his presidency for the principle of government regulation of "big business."

Roosevelt had not always been so open to displays of raw courage. The son of a well-to-do glass merchant and a former southern belle, he had grown up under extremely comfortable circumstances in New York City around the time of the Civil War. Something of a momma's boy, he became the target of bullies on at least one occasion. "I was nervous and timid," he later confessed. Plagued by asthma and poor eyesight, he was content to while away his youthful days reading books and gathering animal specimens for his private natural science collection. "I have got four mice," he excitedly wrote his sister at the age of nine, "two white skinned, red eyed velvety creatures, very tame for I let them run all over me, they trie to get down the back of my neck and under my vest, and two brown skinned, black eyed, soft as the others, but male and female. I keep them in different cages."

As his health worsened, Roosevelt's father, Theodore Sr., sternly advised him to take matters into his own hands. "Theodore," he instructed his son, "you have the mind but not the body, and without the help of the body the mind cannot go as far as it should. You *must* make your body. It is hard drudgery to make one's body but I know you will do it." According to one family account, young "Teedie" reportedly looked up at his father in agreement and exclaimed, "*I'll make my body!*"

He proved as good as his word. Embarking on a strenuous physical regimen that included weight lifting and boxing, Roosevelt was able to work himself into robust shape. "He came out of his shell, made friends, became sociable toward girls, and showed the first signs of leadership," records his biographer John Milton Cooper. "Even without embellishment, his boyhood did lend itself to an exemplary tale of self-improvement."

This uplift continued at Harvard where Roosevelt enrolled as a freshman in 1876. Not only did he become an academic standout, earning Phi Beta Kappa and magna cum laude honors upon graduation, he also excelled at a wide variety of extracurricular activities: secretary for the Hasty Pudding Club, editor of the *Harvard Advocate*, librarian for the Porcellian Club, vice president of the Natural History Club, and runner-up for the campus lightweight boxing championship. More important, he began research on a book about naval warfare during the War of 1812 that would later be published to widespread critical acclaim. But whatever measure of personal satisfaction Roosevelt derived from these accomplishments was leavened by the fact that his beloved father could not be there to share in them. For Theodore Sr. had died unexpectedly of stomach cancer during the fall semester of his son's sophomore year.

"He has just been buried," Roosevelt anguished after the funeral. "I shall never forget . . . the dull inert sorrow, during which I felt as if I had been stunned, or as if part of my life had been taken away, and the two moments of sharp, bitter agony, when I kissed the dear, dead face and realized that he would never again on this earth speak to me or greet me with his loving smile, and then when I heard the sound of the first clod dropping on the coffin holding the one I loved dearest on earth. . . . I feel that if it were not for the certainty, that as he himself has so often said, 'he is not dead but gone before,' I should almost perish. With the help of my God I will try to lead such a life as he would have wished."

As intense as these feelings of grief were, Roosevelt was able to set them aside in 1878 when he met the girl of his proverbial dreams. Alice Hathaway Lee was the daughter of a socially prominent Boston banker and by all accounts intelligent, warm, charming, and physically attractive. Establishing herself as "the light" in Roosevelt's life, she would formally become his wife in 1880. "I never conceived it possible that there could be such a bright, sunny, unselfish girl," Roosevelt wrote in his diary. "I can never express how I love her, and that if I should love her as much and as tenderly it would not be nearly as much as she deserves; I never can understand how I won her!"

Yet the hand of this vivacious young woman was not the only thing Roosevelt won during this period. In 1881 he was elected to the New York state legislature as a Republican assemblyman representing a "silk stocking" district in Manhattan. He later claimed that his decision to enter politics was based on the desire "to belong to the governing class, not to be governed." In any event, Roosevelt wasted no time in making a dramatic impression upon his fellow lawmakers. "All of a sudden the door opened and in rushed Mr. Roosevelt," remembered one bemused colleague of an early legislative meeting he attended with the future commander-in-chief. "He made his way up and sat right down in front of the chairman of the conference. He had on an enormous overcoat and had a silk hat in his hand. As soon as opportunity was given, he addressed the chairman and he pulled off his overcoat and he was in full dress. He had been to a dinner. He had on his eyeglasses and his gold fob.

His hair was parted in the middle. . . . We almost shouted with laughter to think that the most veritable representative of the New York dude had come to the chamber."

Notwithstanding his dandy appearance, Roosevelt established himself as a tough but effective legislator, someone who was willing to take on New York's powerful Tammany Hall machine and survive politically to talk about it. Largely due to his tenacious efforts, a bill creating the state's first civil service system earned passage through the legislature. "If efficiency is left solely to bad men and if virtue is confined solely to inefficient men, the result cannot be happy," Roosevelt later wrote. "When I entered politics there were, as there always had been—and as there always will be—any number of bad men in politics who were thoroughly efficient, and any number of good men who would like to have done lofty things in politics but who were thoroughly inefficient. If I wished to accomplish anything for the country, my business was to combine decency and efficiency; to be a thoroughly practical man of high ideals who did his best to reduce those ideals to actual practice. This was my ideal, and to the best of my ability I strove to live up to it."

All the ideals in the world could not prepare him for the immense personal loss he was about to experience, however. In 1884 his wife suddenly died from Bright's disease after giving birth to a healthy eight-pound daughter named Alice at the couple's Manhattan home. Just a few hours later his mother, the former Martha Bulloch, succumbed to typhoid fever in the very same room. "There is a curse on this house," his brother Elliot declared.

Devastated by these twin tragedies, Roosevelt gave up his legislative seat and trekked westward into the untamed wilderness of the Dakota Territory, where he became a cattle rancher. This abrupt move, which necessitated that his infant daughter be temporarily placed in the care of his sister Bamie, won him no popularity contests. As he confided to a family member, "I suppose all of our friends the unco' good are as angry as ever with me; they had best not express their discontent to my face unless they wish to hear very plain English. I am sorry my political career should be over, but after all it makes very little difference."

In spite of the emotional baggage he was carrying, Roosevelt quickly acclimated himself to the rugged ways of the Badlands. "We led a free and hardy life with horse and rifle," he later recalled. "We worked under the scorching midsummer sun, when the wide plains shimmered and wavered in the heat, and we knew the freezing misery of riding night guard around the cattle in the late fall roundup. . . . There were monotonous days, as we guided the trail cattle, or the beef herds, hour after hour at the slowest of walks; and minutes or hours teeming with excitement as we stopped stampedes or swam the herds across rivers treacherous with quicksand, or brimmed with running ice. We knew toil and hardship and hunger and thirst; and we saw men die, violent deaths as they worked among the horses and cattle, or fought in evil feuds with one another, but we felt the beat of hardy life in our veins, and ours was the glory of work and the joy of living."

Still, as much as Roosevelt relished this new cowboy lifestyle, he could not resist the temptation to seek elective office once more. In 1886 he returned home to run for mayor of New York City as the official Republican nominee. He hit the campaign trail with his usual high energy and enthusiasm, claiming he was a candidate for clean government and civil service reform. "Though I am a strong party man," he averred, "if I find a corrupt public official, if he were the most prominent politician in the Republican party, I would take off his head." As it turned out, it was Roosevelt who had his head handed to him politically: he finished third in a three-way race with Tammany

Democrat Abram S. Hewitt and the social reformer Henry George.

To pile insult upon injury, the following spring Joseph Keppler's *Puck* magazine, a publication dedicated to putting the rich and powerful in their place, printed an archly humorous piece calling for Roosevelt's retirement from politics. "Be happy, Mr. Roosevelt, be happy while you may," the magazine submitted. "You are young—yours is the time of roses—the time of illusions. You see not the rouge on old cheeks, the powder on the wrinkled forehead. Do not let it annoy you if we smile. You have heard of Pitt, of Alexander Hamilton, of Randolph Churchill, and of other men who were young and yet who, so to speak, go there just the same. Bright visions float before your eyes of what the Party can and may do for you. We wish you a gradual and gentle awakening. We fear the Party cannot do much for you. You are not the timber of which Presidents are made."

Meanwhile Roosevelt married his former childhood sweetheart and next-door neighbor Edith Kermit Carow in London. Their union would produce four sons and another daughter. "She is the most cultivated, best-read girl I know," he once said of his second wife. Roosevelt also spent the next several years in a series of high-profile bureaucratic positions, beginning with his appointment as a U.S. civil service commissioner in 1889. "You can guarantee that I intend to hew to the line and let the chips fall where they will," he told a reporter upon accepting the job. Making good on that promise, Roosevelt had a significant hand in doubling the number of federal jobs that were placed under the protected civil service list during his tenure. In the process he proved himself a scourge to political timeservers everywhere. "I do not see how any man can watch the effects of the spoils system," he wrote, "both upon the poor unfortunates who suffer from it and upon the almost equally unfortunate men who deem that they benefit by it, without regarding the whole thing in its entirety as a curse to our institutions. It is a curse to the public service and it is a still greater curse to Congress, for it puts a premium upon every Congressman turning spoilsmonger instead of statesman."

Hungering for still greater challenges, in 1895 Roosevelt accepted an offer to become New York City police commissioner. Charged with "cleaning up" a notoriously corrupt police force, Roosevelt substantially raised professional standards, improved staff morale, and generally rooted out malcontents from positions of authority. To ensure that his directives were being carried out, he would frequently journey out into the city streets to monitor his officers in action. "Policemen were soon watching nervously over their shoulders at night for a dark-cloaked figure with blinding white teeth," one friendly biographer later noted. Nor was Roosevelt above igniting public controversy. Although he professed to be no prohibitionist, he rigidly enforced a local law banning the sale of alcoholic beverages on Sunday. "I do not deal with public sentiment," he explained. "I deal with the law. I am going to see if we cannot break the license forthwith of any saloon keeper who sells on Sunday. This applies just as much to the biggest hotel as to the smallest grogshop. To allow a lax enforcement of the law means to allow it to be enforced just as far as the individual members of the police force are willing to wink at its evasion. Woe to the policeman who exposes himself to the taint of corruption."

In 1897 Roosevelt was tapped by President William McKinley to serve as assistant secretary of the navy in his new administration. While he demonstrated exceptional competence in the day-to-day running of the department, his personal exuberance sometimes rubbed his boss, Secretary of the Navy John D. Long, the wrong way. "He is full of suggestions," Long assessed, "many of which are of great value, and his spirit and forceful habit is a good tonic; but the very devil seems to possess him—distributing ships, ordering ammunition which there is no means to move to places where there is no means to store it; sending messages to Congress for immediate legislation authorizing the enlistment of an unlimited number of seamen."

As armed conflict threatened to erupt between the United States and Spain over the sinking of the *USS Maine* in Havana Harbor in 1898, Roosevelt played a key role in preparing the navy for eventual action. "In the event of declaration of war [against] Spain," he cabled Commodore George Dewey in the Pacific on February 25, "your duty will be to see that the Spanish squadron does not leave the Asiatic coast, and then offensive operations in the Philippines." After hostilities were declared on April 11, Dewey did as instructed and was able to deliver a decisive blow against the Spanish fleet in Manila Bay.

But Roosevelt was not satisfied with sitting out the duration of the war at a safe desk job in the Navy Department. He resigned his post as assistant secretary and proceeded to raise a volunteer cavalry unit to fight against the Spaniards in Cuba. Dubbed the Rough Riders, this colorful ragtag outfit of cowboys, Native Americans, Texas Rangers, Ivy Leaguers, and lumberjacks drew national attention on July 1 when it successfully stormed an entrenched enemy position at Kettle Hill along the San Juan Ridge near Santiago. "I think we suffered more heavily than the Spanish did in killed and wounded (though we also captured scores of prisoners)," Roosevelt later wrote of the famous attack he led. "It would have been very extraordinary if the reverse was the case, for we did the charging, and to carry earthworks on foot with dismounted cavalry, when these earthworks are held by unbroken infantry armed with the best modern rifles, is a serious task."

At war's end Roosevelt returned home a full-fledged military hero and immediately put himself up as a candidate for governor of New York. He had little difficulty in securing the Republican party's nomination as his war record, personal charm, and celebrity status made him appear a sure winner. And come the fall election he was, as he defeated Democrat Augustus van Wyck by a comfortable margin. "I have played it in bull luck this summer," he wrote afterward. "First, to get into the war; and then to get out of it; then to get elected."

In his brief tenure as governor, Roosevelt did his utmost to steer an independent course, which got him into hot water with state GOP boss Thomas C. Platt. Platt had strongly endorsed Roosevelt during his gubernatorial run and for his trouble was expecting patronage and various other political favors. Unwilling to play along, Roosevelt unwittingly set in motion a chain of events that would ultimately make him president. Platt, furious that the new governor was paying him so little heed, plotted to remove Roosevelt from the statewide political scene by maneuvering him into the vice presidency.

Platt's machinations paid off at the 1900 Republican National Convention in Philadelphia when Roosevelt was picked as William McKinley's running mate against a Democratic ticket of William Jennings Bryan and Adlai E. Stevenson. But not everyone embraced his selection. "Doesn't any of you realize that there's only one life between that madman and the Presidency?" asked Senator Mark Hanna of Ohio. Although underwhelmed at the prospect of becoming vice president considering the constitutional restrictions placed on the office, Roosevelt resigned himself to acting for the good of the party. "I am completely reconciled and I believe it all for the best," he informed his longtime friend and political confidant Henry Cabot Lodge. "I should be a conceited fool if I was discontented with the nomination when it came in such a fashion."

To show that he meant it, Roosevelt immersed himself in the campaign, stumping with considerable vigor around the country on McKinley's behalf. In fairness, the incumbent president did not require much assistance. The combination of the recent victory over Spain and a prosperous domestic economy was more than enough to ensure defeat for the Democrats in November. The final poll numbers tell the story: McKinley won 52 percent of the popular vote while carrying 28 states for a grand total of 292 electoral votes. In contrast, Bryan could claim only 17 states for 155 electoral votes and 46 percent of the popular vote. "I am delighted to have been on the national ticket in this great historic contest," Roosevelt enthused after the victory.

Having thus loyally served McKinley in his successful bid for a second term, Roosevelt settled into his new position with a notable lack of enthusiasm. "I have now . . .," he dejectedly wrote, "'taken the veil.'" So bored was he with the vice presidency that he immediately began preparing to become a lawyer after he left office. "Of course, I may go on in public life," he allowed, "but equally of course it is unlikely, and what I have seen of the careers of public men has given me an absolute horror of the condition of the politician whose day has passed, who by some turn of the kaleidoscope is thrown into the background; and who then haunts the fields of his former activity as a pale shadow of what he once was; or else who finds himself adrift in the hopeless position of the man who says he can do anything but who therefore can do nothing."

An assassin's bullets would force him to abandon these plans prematurely. On September 6, 1901, President McKinley was shot point-blank in the chest and in the stomach by an unemployed steelworker and anarchist named Leon Czolgosz while visiting the Pan-American Exposition in Buffalo, New York. The president died of his wounds eight days later. "It is a dreadful thing to come into the Presidency this way," Roosevelt later admitted, "but it would be a far worse thing to be morbid about it. Here is the task, and I have got to do it to the best of my ability; and that's all there is about it."

Roosevelt immediately engaged in a flurry of activity, issuing executive orders, holding informal press conferences, and meeting with various constituent groups. "His offices were crowded with people, mostly reformers, all day long, and the President did his work among them with little privacy and much rejoicing," remembered the muckraking journalist and close personal friend Lincoln Steffens. "He strode triumphant around among us, talking and shaking hands, dictating and signing letters, and laughing. Washington, the whole country, was in mourning, and no doubt the President felt he should hold himself down; he didn't; he tried to, but his joy showed in every word and movement. . . . With his feet, his fists, his face and his free words he laughed at his luck."

That his presidency was destined to stand apart seemed a given, especially after Roosevelt played host to the famed African-American educator and social activist Booker T. Washington at a White House dinner on October 16. Labeling it "the most damnable outrage that has ever been perpetrated by any citizen of the United States," white Southerners lashed out in anger. They felt the gesture undermined the system of racial segregation that had been in place in their region since Reconstruction. "White men of the South, how do you like it?" the *New Orleans Times-Democrat* asked sarcastically. "When Mr. Roosevelt sits down to dinner with a Negro, he declares the Negro is the social equal of the 'white.'" Anticipating a negative reaction, Roosevelt had gone ahead with the dinner anyway, thereby reinforcing his image as a leader willing to challenge the status quo. "I respect [Washington] greatly and believe in the work he has done," he later explained. "I have consulted so much with him it seemed to me that it was natural to ask him to dinner to talk over his work, and the very fact that I felt a moment's qualm on inviting him because of his color made me ashamed of myself and made me hasten to send the invitation. . . . As things have turned out, I am very glad that I asked him, for the clamor aroused by the act makes me feel as if the act was necessary."

More controversy awaited Roosevelt when he decided to take on the issue of economic concentration in American society. Since the industrial expansion following the Civil War, a number of giant corporations had come into being, now accounting for 40 percent of the nation's manufacturing capital. With Darwinian precision, companies like John D. Rockefeller's Standard Oil had managed to establish near monopolies in their fields. They employed such practices as price-fixing, stock manipulation, and pooling agreements to eliminate their competition. "The growth of these large companies during the 1890s," observes the historian Lewis L. Gould, "renewed fears that the growth of trusts and holding companies might stifle economic opportunity for the middle class."

Attuned to these concerns, Roosevelt made a point of addressing them in his first State of the Union message to Congress on December 3. After a lengthy tribute to his slain predecessor, a man he described as "a good and great President," Roosevelt called for greater government supervision of corporations. "There is a widespread conviction in the minds of the American people that the great corporations known as trusts are in certain of their features and tendencies hurtful to the general welfare," he contended. "This springs from no spirit of envy or uncharitableness, nor lack of pride in the great industrial achievements that have placed this country at the head of the nations struggling for commercial supremacy. . . . It is based upon sincere conviction that combination and concentration should be, not prohibited, but supervised and within reasonable limits controlled; and in my judgment this conviction is right."

He continued: "It is no limitation upon property rights or freedom of contract to require that when men receive from Government, the privilege of doing business under corporate form, which frees them from individual responsibility and enables them to call into their enterprises the capital of the public, they shall do so upon absolutely truthful representations as to the value of the property in which the capital is to be invested. Corporations engaged in inter-state commerce should be regulated if they are found to exercise a license working to the public injury. It should be as much the aim of those for social betterment to rid the business world of crimes of cunning as to rid the entire body politic of crimes of violence. Great corporations exist only because they are created and safeguarded by our institutions, and it is therefore our right and our duty to see they work in harmony with these institutions."

While Roosevelt received praise in many quarters for his perceived "safe" and "temperate" approach to the trust question, others were not at all satisfied. On the far right of the political spectrum the president was accused of promoting "government ownership" of private property, while on the far left he was ridiculed for being too accommodating to corporate interests. As the humorist Finley Peter Dunne's "Mr. Dooley" interpreted the message, "Th' trusts are heejoous monsthers built up be th' enlightened intherprise iv th' men that hae done so much to advance progress in our beloved country. On wan hand I wud stamp thim undher fut; on th' other hand not so fast."

Regardless of the reaction, in confronting the controversial issue head-on Roosevelt had placed himself at the head of a growing reform movement taking hold in American society at the turn of the century. Called progressivism, this politically moderate agglomeration of mostly young middle-class professionals sought to remove the rougher edges from urban industrial life and promote greater democratization at federal, state, and local levels. Among the major reforms progressives advocated were the elimination of child labor, improved factory conditions, environmental conservation, the right to recall public officials, the direct primary election, tariff relief, the elimination of secret railroad rebates, and federal oversight of trusts. "Struggling to redefine the meaning of American democracy in the age of corporate capitalism," writes the historian Stephen J. Diner, progressives "asked how government could protect its citizens against the negative effects of industrialism and economic concentration and how the polity could use government to regain control of the nation's destiny."

On this latter point Roosevelt was only too willing to lead. For, in his opinion, "malefactors of great wealth" like Andrew Carnegie, John D. Rockefeller, and Morgan held too great an influence on the economic and political affairs of the nation. "In no other country in the world had such enormous fortunes been gained," he noted. "In no other country in the world was such power held by the men who had gained these fortunes; and these men almost always, worked through, and by means of, the giant corporations which they controlled. The power of the mighty industrial overlords of the country had increased with giant strides, while the methods of controlling them, or checking abuses by them, on the part of the people, through the Government, remained archaic and therefore practically impotent."

Seeking to balance the scales, Roosevelt patiently awaited the right opportunity to reassert federal authority. The Northern Securities case provided him with just such an opening.

A vast holding company that had been formed by Morgan and fellow magnates Edward H. Harriman and James J. Hill to monopolize rail traffic in the Northwest, Northern Securities appeared poised to extend its financial tentacles still further. As one newspaper editor warned, "One railroad after another will

A Robust Fight: TR takes on the railroads.

slide gently into their grasp until any passenger anywhere who objects to traveling on their lines can take a trolley car or walk."

Determined to prevent this scenario from occurring, Roosevelt instructed his attorney general, Philander C. Knox, to begin legal proceedings against the company for being in noncompliance with the Sherman Anti-Trust Act, a landmark piece of legislation that an earlier generation of reformers had persuaded Congress to pass in 1890. The act deemed it illegal to form a trust or any other business combination that resulted in the restraint of trade or commerce. Due to vague phrasing in the law and the apparent unwillingness of federal officials to prosecute, the act proved more a curiosity than an effective instrument in checking the growth of trusts in the decade to follow. But this poor track record would soon be reversed when on

February 19, 1902, Knox publicly revealed the government's intention to prosecute Morgan and his business partners over Northern Securities.

"Some time ago," he said in a released statement to the press, "the President requested an opinion as to the legality of this merger, and I have recently given him one to the effect, that, in my judgment, it violates the provisions of the Sherman act of 1890, whereupon he directed that suitable action should be taken to have the question judicially determined. A bill in equity is now in course of preparation, which will be filed within a very short time, which will ask that the merger effected, through the exchange of shares of the Northern Securities Company for shares of the two railroad companies, be dissolved, and such shares ordered re-exchanged to restore the stocks of the two railroad companies to their original holders.

"The two railroad companies, the Northern Securities Company, J. Pierpont Morgan, and James J. Hill, and their associates, stockholders in the two companies, will be the defendants in the bill."

Word of the legal action caught Wall Street completely by surprise. As the *Hartford Daily Courant* noted, "There has been an assumption . . . which was carefully fostered in the interest of a revival of speculation, that the public opposition to financial combinations was more apparent than real, and that a demonstration of the public utility of these combinations would secure them against interference even where technically open to construction of illegality. This morning's announcement from Washington was, therefore, a rude shock to all this optimistic sentiment that has been carefully nurtured in the financial districts."

Still, many in the business community chose to adopt a subdued wait-and-see attitude. "There is no occasion for any alarm over what may be accomplished by the President's proposed action," reported one insider. "The fact remains that, no matter what is done, this consolidation is going to become an accomplished fact in one form or another. If the present merger is contrary to law, a merger which obeys the law will be effected. It is absolutely impossible to stop these consolidations so long as they are formed for legitimate purposes."

As for the main target of the federal anti-trust suit, J. P. Morgan saw fit to air his displeasure in person at a tense White House meeting on February 23. "If we have done anything wrong," he told Roosevelt, "send your man to my man and they can fix it up." Annoyed by Morgan's dismissive attitude, Roosevelt informed the tycoon that such a tactic "was impossible" and that his primary goal in this instance was "to stop illegal mergers." Ever the shrewd business operator, Morgan asked whether his "other interests" would be threatened by similar legal action. "Certainly not," answered Roosevelt, "unless we find out they have done something that we regard as wrong." Doubtless dissatisfied with this response, Morgan departed from the executive mansion empty-handed, leaving the president to muse over what had just transpired. "Mr. Morgan," Roosevelt concluded, "could not help regarding me as a big rival operator, who either intended to ruin all his interests or else could be induced to come to an agreement to ruin none."

As events unfolded, the "rival operator" would have the last laugh. On March 14, 1904, the U.S. Supreme Court sided with Roosevelt and the government when it handed down a 5-to-4 decision affirming a lower court ruling dissolving the Northern Securities Company. In presenting the majority opinion, Justice John M. Harlan asserted that the company was in clear violation of the Sherman Anti-Trust Act and therefore had to be dealt with to the fullest possible extent of the law. "The mere existence of such a combination," he wrote, "and the power acquired by the holding company as trustee for the combination, constitute a menace to and a restraint upon that freedom of commerce which Congress intended to recognize and protect, and which the public is entitled to have protected."

Morgan did as the high court instructed, dissolving the Northern Securities Company in an expeditious manner. While unhappy with the final verdict, he successfully avoided further run-ins with Roosevelt over his vast business empire. Still, part of him could never quite get over the humiliation Roosevelt had dealt him with Northern Securities. After Roosevelt had stepped down from the presidency and journeyed to Africa for a well-publicized hunting expedition, Morgan was reported to have remarked, "America expects that every lion will do his duty."

Having thus achieved a great victory, Roosevelt acquired the reputation for being a "trustbuster." While his administration did go on to prosecute several other combinations, including Standard Oil and the American Tobacco Company, it would be inaccurate to apply such a label to him. Roosevelt had no strong desire to see large corporations broken up. He believed such a course of action to be foolishly impractical, given the complex nature of the country's burgeoning industrial economy. "Under present-day conditions it is as necessary to have corporations in the business world as it is to have organizations, unions, among wage workers," he told an audience in Providence, Rhode Island, in 1903. "Exactly as labor organizations, when managed intelligently and in a spirit of justice and fair play, are of very great service not only to the wage-workers, but to the whole community, as has been shown again and again in the history of many such organizations; so wealth, not merely individual, but corporate, when used aright is not merely beneficial to the community as a whole, but is absolutely essential to the upbuilding of such a series of communities as those whose citizens I am now addressing."

Yet when big business grew corrupt or worked at cross-purposes with society's common good, Roosevelt maintained that the federal government was morally and legally obligated to step in and provide swift remedial action. "The great corporations which we have grown to speak of rather loosely as trusts are the creatures of the State, and the State not only has the right to control them, but it is duty bound to control them wherever the need of such control is shown. There is clearly need of supervision—need to possess the power of regulation of these great corporations through the representatives of the public—wherever, as in our country at the present time, business corporations become so very powerful alike for beneficent work and for work that is not always beneficent. It is idle to say that there is no need for such supervision."

As a further sign of how seriously Roosevelt was committed to regulation, his administration successfully pushed through legislation that expedited the cumbersome manner in which anti-trust cases were then being tried in federal courts. It also established a Bureau of Corporations to investigate possible misdeeds committed by businesses engaged in interstate commerce. "I wish to do everything in my power to aid every honest businessman, and the dishonest businessman I wish to punish simply as I would punish the dishonest man of any type," Roosevelt said.

Due in part to the popularity of his anti-trust actions, Roosevelt achieved a landslide reelection victory in 1904. He carried the majority of electoral votes in thirty-two states as against thirteen for his overmatched challenger, Democrat Alton B. Parker of New York. "I am stunned by the overwhelming victory we have won," he enthused to his son Kermit. "I had no conception that such a thing was possible. . . . I have the greatest popular majority ever given to a candidate for President."

But in his jubilation over at last winning the presidency in his own right, Roosevelt committed a grave political error. He told reporters that "under no circumstances" would he seek a third term. While he would come to deeply regret this statement, at the time it seemed the perfectly logical thing to do. "I feel very strongly that, at least in our country, a public man's usefulness in the highest position becomes in the end impaired by the mere fact of too long continuance in that position," he wrote a British acquaintance. "After eight years in the Presidency, not only is it unwise for other reasons to re-elect a man, but it is inadvisable because it is almost certain that someone can be found with the same principles, who, from the mere fact that he is someone else, can better succeed in putting those principles into practice."

That special "someone" whom Roosevelt was counting on to continue his progressive political policies was William Howard Taft of Ohio. A former U.S. solicitor general and governor-general of the Philippines, Taft was considered Roosevelt's most able and trusted lieutenant. But he had little ambition for attaining high elected office. Taft's lifelong dream was to sit on the Supreme Court, much to the chagrin of his politically ambitious wife Nellie. She wanted to become First Lady, whether Taft liked the idea or not. Thus pressured by both his wife and Roosevelt into accepting the 1908 Republican nomination for the presidency, Taft reluctantly acceded. And with Roosevelt's "full backing" he went on to crush perennial Democratic presidential candidate William Jennings Bryan in the November election.

It didn't take long for Roosevelt to sour on his successor. Lacking the political acumen and skill that Roosevelt so deftly employed in his presidency, Taft soon alienated the entire progressive wing of the Republican party. Specifically he torpedoed a progressive-led effort in Congress to lower tariff rates and aligned himself politically with conservative business elements. "The truth is," Roosevelt complained, "that we have had no national leadership of any kind since election day 1908." To remedy the situation, Roosevelt publicly announced his intention to challenge Taft for the GOP presidential nomination in 1912. "My hat is in the ring!" he thunderously proclaimed. "The fight is on and I am stripped to the buff."

While Roosevelt easily bested Taft in popularity among rank-and-file Republicans nationwide, he did not control the party's ruling national committee, which threw its support behind the incumbent president. Thus Roosevelt was denied the nomination at the Republican convention in Chicago. Feeling cheated, he decided to switch his political allegiance to the newly formed Progressive party, under whose banner he launched a spirited campaign to recapture the White House. "We stand at Armageddon," he told supporters, "and we battle for the Lord!"

Even before he officially bolted from the GOP, Roosevelt had articulated a bold new vision for political and economic reform he called the "New Nationalism." Drawing from his earlier experiences with Morgan and the trusts, his proposed program called for selfless individual behavior and greater government supervision of big business. "The struggle for liberty has always been, and must always be to take from some one man or class of men the right to enjoy power, or wealth, or position, or immunity, which has not been earned by service," he said. "The man who wrongly holds that every human right is secondary to his profit must now give way to the advocate of human welfare. . . . The New Nationalism puts the national need before sectional or personal advantage."

His message failed to register with enough voters on election day. A reformist Democrat named Woodrow Wilson held on to the bulk of his party's base to score a resounding 435-to-88 victory over Roosevelt in the electoral college. Despite the loss, Roosevelt recorded the greatest showing for a third-party presidential candidate in modern American history, securing 27 percent of the popular vote to Wilson's 42 percent. Taft meanwhile could muster only eight electoral votes and 23 percent of the popular vote in his own lackluster reelection bid. In retrospect it seems probable, as the historian James Chace has pointed out, that the "vote totals for Roosevelt and Taft together indicate a Republican victory over Wilson had TR received the Republican nomination in Chicago." But the Republican split over progressivism rendered the issue moot. As Roosevelt magnanimously declared, "We have fought the good fight, we have kept the faith, and we have nothing to regret."

Roosevelt's remaining years were devoted largely to the issue of military preparedness. "I advocate military preparedness not for the sake of war," he stated, "but for the sake of safeguarding this nation against war, so long as that is possible, and of guaranteeing its honor and safety if war should nevertheless come. We hope ultimately the day will come on this earth when wars will cease. But at present the realization of that hope seems as far in the future as the realization of that other hope, that some day in the future all crime shall cease."

When the United States declared war on Germany and the Central Powers in 1917, Roosevelt approached President Wilson with an offer to organize and lead a volunteer army unit in France. But Wilson flatly turned him down. He recoiled at the notion of a fifty-eight-year-old former commander-in-chief dodging enemy bullets at the front lines. "I need not assure you," Wilson informed Roosevelt, "that my conclusions were based entirely upon imperative considerations of public policy and not upon personal or private choice."

Although bitterly disappointed, Roosevelt took some measure of solace by closely following the military exploits of his four sons, all of whom volunteered for combat service. "You are having your crowded hours of glorious life," he wrote Theodore Jr., "you have seized the great chance, as it was seized by those who fought at Gettysburg, and Waterloo, and Agincourt, and Arbela and Marathon." Tragically, not all of his sons would return home alive. Quenten, the youngest, was killed in action when the plane he was piloting was shot down in a dog-fight with seven German Fokkers. For Roosevelt, Quenten's passing represented a crushing personal loss that no passage of time could heal. "I would not for all the world have had him fail fearlessly to do his duty, and to tread his allotted path, high of heart, even though it led to the gates of death," he maintained. "But it is useless for me to pretend that it is not very bitter to see that good, gallant, tender-hearted boy, leave life at its crest . . . and such happiness, and certainly an honorable and perhaps distinguished career."

Roosevelt himself would meet his final reward at his Long Island estate in the early morning hours of January 6, 1919, the victim of a coronary embolism. "The old lion is dead," his son Archie somberly announced. During his presidency Roosevelt's distinct roar could be heard in every corner of American society, including the opulent boardrooms of Wall Street, where J. P. Morgan presided. "I greatly enjoy the exercise of power," Roosevelt once stated. And he meant it. By successfully taking Morgan to court over the Northern Securities merger, Roosevelt demonstrated that the federal government was "more powerful" than any single corporation and that "rich man and poor man were held equal before the law." It was exactly this kind of bold assertion of executive leadership that would prompt a family friend to observe, "There is no one like Theodore."

Indeed, there wasn't.

---★---

CHAPTER SIX

Saving Democracy

Franklin Roosevelt and the Destroyers-for-Bases Deal

A s a leader, Franklin Delano Roosevelt frowned upon rash impulsiveness. He preferred instead to weigh carefully the pros and cons of a considered action before arriving at a final decision—often, his political enemies charged, in a dissembling and manipulative way. "I am a juggler," Roosevelt once boasted. "I never let my right hand know what my left hand does." But the crush of events appeared to be conspiring against the usually buoyant commander-in-chief in the frenzied summer of 1940. France had fallen to the marauding armies of Adolf Hitler in June, and a Nazi invasion of Great Britain appeared imminent as the Luftwaffe was on the verge of delivering a knockout blow against the badly outgunned and outnumbered Royal Air Force (RAF). "A few more weeks of this," wrote one American observer, "and Britain would have no organized defense of its skies. The invasion could almost certainly succeed." British Prime Minister Winston Churchill spent most of these critical days frantically pleading with Roosevelt to provide whatever arms and materiel he could spare to ward off the expected German military onslaught.

In particular, Churchill requested that a number of older American naval destroyers be handed over to his country immediately to help protect the English coastline and prevent German U-boats from sinking merchant ships carrying vital war supplies. "Destroyers are frighteningly vulnerable to air bombing," Churchill wrote Roosevelt in late July, "and yet they must be held in the air bombing area to prevent a seaborne invasion. We could not keep up the present [high] rate of casualties for long, and if we cannot get a substantial reinforcement, the whole fate of the war may be decided by this minor and easily remediable factor. I cannot understand why, with the position as it is, you do not send me at least 50 to 60 of your oldest destroyers."

For Roosevelt the stakes could not have been higher. If Britain fell, all of Western Europe would be under Hitler's iron heel, with the United States and the Western Hemisphere next in line as targets for conquest. "In times like these—in times of great tension, of great crisis—the compass of the world narrows to a single fact," Roosevelt told a nationwide radio audience in July. "The fact which dominates our world is the fact of armed aggression, the fact of successful armed aggression, aimed at the form of Government, the kind of society that we in the United States have chosen and established for ourselves. It is a fact which no one longer doubts—which no one is longer able to ignore."

Yet to come so openly to Britain's aid with the destroyers risked violating existing neutrality laws while seriously jeopardizing Roosevelt's chances at winning reelection for an unprecedented third term that fall, as Americans overwhelmingly favored staying out of the war. Nevertheless a decision had to be made and made quickly. The fate of Britain and "the institutions of democracy in the Western World" hung precariously in the balance. The time for juggling had clearly passed.

Long derided as an individual with "a first-class temperament" but "a second-class intellect," Roosevelt spent his entire life defying these low expectations. Born on January 30, 1882, he enjoyed a relatively happy childhood on his family's rural estate in Hyde Park, New York. With his every whim catered to by his doting parents, James and Sara Delano, Roosevelt came across to many observers as a callow youth. "He is a well meaning, nice young fellow, but light . . .," remarked Senator Henry Cabot Lodge of Massachusetts. This surface immaturity, however, masked a fierce personal determination to become, in his mother's words, "an upstanding American." Modeling himself after his distant cousin Theodore Roosevelt, the twenty-sixth president of the United States, young Franklin hoped someday to excel in the world of politics. In his zeal to be like the Rough Rider, he often went to extremes, punctuating his speech with words like "Bully!" and wearing a pince-nez. All the same, he wasn't a new version of his Republican cousin, and this became abundantly clear when in 1910 he won election to the New York State Senate as a Democrat.

Preferring to keep his own counsel, Franklin conveyed the unfortunate impression that he was "looking down his nose" at his fellow lawmakers. "Awfully arrogant fellow, that Roosevelt," complained one political insider. Despite this standoffish behavior, he was able to establish a noteworthy record as a progressive reformer, supporting women's suffrage, farm-improvement loans, and the direct election of U.S. senators. As he gained experience, he shed his earlier reticence and came to be more outgoing in his dealings with his political peers. In the process of doing so, he became "a prime mover" in state Democratic circles. So impressive was his performance that in 1913 he caught the eye of new President Woodrow Wilson. The former New

Jersey governor appointed Roosevelt assistant secretary of the navy, the same position his illustrious cousin had held at the start of the Spanish-American War in 1898. Now seated at a major center of power in the federal government, Roosevelt gained invaluable knowledge about how to run a large bureaucracy. "He became keenly aware, like so many young progressive administrators, of the need for greater efficiency in government, and it was to become a major theme in his political speeches," noted his biographer Frank Freidel.

All the while Roosevelt was attempting to raise a family of five children with his independent-minded wife Eleanor, a fifth cousin whom he had married in 1905. "Nothing like keeping the name in the family," joked Theodore Roosevelt at their wedding ceremony. Unfortunately theirs was not a happy union. Differences in style, temperament, and interests compelled the two to live separate lives. Nor was it conducive to marital harmony that Eleanor was quite forward in expressing her political views. A staunch liberal activist, she did not hesitate to criticize her husband when she felt he had failed to live up to his stated commitments to minorities, workers, or the poor. "He might have been happier with a wife who was completely uncritical," she later confessed. "That I was never able to be, and he had to find it in some other people. Nevertheless, I think I sometimes acted as a spur, even though the spurring was not always wanted or welcome."

Franklin required no such goading when he accepted the Democratic nomination for the vice presidency in 1920. A surprise candidate, he was selected chiefly "to lure progressive Republicans attracted by the Roosevelt name." His famous last name commanded considerable national attention during the race, but it did not translate into votes. On election day Roosevelt and his running mate, Governor James Cox of Ohio, were swamped by the GOP ticket of Warren Harding and

Calvin Coolidge, 404 to 127 in the electoral college. Following the crushing defeat, Roosevelt left the public stage and dabbled for a year in a series of moderately successful business enterprises. Although this less hectic way of life had its rewards, his heart remained in politics. He looked forward to running again, either for a U.S. Senate seat in 1922 or some other high-profile office. The vicissitudes of fate, however, had something else in store for him.

In August 1921, while vacationing with his family in Maine, Roosevelt was stricken with polio. The dreaded disease, which can cause severe pain and permanent paralysis of skeletal muscles, left him without full use of his legs for the rest of his life. "I'll never forget the terror I felt," his son Elliot later recalled. "I fully expected Father to die at any moment. He was so still— so very still—and it seemed that my world was coming to an end." While such a malady might have caused lesser men to fall into a pit of despair and self-pity, Roosevelt stubbornly refused the temptation. Instead he embarked on a program of intense physical rehabilitation that allowed him to stand on his feet with metal braces for extended periods of time. The steady improvement in his health also allowed him to reenter politics.

In 1928 he sought the governorship of New York and won a close race against the state's popular attorney general, Albert Ottinger. During the contest Roosevelt was able to persuade the press not to report on his disability, fearing that voters would instinctively shy away from a candidate in a wheelchair. Owing to the more congenial journalistic standards of the day, the national media obligingly adopted a similar policy when FDR entered the White House four years later. Henceforward there would be no depictions of him either in print or on film being carried off a boat "like a child" or requiring substantial assistance in getting down from a stage. "No sob stuff for me," Roosevelt said.

There would be sobbing of a different sort when the New York Stock Exchange crashed in October 1929. This heralded the cataclysmic economic event we now know as the Great Depression. It eventually led to the collapse of the nation's economy, the failure of 85,000 businesses, and 40 percent of the country's workforce without a job. Mass hunger and homelessness inevitably followed. Soup kitchens, organized by secular and religious charitable groups, became familiar sights in most American cities. But a lack of money and other essential resources made it impossible for these institutions to service everyone in need. Describing the scene at one of these soup kitchens in New York City, one observer wrote, "There is a line of men, three to sometimes four abreast, a block long and wedged tightly together—so tightly that no passerby can break through. For this compactness there is a reason: those at the head of the grey-black human snake will eat tonight; those further back probably won't."

Perhaps due to his own personal experience with human suffering, Roosevelt demonstrated tremendous compassion and empathy for those caught in the grip of the depression. As governor he successfully pushed through the New York legislature a bill that established the Temporary Emergency Relief Administration, an agency that provided needed aid for the growing number of unemployed. He enacted tax relief for financially hard-pressed farmers upstate and committed his administration to bold reform efforts in workmen's compensation and unemployment insurance. All the while he rejected the laissez-faire approach to government that many of his political contemporaries had embraced in the 1920s under conservative Republican presidents Calvin Coolidge and Herbert Hoover. "More and more," he said, "those who are victims of dislocations and defects of our social and economic life are beginning to ask . . . why government can not and should not act to protect its citizens from disaster."

Roosevelt carried this activist spirit with him to the Oval Office in 1933, after posting a lopsided 472-to-59 electoral victory over Hoover the preceding November. He had entered the presidential contest promising a "New Deal" to his fellow countrymen, one in which their fading hopes and dreams for a better economic future would be restored. Now newly sworn in as chief executive, he intended to follow through on that campaign pledge. "Our greatest primary task is to put people to work," he said. "This is no unsolvable problem if we face it wisely and courageously. It can be accomplished in part by direct recruiting by the Government itself, treating the task as we would treat the emergency of a war, but at the same time, through this employment, accomplishing greatly needed projects to stimulate and reorganize the use of our natural resources."

To accomplish this goal, Roosevelt embarked on a frenzied period of legislative activity. In short order he steered bills through Congress that bailed out the country's floundering banking and housing industries while establishing massive federal public works programs that provided jobs for the unemployed. In farm policy Roosevelt was also active, creating the Agricultural Adjustment Agency that helped farmers gain greater profits and purchasing power by restricting their overall production. And Roosevelt was not content to stop there. To bring economic development to the traditionally depressed region of southern Appalachia, he hit upon the idea of establishing the Tennessee Valley Authority. A sponsored federal agency, the TVA set up a series of power plants, dams, and transmission lines along the floodwaters of the Tennessee River to deliver cheap electrical power to poor rural communities in a seven-state area. Yet the undisputed crown jewel of Roosevelt's reform efforts was the Social Security Act of 1935, which provided federally funded old-age pensions and unemployment compensation. "It is a sound idea—a sound ideal," Roosevelt said. "Most

of the other advanced nations of the world have adopted it, and
their experience affords the knowledge that social insurance can
be made a sound and workable project." Taken in full, these
measures saved millions from falling into poverty and helped
stabilize the ailing manufacturing and agricultural sectors of the
economy.

Regardless of the brighter economic picture, however, Roosevelt was unable to raise the country out of the depression.
High unemployment persisted along with sluggish business expansion and investment. Not until World War II did the economy fully recover, thanks to the high demand for war-related
goods and services. Nevertheless Roosevelt had no difficulty
getting himself reelected in 1936, registering an historic landslide victory against Republican Governor Alf Landon of
Kansas. The president carried every state in the union except
Vermont and Maine while trouncing his opponent in the popular vote, 61 to 31 percent. While the win undoubtedly filled
Roosevelt with an enormous sense of pride and personal accomplishment, he knew there was much work still to be done.
"I see millions of families trying to live on incomes so meager
that the pall of family disaster hangs over them day to day,"
Roosevelt solemnly declared in his second inaugural address. "I
see millions whose daily lives in city and on farm continue under conditions labeled indecent by a so-called polite society half
a century ago. . . . I see one-third of a nation ill-housed, ill-clad,
ill-nourished. It is not in despair that I paint you that picture. I
paint it for you in hope—because the nation, seeing and understanding the injustice in it, proposes to paint it out."

Alas, Roosevelt was destined to be disappointed in his second term. Standing in the way of his ambitious new reform efforts was the U.S. Supreme Court, which had made a distress-
ing habit of declaring a number of important New Deal
measures unconstitutional. Determined to see this judicial

trend reversed, Roosevelt embraced a radical notion: he asked for legislative approval of a proposal to increase the size of the Court from nine to fifteen members. Moreover he sought sweeping authority to appoint additional judges to the federal bench when an incumbent failed to "avail himself" of the opportunity to retire at the age of seventy. "By bringing into the judicial system a steady and continuing stream of new and younger blood," Roosevelt explained, "I hope, first, to make the administration of all federal justice speedier and, therefore, less costly; secondly, to bring to the decision of social and economic problems younger men who have had personal experience and contact with modern facts and circumstances under which average men have to live and work."

Condemned by Democrats and Republicans alike as a transparent attempt to arrogate the independence of the judiciary, Roosevelt's "Court-packing" scheme went down with a resounding thud in the halls of Congress. He fared no better two years later when he unsuccessfully attempted to purge the Democratic party of conservatives during congressional midterm elections. Roosevelt had hoped such a move would initiate a long-overdue reconfiguration of the two major political parties into predominantly liberal and conservative alignments. But members of his own party saw things differently. "There was a time when I would have bled and died for him," remarked Senator James Murray of Montana, "but in view of the way he has been acting I don't want to have any dealings with him and I just intend to stay away from him and he can do as he pleases."

In the midst of dealing with these embarrassing political setbacks, Roosevelt also had to contend with the tumultuous events occurring in Europe. The fascist dictators Adolf Hitler of Germany and Benito Mussolini of Italy had engaged in a series of aggressive military actions, shattering the fragile peace that had existed on the Continent since the end of World War I. Mussolini was the first to strike when his armies invaded Ethiopia in 1935. Without a modern army, Ethiopia quickly succumbed. The genie of war was out of the bottle. Emboldened by the ease with which Mussolini had conquered Ethiopia, Hitler marched his troops into Austria and Czechoslovakia, brazenly annexing to Germany these formerly independent nations.

Reacting to these provocative moves, the leading democracies of Europe, Great Britain and France, essentially turned the other cheek. Exhausted militarily and economically by their participation in the First World War, they had no stomach for another conflict. Their reluctance to fight merely encouraged Germany and Italy to seize more territory. "They'll just protest," Hitler said contemptuously. "And they'll always be too late." Notwithstanding, when Germany invaded Poland in September 1939, Britain and France decided they had seen enough. They declared war on Germany, thus touching off the Second World War.

To their everlasting detriment, however, they were woefully unprepared for the Nazi blitzkrieg to follow. Despite holding a slight numerical superiority over the Germans, the British and French forces in the West were made short work of by the more experienced and tactically superior Wehrmacht. By June 1940 France was forced to capitulate to Germany while the bulk of the British Expeditionary Force narrowly avoided disaster by escaping to safety across the English Channel from the port of Dunkirk in northwestern France.

With France now firmly under Nazi occupied rule, Britain found itself the only major European democratic power left standing against Hitler. But it was a wobbly stand, to say the least, for Britain now faced the very real prospect of a German invasion. Hitler had ordered plans drawn up for just such a contingency. Code-named Operation Sea Lion, this highly anticipated military operation was scheduled to begin once air superiority had been achieved over the Royal Air Force. Yet Britain, under the dynamic leadership of new Prime Minister Winston Churchill, had no intention of rolling over. "What has happened in France makes no difference to our actions and purpose," Churchill said. "We have sole champions now in arms to defend the world cause. We shall do our best to be worthy of this high honour. We shall defend our Island home, and with the British Empire we shall fight on unconquerable until the curse of Hitler is lifted from the brows of mankind. We are sure that in the end all will come right."

Roosevelt viewed the deteriorating situation overseas with growing alarm. An unabashed realist when it came to foreign affairs, he was under no illusion regarding what a Nazi triumph in Europe would mean. These "gods of force and hate," he believed, would use the victory as a springboard to conquering the rest of the globe, including the United States. "Your government knows what terms Hitler, if victorious, would impose," Roosevelt said. "They are, indeed, the only terms on which he would accept a so-called 'negotiated peace.' And under those terms, Germany would literally parcel out the world—hoisting the swastika itself over vast territories and populations, and setting up puppet governments of its own choosing, wholly subject to the will and the policy of the conqueror."

Yet Roosevelt was severely constrained politically to do much about this calamitous state of affairs, as the vast majority of Americans abhorred the idea of U.S. military intervention abroad. One Gallup poll from this period indicates that as much as 70 percent of the general public supported staying out of another European war. Still fresh on most people's minds were the horrific American losses incurred during World War I, along with the popular suspicion that unscrupulous bankers and arms dealers, the "merchants of death," had maneuvered the country into the conflict.

It didn't help matters that prominent national figures like Herbert Hoover, John L. Lewis, Joseph P. Kennedy, and Charles A. Lindbergh lent their voices to a swelling isolationist chorus. Lindbergh, the first person to fly nonstop from New York to Paris in 1927 and now a national hero, drew the most attention and controversy. He declared that Germany was justified in pursuing an aggressive foreign policy, owing to the Darwinian principle of "survival of the fittest." "There is," he said, "no adequate peaceful way for a nation to expand its territory and add to its colonies—no international measure for the right of birth rates, virility, skill, and all the innumerable factors that enter into the rise and fall of nations, of empires, of civilizations. And therefore, where a strong people become dissatisfied with its position through negotiation and agreement, it turns to that primeval 'right' of force—as we did with the American Indians and with Mexico, as England did in Africa, India and America, as Italians did in Ethiopia, as Germany is doing today."

Ever responsive to this isolationist tilt in public opinion, Congress in the late 1930s enacted into law a series of stringent neutrality measures. Designed to prevent the United States from becoming entangled in a foreign war, these regulations made illegal the sale of arms or munitions to belligerent powers. They also advised American citizens against traveling on belligerent vessels and forbade outright the extension of loans or credits to the combatants. Bowing to political reality, Roosevelt initially supported the passage of these measures. But as the Nazi juggernaut began its inexorable march across Europe, he decided the legislation needed major revision.

On September 21, 1939, the president convened a special session of Congress and exhorted legislators to lift the imposed embargo and allow arms or munitions to be sold to belligerents on a "cash and carry" basis. He wanted belligerents to be permitted to purchase arms or munitions as long as they agreed to pay for them in cash and provide for the transportation of the materiel out of American ports. Viewed objectively, the measure favored Britain, as her navy had unquestioned control of all vital Atlantic sea lanes. Roosevelt, however, maintained he was not taking sides or attempting to ensnare the country in a bloody war: "I give to you my deep and unalterable conviction, based on years of experience as a worker in the field of international peace, that by the repeal of the embargo the United States will more probably remain at peace than if the law remains as it stands today. I say this because with the repeal of the embargo, this government clearly and definitely will insist that American citizens and American ships keep away from the immediate perils of the actual zones of conflict."

After brief discussion and debate on the issue, Congress acceded to the president's wishes in October. The arms embargo was lifted, and "cash and carry" became an official tenet of U.S. foreign policy. But with Britain militarily cut off and on the brink of collapse by the late summer of 1940, Roosevelt was confronted with an entirely new dilemma. In a presidential election year, should he accede to a request by Britain for fifty aged American destroyers, to defend the island against an impending threat of Nazi invasion? The political risks were enormous. Owing to the nation's continued isolationist mind-set, such a move might swing enough voters away from Roosevelt in November to deny him a third term. For Winston Churchill, who had spent a lifetime in British politics swimming against the stream, the choice was obvious. "Mr. President, with great respect I must tell you that in the long history of the world, this is a thing to do now," he wrote Roosevelt.

After deep soul-searching, Roosevelt reached a similar conclusion. "Cries of 'war monger' and 'dictator' will fill the air," Roosevelt predicted, "but if Britain is to survive we must act." Nor was he apparently alone in this sentiment. At a full Cabinet meeting on August 2 the president noted it "was the general opinion, without any dissenting voice, that the survival of the British Isles under German attack might possibly depend on their getting these destroyers." But persuading Capitol Hill to sign off on this controversial course of action was another matter. Staunch isolationists in the Senate such as David I. Walsh of Massachusetts and Gerald P. Nye of South Dakota were expected to stage a lengthy filibuster against the measure. "Congress is going to raise hell about this," Roosevelt said, "but even another day's delay may mean the end of civilization."

Given this somber assessment, Roosevelt chose to bypass congressional approval and declare the destroyer deal an "Executive Agreement," consonant with his constitutional and statutory authority as commander-in-chief to uphold the security of the United States. In a supporting legal brief written by attorney general and future Supreme Court justice Robert H. Jackson, Roosevelt's actions were deemed appropriate, with ample precedent in international case law for the president "to transfer title and possession of the proposed considerations upon certificate of appropriate staff officers." Quoting verbatim from the 1936 Supreme Court ruling in the *Curtiss-Wright* case, Jackson noted that the president was "the sole organ of the Federal Government in the field of international relations" and as such should be afforded "a degree of discretion and freedom from statutary restriction which would not be admissible were domestic affairs alone involved." Put another way, Roosevelt did not require an act of Congress to give away the destroyers.

As a bone to skeptical legislators, however, Roosevelt arranged for Britain to agree to an additional proviso whereby the United States would receive ninety-nine-year leases to build naval and air bases on several British colonial possessions in the Western Hemisphere, including Newfoundland, Bermuda, the Bahamas, Jamaica, Trinidad, St. Lucia, and British Guiana.

That way, Roosevelt felt he could argue with some justification "to the American people and the Congress" that the destroyers-for-bases deal greatly enhanced "the defense and security of the United States." Although initially reluctant to commit to such an arrangement, Churchill eventually came around to accepting Roosevelt's judgment. "What we want is that you shall feel safe on your Atlantic seaboard so far as any facilities in possessions of ours can make you safe and naturally if you put in money and make large developments you must have the effective security of a long lease," Churchill wrote.

With the negotiations completed, Roosevelt formally announced the destroyers-for-bases deal in a message to Congress on Labor Day, September 3, 1940. While insisting that the exchange was in no way "inconsistent" with "our status for peace," he pointed out that it nevertheless represented "an epochal and far-reaching act of preparation for continental defense in the face of grave danger." Despite these assurances, critics were quick to pounce on the deal. "Mr. Roosevelt today committed an act of war," reproved the *St. Louis Post-Dispatch*. "He also became America's first dictator. Secretly his Secretary of State, Mr. Hull, entered into an agreement with the British Ambassador that amounts to a military and naval alliance with Great Britain . . . [and] may eventually result in the shedding of the blood of millions of Americans." The *Boston Post* pulled no punches either, questioning the legitimacy of the deal. "The giving of our destroyers in return for rights to fortify certain points was done in a manner far removed from our rightful democratic processes. Legally, the deal was as raw a piece of chicanery as has been yet foisted upon a trusting people. The interventionist lawyers dug back into mouldy legislation to find a forgotten statute to enable the deal to be put over. The Congress was flouted. Due process of deliberation was debauched."

A Victory Smoke: **Roosevelt and Churchill.**

One opposition political leader likened the transaction to a "sucker deal." "You must remember," sneered Republican National Committee Vice Chairman Samuel F. Pryor, Jr., "that Great Britain owes us a great deal of money. However, the great issue involved is that it is the first step toward taking us into this war without consulting the representatives of the people. It is the act of a dictator." The isolationist activist John T. Flynn of the "Keep America Out of War Congress" did not disagree, claiming that Roosevelt had been saved the humiliation of impeachment only by the House of Representatives' supposed "long record of servile submission to the executive." Yet it was the remonstrations of formerly avid Roosevelt supporters like Congresswoman Frances Payne Bolton of Ohio that may have cut deepest. "If Mr. Roosevelt can do what he likes with our destroyers without consulting Congress and we give him our boys," she declared, "God alone knows what he will do with them."

Across the Atlantic, relief and jubilation characterized the official British reaction. "I greet with the utmost pleasure and satisfaction the newly announced arrangement whereby a large number of destroyers of the United States navy are made available for the British Navy," exulted A. V. Alexander, first lord of the admiralty. "They come at a time when the strain upon our destroyer fleets has been very great, and they will be of inestimable value to us, not only for escorting convoys, but also for protecting our coasts from threats of invasion." He added that apart from the "immediate advantage" both nations would enjoy by way of improved naval defenses, the event would "strengthen the feeling of good will and friendship between our two great peoples." Churchill took the occasion to personally throw a well-timed jibe his enemy's way. "I have no doubt that Herr Hitler will not like this transference of destroyers," he told the House of Commons, "and I have no doubt that he will pay the United States out, if he ever gets the chance. That is why I am very glad that the army, air, and naval frontiers of the United States have been advanced along a wide arc into the Atlantic Ocean, and that this will enable them to take danger by the throat while it is still hundreds of miles away from their homeland."

Unsurprisingly, the German response was dismissive, if not downright contemptuous. "England's exigency now has mounted to unlimited proportions," the German Foreign Office sniffed. "For the first time since George Washington's war of liberation, England is retreating in the Western Hemisphere. The United States is about to take over the power of hegemony, not with force this time, but as an heir. Washington is naturally elated about this cheap prize. The material price paid was not worth mentioning." Nazi-controlled press organs like the *Berlin Nachtausgabe* piled on further, describing the transaction as "a flagrant breach of neutrality." "Fundamentally this trade is completely one-sided in favor of the United States," the paper maintained. "Therein is expressed the great weakness of Britain's position. It cannot be overlooked, however, that this development was only made possible through the sovereign action of authorized quarters in Washington, who apparently forgot that the American Neutrality Act in its revised form forbids the replacement of outworn war material for the belligerents."

In strictest military terms, the destroyers-for-bases deal was not decisive. The Royal Navy quickly discovered that only nine of the aging fifty destroyers could be placed in service by the end of 1940, too late to influence the final outcome of the Battle of Britain. But on a broader psychological and political level they made a huge difference to the war-ravaged population of Britain, who had been subjected to devastating bombing raids by the Luftwaffe on a daily basis since July. Now they could take stock in the belief that help was on the way, that they would not have to go it alone against Hitler much longer. As Cordell Hull later wrote, the deal "was a demonstration to the world that [the U.S.] government believed that Britain had a real chance to hold fast against Hitler's might. It showed that we were willing to go beyond ordinary methods to find new means to aid the major democracy fighting Nazism." British hopes received a further boost in mid-September when it was learned that Hitler had "postponed" Operation Sea Lion for his failure to achieve air supremacy over Britain. "There was a very broad smile on Churchill's face now as he lit up his massive cigar and suggested we should all take a little fresh air," noted British intelligence officer F. W. Winterbotham, who was with the prime minister when the news arrived.

While Roosevelt received ample political heat for the deal, he was not without his share of enthusiastic backers. Many influential journals of opinion came out in support of his brave decision. "We have made, at last, a down payment on national security," enthused the *Louisville Courier-Journal.* "And we haven't had a better bargain since the Indians sold Manhattan Island and got $24 in wampum and a demijohn of hard liquor. Great Britain is going to get those fifty destroyers. And with them she may live. President Roosevelt acted with firmness and considerable daring in concluding this admirable transaction without consulting the Congress. He had no other course. The peril was too desperate." Echoing this theme of intrepid presidential leadership, the *New Orleans Times-Picayune* suggested that the deal would go down in history "second only in importance" to the 1803 Louisiana Purchase. "For, with the new bases established, equipped and adequately manned, this country will have . . . a defense line we should be able to hold against the strongest naval and air attack that could be sent against it by transatlantic foes if they have no footholds or supply sources in our hemisphere. From these outlying bases, too, a much stronger defense of the other Americas can be organized and supported."

Roosevelt also obtained an unexpected major lift when GOP presidential challenger and political moderate Wendell Willkie publicly supported the deal. "The country will undoubtedly approve of this program to add to our naval and air bases and assistance given to Great Britain," Willkie said. His support proved invaluable as it "drew the sting out of the opposition in Congress" and allowed Roosevelt some needed political elbow room to take further bold action. Two weeks after announcing the destroyers-for-bases deal, Roosevelt declared his intention to create the first peacetime military draft in American history. "In thus providing for national defense," he explained on September 16, "we have not carved a new and uncharted trail in the history of our democratic institutions." On the contrary, he insisted, his government was merely reasserting "an old and accepted principle" of democratic government that stretched back to the early days of the Republic. "In those days," he said, "little was required in the way of equipment and training for the man in arms. The average American had his flintlock and knew how to use it. . . . Today, the art of war calls for a variety of weapons. Modern life does not emphasize the qualities of soldiers." Compulsory military service would therefore provide the citizenry with these missing qualities while producing an effective fighting force "to meet the threat of war."

Remarkably, these highly controversial moves had little impact on Roosevelt's reelection campaign. He easily staved off Willkie's challenge to win a third term with 55 percent of the popular vote and an impressive 449-to-82 showing in the electoral college. Heading into the election-year fight, Roosevelt had planned to retire from politics, but the exigencies of the European crisis soon convinced him to forgo this decision. "Like most men of my age," he told supporters, "I had made plans for myself, plans for a private life of my own choice and for my own satisfaction, a life of that kind to begin in January, 1941. These plans, like so many other plans, had been made in a world which now seems as distant as another planet. Today all private plans, all private lives, have been in a sense repealed by an overriding public danger. In the face of that public danger all those who can be of service to the Republic have no choice but to offer themselves for service in those capacities for which they may be fitted. Those . . . are the reasons why I have had to admit to myself . . . that my conscience will not let me turn my back upon a call to service."

Despite his earlier endorsement of the destroyers-for-bases deal, Willkie tried throughout the campaign to make an issue of the administration's greater military ties to Britain by suggesting that a vote for Roosevelt was a vote for war with Germany. As one of his party's radio ads fulminated, "When your boy is dying on some battlefield in Europe—or maybe in Martinique—and he's crying out, 'Mother! Mother!'—don't blame Franklin D. Roosevelt because he sent your boy to war—blame YOURSELF, because YOU sent Franklin D. Roosevelt back to the White House!" Roosevelt skillfully repelled these allegations by famously declaring "to the mothers and to the fathers of America" that their sons were "not going to be sent into any foreign wars." While Roosevelt would come under heavy fire in later years for making such a brazen statement, at the time he saw nothing improper about it. "It's not necessary," he told his speechwriters when they suggested he qualify his words with the add-on phrase "except in cases of attack." "If we're attacked," Roosevelt reasoned, "it's no longer a foreign war."

Such parsing of the English language was not unfamiliar to Winston Churchill, but a month after Roosevelt's electoral triumph the British prime minister saw fit to communicate with his fellow chief executive in a more straightforward manner. "My Dear Mr. President," he wrote, "As we reach the end of this year, I feel you will expect me to lay before you the prospects for 1941. I do so with candour and confidence, because it seems to me that the vast majority of American citizens have recorded their conviction that the safety of the United States, as well as the future of our two Democracies and the kind of civilization for which they stand, is bound up with the survival and independence of the British Commonwealth of Nations." Churchill proceeded to paint a grim picture of the challenges both nations faced. Specifically he mentioned the exceedingly poor financial condition of the British government. "The moment approaches when we shall no longer be able to pay cash for shipping and other supplies," he warned. To improve the situation, he appealed to Roosevelt to provide a program of massive economic assistance for his embattled homeland. "If, as I believe, you are convinced, Mr. President, that the defeat of the Nazi and Fascist tyranny is a matter of high consequence to the people of the United States and to the Western Hemisphere, you will regard this letter not as an appeal for aid, but as a statement of the minimum action necessary to achieve our common purpose."

As he had done earlier in the destroyers-for-bases deal, Roosevelt did not waver in responding to this latest request for assistance. Arguing that it was in America's long-term interest to keep Britain in the war effort against Hitler, Roosevelt successfully pushed through Congress the Lend-Lease Act of 1941, which gave the president the legal authority to sell, lease, exchange, or transfer defense materials to the United Kingdom and her allies, regardless of their ability to pay immediately.

To sell his plan to Congress, Roosevelt brilliantly related a parable about two neighbors who found themselves in a rather sticky situation. "Suppose the house of the President's neighbor catches fire and he has a length of garden hose," Roosevelt conjectured. "If he can take the hose and connect it to the neighbor's hydrant, he may be able to put out the fire. He does not say his hose cost $15, pay me $15. He doesn't want $15, but his hose back when the fire is over. The neighbor gives back the hose and pays him for the use of it." Similarly, Roosevelt concluded, "if we take over not all but a large part of British war orders when they come off the production line and come to an arrangement for their use by the British and get repaid in kind when the war is over, that would be satisfactory."

Lend-lease would also be extended to the Soviet Union when Hitler launched a full-scale invasion against the Communist nation in June 1941. While Germany recorded impressive early victories, advancing all the way to the outskirts of Moscow, the tide of battle would turn against the Nazis by 1943, thanks to the combination of a harsh Russian winter and the resiliency of the Red Army. The once invincible Nazi war machine would never be the same. In the throes of victory, Soviet leader Joseph Stalin magnanimously credited Roosevelt and his program of lend-lease assistance for helping "win the war." "The most important things in this war are machines. The United States has proven that it can turn out from 8,000 to 10,000 airplanes per month. Russia can only turn out, at most 3,000 a month. . . . The United States, therefore, is the country of machines. Without the use of these machines, through Lend-Lease, we would lose the war." America truly became what Roosevelt had called the "arsenal of democracy" for countries opposing Hitler.

Yet providing military and economic aid to Britain and Russia was not the only issue occupying Roosevelt's thoughts during this crucial period. He believed that as leading democracies, both the United States and Great Britain had a special duty to articulate the kind of world they wished to see emerge from their current struggle with Nazi Germany. The end result was the Atlantic Charter of 1941. In this broad statement of postwar aims that Roosevelt and Churchill agreed upon at a secret four-day summit meeting off the coast of Newfoundland in early August, the two leaders spelled out what they considered to be the essential "principles of freedom": national self-determination, freedom of the seas, open trade agreements, and liberal labor practices. "No society of the world organized under the announced principles could survive without these freedoms which are a part of the whole freedom for which we strive," Roosevelt said.

Given the lavish attention paid to the Nazi threat, it is no small irony that the triggering event that propelled the United States into active participation in World War II was the surprise Japanese attack on American naval and air installations at Pearl Harbor, Hawaii, on December 7, 1941, a "date which will live in infamy," Roosevelt said. The United States and Japan had been at loggerheads for almost two decades over control of the Pacific Ocean and East Asia. But when Roosevelt imposed crippling economic sanctions on Japan during the summer of 1941, in response to Japan's military invasion of Indochina, armed conflict became inevitable. Tokyo became convinced that a quick and lethal air strike against Pearl Harbor would so incapacitate the American Pacific Fleet that the United States would be forced to sue for a compromise peace while presumably dropping its economic sanctions. What the Japanese leaders failed to take into serious account was their country's inability to prevail in a protracted conflict with the United States, for Japan lacked the industrial capacity to win such a fight. "You have to plunge into war if there is some chance, however slight, of winning victory," reasoned Japanese Premier Hideki Tojo. Unfortunately for Tojo, the surprise air strike wasn't nearly as decisive as first hoped, and the seeds were thus sown for Japan's eventual defeat in 1945.

Owing to the terms of an earlier treaty that Hitler had unwisely signed with Japan and Italy in 1940—the Tripartite Pact—Germany was forced to declare war on the United States on December 11, 1941. For the first time in its history, the United States would have to fight a war simultaneously on two fronts, in Europe and in the Pacific. Unfazed by the supreme task confronting him, Roosevelt threw his heart and soul into the war effort, plotting grand military strategy, conducting high-level diplomatic talks, coordinating civilian relief efforts, and making sure the federal government provided American GIs with the necessary leadership, equipment, and training to defeat the combined armies of the Axis. "We cannot wage this war in a defensive spirit," he said. "As our power and resources are fully mobilized, we shall carry the attack against the enemy—we shall hit him and hit him again wherever and whenever we can reach him."

In the process, Roosevelt became the most celebrated wartime commander-in-chief since Abraham Lincoln. But sadly, he was denied the opportunity of witnessing final victory. On April 12, 1945, the president died at a vacation retreat in Warm Springs, Georgia, the victim of a cerebral hemorrhage. His death set off an outpouring of grief and sadness that stretched across the globe. "I can remember the President ever since I was a little kid," lamented Private Albert M. Osborn of Bowling Green, Ohio, who was serving with the American Third Army in Germany. "America will seem a strange, empty place without his voice talking to the people whenever great events occur. He died fighting for democracy, the same as any soldier."

Soviet ruler Joseph Stalin described the event as "a great loss" and praised Roosevelt as "a great politician of world significance and a pioneer in the organization of peace and security after the war." Stalin's ultra paranoid mind also held out the possibility that Roosevelt might have been "poisoned"—no doubt part of a larger nefarious scheme to sour East-West relations. He thus discreetly sent a communiqué to the State Department requesting that an autopsy be performed on the deceased president. The London *Daily Telegraph* chose to focus on Roosevelt's substantial legacy as a world statesman: "This country, in particular, owes him a debt which can never be repaid for his understanding, help and confidence in its darkest hours. When we had few confident friends he was an unremitting and undespairing one." But perhaps the most poignant and heartfelt testimonial of all came from Roosevelt's trusted friend and comrade-in-arms. "He died on the eve of victory," Winston Churchill said, "but he saw the wings of it. And he heard them."

To be sure, Roosevelt became a driving force for this victory when he threw aside political caution five years earlier and began directly to support Britain militarily with the destroyers-for-bases deal. Although the venerable island nation might have survived the Battle of Britain without the destroyers, it could not have done without the substantive flow of American aid that followed. The destroyers-for-bases deal made possible this assistance while forging a "special relationship" between the two great democratic powers that prevented Hitler and his minions from dictating the future direction of the world. Churchill characterized these years as Britain's "finest hour." They were Roosevelt's as well.

★

CHAPTER SEVEN

Slaying an American Caesar

HARRY TRUMAN AND THE
FIRING OF DOUGLAS MACARTHUR

Tough decisions never bothered this former dirt farmer from Missouri. He once said that presidents had to make them if they hoped to go anywhere, and those who didn't were the ones doomed to cause "all the trouble." On April 6, 1951, Harry S Truman left no doubt he belonged among the most stouthearted of chief executives when he conferred with his top advisers at Blair House, his temporary home while renovations on the White House were being completed. The intended purpose of the gathering: to discuss removing General of the Army Douglas MacArthur from his post as head of the United Nations force in South Korea fighting the Communist North and China. Truman and many in his administration believed that MacArthur had brazenly exceeded his reach as field commander, to the point where he was imperiling the foundations of representative democracy in America. The general had already scuttled a Truman peace initiative to the Chinese by directly violating a presidential gag order. If the president allowed such "rank

152

insubordination" to go unchallenged, the founders' precept of the military being subordinate to civilian authority stood to be irretrievably compromised. "He thought he was a bigger man than the President of the United States," Truman later explained. If "his brigadier generals or his colonels had treated him the same way, under the same circumstances, what would have happened to them? They'd have been court-martialed. . . ."

But on this somber day many of Truman's aides were counseling caution, given MacArthur's immense popularity with the American public as a revered military hero from World War II and his close personal ties to many of the president's domestic political enemies. "If you relieve MacArthur," Secretary of State Dean Acheson warned, "you will have the biggest fight of your administration." Secretary of Defense George Marshall offered a similar warning. But Truman was having none of it. Unconcerned with the political risks involved, bucked up by the belief he was acting well within his powers as commander-in-chief, he decided to lower the boom on his wayward commanding general. "The time had come to draw the line," he later wrote in his memoirs.

Drawing the line was something Truman had striven to do his entire life. The son of a mule trader, he had spent most of his youth in Independence, Missouri, a small rural farming community ten miles east of Kansas City. A shy boy with thick Coke-bottle glasses and an introspective personality, Truman had difficulty fitting in with his peers while growing up. "Why no, I was never popular," he once admitted. "The popular boys were the ones who were good at games and had big, tight fists. I was never like that. Without my glasses I was blind as a bat, and to tell the truth, I was kind of a sissy. If there was any danger of getting into a fight, I always ran."

As he matured into a physically fit and morally upright young man, Truman was able to overcome his poor self-image and assert himself. But he did experience a number of personal setbacks during these impressionable years, including a rejection by West Point for admission into that school's elite corps of cadets. Undaunted, Truman tried his hand at business, working in a series of nondescript office jobs following his graduation from high school in 1901. He quickly grew dissatisfied with this line of work, and when his father suggested he "help out" on the family farm, Truman jumped at the opportunity. "It was a great experience," he related. "It was my job to help my father and brother feed the livestock, sometimes milk a couple of cows, then help my mother get breakfast. After breakfast we'd go to the fields. In spring and fall there'd be planting to do. . . . It was always my job to plant the corn, sow the wheat and run the binder to cut the wheat and oats. I usually pitched hay to my father on the stack also."

Alas, these idyllic days on the farm ended abruptly. In 1917 the United States declared war on Germany, and Truman enthusiastically signed up for active military duty. "I was stirred in heart and soul by the war messages of Woodrow Wilson, and since I'd joined the National Guard at twenty-one I thought I ought to go," he wrote. Commissioned as a first lieutenant in the Artillery Corps, Truman was quickly promoted to captain and sent overseas to fight in France. Soon after his arrival, he was placed in command of a poorly disciplined artillery company and told to whip it into combat-ready shape. This he accomplished with remarkable speed and efficiency, impressing both his superiors and those under him with his ability to lead men. "We were a pretty rough bunch of boys; anyway, we thought we were," remembered one veteran of the outfit. "We'd already got rid of four commanding officers when Harry came along. He looked like a sitting duck to us. He was sort of small and with four eyes. And then he called all the noncoms together, and he said, 'Now, look, I didn't come here to get along with you guys. You're going to have to get along with me, and if any of you thinks he can't, why, speak right up, and I'll give you a punch in the nose.' He was tough, but he was fair; he was a good officer."

These qualities stood him in good stead, especially when circumstances compelled Truman to lead his men into several major engagements, including the Meuse-Argonne campaign of 1918. During that decisive battle, which resulted in an Allied victory, a regimental runner recounted how impressively Truman handled himself under fire: "He was a banty officer in spectacles. . . . I never heard a man cuss so well or so intelligently, and I'd shoed a million mules. He was shouting back ranges and giving bearings. The battery didn't say a word. They must have figured the cap'n could do the cussin' for the whole outfit. It was a great sight, like the center ring in Barnum and Bailey at the close of the show, everything clockwork, setting fuses, cutting fuses, slapping shells into breeches and jerking lanyards before the man hardly had time to bolt the door. . . . He really broke up [an enemy] counterattack." Truman too was satisfied with his performance. "I am so pleased that I was lucky enough to get in on the drive that made the Boche squeal for peace that I sometimes have to pinch myself to see if I am dreaming or not," he wrote. "It really doesn't seem possible that a common old farmer boy could take a battery in and shoot it on such a drive, and sometimes I think I just dreamed it."

Returning home more confident and self-possessed, Truman married his longtime sweetheart, Bess Wallace, and decided to give business another try. He opened a haberdashery in Kansas City with an acquaintance he had made in the army. Unlike his marriage, which would last a robust five decades, Truman's foray into men's clothing proved short-lived. He and his partner were forced to close up shop after only two and a half years. Stung by the economic reversal, Truman turned to politics as a way to support himself and his wife. I "liked the political game and I knew personally half the people [in my district]," he later explained. "I also had kinfolks in nearly every precinct. . . ." Taking advantage of these long-standing family ties and his own standout record in the military, he successfully ran for county judge for the eastern district of Jackson County, winning by a plurality of five hundred votes. "I was sworn in on January 1, 1923, and went to work trying to learn everything I could about the law and the duties attached to my new job," Truman recalled. "I had an old Dodge roadster, the roughest-riding car ever built, but sturdy enough to take the gullies and mudholes of every crossroads in the county. Every road, bridge, lane and every county institution was thoroughly examined. County court procedure was studied in every detail. All this was useful some years afterward."

Truman used this nuts-and-bolts knowledge to become a competent judge and to build a network of loyal political supporters that in 1934 helped him win election to the U.S. Senate. Playing an equally vital role in his rise to electoral prominence was Tom Pendergast, the Democratic boss of Kansas City. Pragmatic, shrewd, and reticent, Pendergast was a kingmaker in Missouri politics, and in Truman he saw someone who could provide "a cover of respectability" to the seamier aspects of his political organization. He gave the former haberdasher invaluable support in the formative stages of his political career. In his defense, Truman insisted Pendergast never interfered with how he chose to conduct his affairs while in office, outside of one notable exception that occurred in the early 1930s. "The Boss wanted me to give a lot of crooked contractors the inside [on a road construction project] and I couldn't," Truman said. While initially irked at Truman's attitude, Pendergast quickly cooled down and told him to "run things as he thought best." "Didn't I tell you boys," Pendergast boasted to his friends.

"He's the contrariest cuss in Missouri." Truman would have it no other way. Pendergast, Truman maintained, "was an able clear thinker and understood political situations and how to handle them better than any man I have ever known. His word was better than the contracts of most men, and he never forgot his verbal commitments."

Truman's loyalty to Pendergast never wavered, even when his political mentor was jailed in the late 1930s on charges of corruption and graft. When the broken and disgraced power broker died in 1945, Truman made a point of attending his funeral as vice president. "You should have seen the headlines and the carrying-on when I did that," Truman later told Dean Acheson, "but Tom Pendergast was a good and loyal friend, and he never asked me to do a dishonest deed, and so I went to his funeral, and, eventually, it all blew over. . . ."

As senator, Truman distinguished himself as a dyed-in-the-wool supporter of President Franklin Roosevelt's New Deal, voting for the Wage and Hour Law, the Works Progress Administration, the Agricultural Adjustment Act, the Social Security Act, and the Wagner Labor Relations Act. He also had a hand in crafting several major pieces of legislation, such as the Civil Aeronautics Act of 1938, which enhanced federal authority over the civil aviation industry. Yet national fame eluded him until World War II when he chaired the Senate Special Committee to Investigate the National Defense Program. It became known as the Truman Committee.

Charged with examining "all aspects of war production," the committee uncovered several examples of corruption and mismanagement. "We saw the seamier side of the war effort," Truman once said. "We had to investigate crooked contractors on camp construction, airplane engine manufacturers who made faulty ones, steel plate factories which cheated, and hundreds of other such sordid and unpatriotic ventures. We investigated procurement, labor hoarding, army and navy waste in food and other supplies." All told, the Truman Committee saved American taxpayers billions of dollars, which did not go unnoticed by the nation's media. In 1944 Truman was singled out by a *Look* magazine survey of newsmen as being "one of the ten most valuable officials in Washington."

With the high-profile success of his committee, Truman's political stock rose in national Democratic circles, to the point where he was mentioned as a serious contender for the party's vice-presidential nomination in 1944. Bemused by the speculation, Truman paid it no serious mind. "I liked my job as senator and I wanted to stay with it," Truman later recounted. "It takes a long time for a man to establish himself in the Senate. I was a member of three very important standing committees— Appropriations, Interstate Commerce, and Military Affairs— and was well up on the list in all of them for seniority, which is very important. My Special Committee was doing good work and I wanted to stay with it." But Truman did not count on the persistence of Franklin Roosevelt.

Facing a tough reelection fight for his fourth term, and in sore need of the kind of Midwestern electoral support the popular Missourian could deliver, Roosevelt was easily persuaded by party leaders to take on the reluctant Truman as his running mate. "You tell him that if he wants to break up the Democratic party in the middle of a war, that's his responsibility," Roosevelt told a top party official. Unwilling to buck his commander-in-chief, Truman caved in. "Well," he said, "if that is the situation I'll have to say yes, but why the hell didn't [Roosevelt] tell me in the first place?"

The Roosevelt-Truman ticket went on to score a comfortable victory at the polls, but Truman was less than enthusiastic about becoming vice president. He viewed the office as strictly honorific, with no real power or influence. "You know," he confessed at a Senate press conference on April 11, 1945, "right here is where I've always wanted to be, and the only place I ever wanted to be. The Senate—that's just my speed and my style. I did what I could. I did my best. I was getting along fine, until I stuck my neck out too far and got too famous. And then they made me VP and now I can't do anything." Just one day after uttering this statement, Truman had the mantle of presidential leadership thrust upon him as Franklin Roosevelt died in Warm Springs, Georgia. "I don't know whether you fellows ever had a load of hay fall on you," he informed a group of reporters on April 13, "but when they told me yesterday what had happened, I felt like the moon, the stars, and all the planets had fallen on me. I've got the most terribly responsible job a man ever had."

In the difficult months that followed, Truman had the daunting task of ending World War II and putting American society back on a peacetime footing. To seal the Allied victory and avoid a costly invasion of the Japanese mainland, the new president chose to use the most destructive weapon ever devised in the history of warfare: the atomic bomb. On August 6 and 9, 1945, following the president's orders, the army air force dropped two of the bombs on the Japanese cities of Hiroshima and Nagasaki. More than 200,000 people perished in the destruction, but a heretofore recalcitrant Japanese government surrendered unconditionally, just as Truman had hoped. "The final decision of where and when to use the atomic bomb was up to me," he later wrote. "Let there be no mistake about it. I regarded the bomb as a military weapon and never had any doubt that it should be used. The top military advisors to the President recommended its use, and when I talked to [British Prime Minister Winston] Churchill he unhesitatingly told me that he favored the use of the atomic bomb if it might aid to end the war."

Turning to domestic affairs, Truman faced a bewildering set of political and economic challenges following VJ-day. High inflation, massive labor unrest, and an acute housing shortage threatened to sink the nation's economy into deep recession. Nonetheless Truman was able to bring order to the chaotic situation through strong executive action. For example, when railroad workers staged a paralyzing nationwide strike for higher wages in 1946, Truman told them in no uncertain terms that he would draft them into the army and have the government take over the railway system. "You are not going to tie up the country," he bluntly remarked. "If this is the way you want it, we'll stop you." Impressed by Truman's resolve, the union backed down and agreed to a settlement.

But taking such bold and uncompromising action did not come without a political price. "As 1946 ended," noted the historian Eric Goldman, "Harry Truman sat in the President's chair a perfect target. Not since another simple man, Andrew Johnson, tried to fill the place of another strong President in another postwar had such a fury of unpopularity lashed the White House." Indeed, Truman's standing among prospective American voters fell so low that he soon began entertaining thoughts of stepping aside as the Democratic standard-bearer in the 1948 presidential election. Yet, as he had done in so many previous crises in his life, he set aside his personal doubts and pushed ahead. Portraying himself as "a man of the people" and a defender of democratic values around the globe, he staged a stunning come-from-behind victory over GOP front-runner Thomas E. Dewey in the presidential race. "In retrospect," his biographer Donald R. McCoy has argued, "[the victory] is not so unbelievable. Roosevelt had built a coalition of Democratic voters that only a disaster could have dismantled rapidly, and Truman was no bringer of disaster. He had found ways to appeal to most of the New Deal voters as well as regular Democrats."

One of the major themes Truman raised during the campaign, and one that resonated strongly among his fellow countrymen, was anti-communism. By the late 1940s relations between the United States and the Soviet Union, wartime partners in the "Grand Alliance" against German fascism, had hit rock bottom. Disputes over the organization of postwar governments in Germany and Eastern Europe, in addition to quarrels over war reparations, arms control, and unsettled national boundaries, had resulted in a "cold war" state of affairs. Americans now saw their former allies "not as trusted friends but as ruthless purveyors of 'Red Fascism,' a popular notion that suggested Russian expansionism was no different from the acts of aggression Nazi Germany had performed on Europe a decade earlier."

By 1949 the cold war had spread into East Asia, where Chinese Communists under the dynamic leadership of Mao Zedong had expelled the corrupt Nationalist regime of Chiang Kai-shek from the mainland and into permanent exile on the island of Formosa. Almost immediately Truman's political enemies wanted to know "who lost China?" According to many of his Republican critics, who were looking for a hot-button issue to regain the White House, responsibility lay squarely on the president's shoulders. He was blamed for being "soft" on communism and pursuing "a willful, do-nothing policy which has succeeded only in placing Asia in danger of Soviet conquest."

Truman, however, had already gone to considerable lengths to curb the perceived Communist threat. Beginning in 1947 his administration had charted an aggressive and farsighted foreign policy that sought to nip in the bud what Truman saw as the expansionistic tendencies of Soviet communism. Called "containment," this policy relied on a successful combination of diplomatic, economic, and military pressures to prevent the Soviets from gaining control of Western Europe and the Mediterranean. "The free peoples of the world look to us for support in maintaining their freedoms," declared Truman in launching this new strategic doctrine. "If we falter in our leadership, we may endanger the peace of the world—and we shall surely endanger the welfare of our own Nation."

Despite this firm and unequivocal stance, Truman could not shake partisan charges that he had surrendered China to the communists. Even members of his own party, people like the up-and-coming congressman John F. Kennedy of Massachusetts, couldn't resist taking a dig. In January 1949 Kennedy, addressing the House of Representatives, railed against Truman's alleged perfidy in allowing China to go "red." "The responsibility for the failure in our foreign policy rests . . . in the White House and in the Department of State," he thundered. Stung by the criticism, the president and his advisers purposively steeled themselves against allowing any further loss of territory to the Communists. Their resolve was soon tested in Korea, setting the stage for the events leading to MacArthur's ouster.

On June 24, 1950, Soviet-backed North Korean forces invaded south of the thirty-eighth parallel in "a bold attempt" to overturn the militarily weak Republic of Korea, a staunch ally of the United States. Truman first learned of these developments while enjoying what had been a quiet Saturday evening at his Missouri home. "The phone rang," he remembered, "and it was Dean Acheson calling from his home in Maryland. He said, 'Mr. President, I have serious news. The North Koreans are attacking across the thirty-eighth parallel.'" Angered by the turn of events, Truman vowed not to let the aggressive action stand. "We've got to stop the sons of bitches," he exclaimed. He ordered U.S. combat troops into the war zone while seeking and receiving a United Nations resolution authorizing military force to remove the Communists from South Korea.

Named commander of the UN defense force was General Douglas MacArthur, one of the most celebrated military leaders of the twentieth century. A graduate of West Point, MacArthur had risen rapidly through the ranks. In 1919 he was named superintendent at the military academy, where he distinguished himself as an innovative thinker and motivator. He went on to serve several years in the Philippines before being tapped as army chief of staff by President Herbert Hoover in 1930. During World War II he reached the pinnacle of his fame as supreme Allied commander of the Pacific theater. So crucial were MacArthur's contributions to the final victory over the Japanese that he was given the honor of receiving their surrender onboard the *USS Missouri* in Tokyo Bay on September 2, 1945. Not content to remain idle after the war, he immediately accepted command of the occupying Allied powers in Japan. From this position of unprecedented authority, he played a pivotal role in rebuilding and democratizing Japanese society.

Yet with all these electrifying accomplishments came an unbearable hubris that often alienated MacArthur from his military and civilian superiors. One former aide, future president Dwight Eisenhower, went so far as to compare him to a "baby," overly smitten with the limelight. Truman himself was aware of these less than attractive personal qualities, derisively referring to him as "Mr. Prima Donna, Brass Hat, Five Star MacArthur." But as a former army officer himself, he could appreciate the general's undeniable leadership qualities. So it was with little trepidation that Truman appointed him to head the UN defense force in South Korea. And from the outset the Congressional Medal of Honor winner seemed like an inspired choice.

Not only did MacArthur halt the Communist advance in the south, he was able to roll back their lines to well north of the thirty-eighth parallel, due in part to his brilliantly conceived amphibious landing at Inchon in September 1950. With apparent victory in sight, Truman fatefully gave MacArthur the green light to pursue the retreating enemy into the north. This

MacArthur did with relish, marching his army all the way to the outer reaches of the Yalu River, the natural border that divides Korea from China. From this forward position he hoped to mop up whatever military opposition remained and unify both Koreas under the protective sponsorship of the UN.

But throughout this crucial period there were ominous signs that all was not right between the president and his commanding general. The first indication of trouble occurred in early August when MacArthur paid an unauthorized visit to Chiang Kai-shek in Formosa. The generalissimo had been eager to join the United States and her UN allies in Korea, but because of the anticipated diplomatic furor such a move would inevitably arouse, particularly among the Red Chinese who feared a Nationalist invasion of the mainland, official administration policy was to say thanks, but no thanks. Yet Chiang persisted, and in MacArthur he clearly found a receptive audience. For MacArthur believed Chiang's army could provide a valuable military counterweight to the Communists in Asia. Upon conclusion of their private meeting, MacArthur gave open assurances that "effective military cooperation" existed between the two countries and that he was sending three squadrons of jet fighters to Formosa as a gesture of goodwill.

Alarmed that this action might be misinterpreted by friend and foe alike as a sign that Chiang was about to enter the war and thus unnecessarily broaden the conflict, Truman dispatched former ambassador to the Soviet Union Averell Harriman to Asia to set things straight with MacArthur. "Tell him two things," Truman enjoined his personal envoy. "One, I'm going to do everything I can to give him what he wants in the way of support; and secondly, I want you to tell him that I don't want to get into a war with the Chinese Communists." Harriman dutifully carried out his instructions. "The President wanted me to tell you," he informed MacArthur, "that you must not permit

Chiang to be the cause of starting a war with the Chinese Communists on the mainland, the effect of which might drag us into a world war." Professing loyalty to the president, MacArthur said he would fully comply with his orders.

But the issue did not die there. MacArthur took it upon himself to publicly reveal his views on Formosa in a statement to be read at a Chicago Veterans of Foreign Wars convention on August 28, 1950. Comparing Formosa to "an unsinkable aircraft carrier and submarine tender," he said the island was "ideally located" to accomplish an "offensive strategy" against a "hostile power" on the Asian mainland. He continued: "Nothing could be more fallacious than the threadbare argument by those who advocate appeasement and defeatism in the Pacific that if we defend Formosa we alienate continental Asia. Those who speak thus do not understand the Orient. They do not grant that it is in the pattern of Oriental psychology to respect and follow aggressive, resolute and dynamic leadership—to quickly turn on a leadership characterized by timidity or vacillation—and they underestimate the Oriental mentality."

Despite this obvious dig at Truman and his foreign policy team, MacArthur professed to be "utterly astonished" when the president ordered him to retract the statement. More pliant occupants of the White House had given MacArthur an exceptionally wide berth when it came to his comments on policy. Now he faced a tough, no-nonsense chief executive who did not take kindly to military commanders who publicly questioned administration policy. It was a rude awakening. Backpedaling, MacArthur said he was only too willing to pull the statement, but at the same time he expressed annoyance that his words had somehow been construed as critical. "My message was most carefully prepared to fully support the President's policy position," he sheepishly claimed in a letter to an administration official. "My remarks were calculated only to support his declaration, and I am unable to see wherein they might be interpreted as otherwise."

Truman had a different view of the affair: "It was my opinion that this statement could only serve to confuse the world as to just what our Formosa policy was . . . and it also contradicted what I had told the Congress." The president felt strongly that when dealing in foreign relations, where qualities of precision and accuracy were at a premium, there could be "only one voice stating the position of the United States." That voice would be Truman's.

To ensure MacArthur understood this, Truman arranged to fly to Wake Island on October 15 and confer with his Far East commander. While the private meeting on the tiny Pacific island lasted fewer than two hours, both principals expressed satisfaction with the conversation. "I got from him a clear picture of the heroism and high capacity of the United Nations forces under his command," Truman said afterward. "We also discussed the steps necessary to bring peace and security to the area as rapidly as possible in accordance with the intent of the resolution of the United Nations General Assembly and in order to get our armed forces out of Korea as soon as their United Nations mission is accomplished." MacArthur, who flew from his military headquarters in Tokyo to the meeting, also contributed a favorable appraisal. He characterized his encounter with the president as "very pleasant" and told reporters it would not be long before UN troops scored a decisive victory in North Korea. "Come on up to Pyongyang [the North Korean communist capital]," he joked half-seriously.

But the last laugh would be on him. As he was concluding his conference with Truman, more than 100,000 Chinese troops were crossing the Yalu River and slipping largely undetected into North Korea. Another 100,000 soon followed. The Chinese government had concluded that the rapidly advancing

UN force under MacArthur's command represented a major threat to its security, especially since the general had done little in previous months to disguise his desire that the Marxist regime be overthrown. Better to strike now preemptively, the Chinese reasoning went, than wait for a military invasion down the road.

What followed in the weeks ahead was the greatest military disaster in modern American history. Taken by surprise, MacArthur's army was nearly annihilated as these Chinese "volunteers" proved to be a formidable fighting force. At one crucial point it looked like the entire UN force might be driven into the sea. MacArthur's "in very serious trouble," Truman noted grimly in his personal journal on December 2. "We must get him out of it."

Thanks largely to the brilliant leadership of Eighth Army commander Matthew Ridgway, Truman's hope was realized. Rallying the dispirited remnants of MacArthur's shattered command, Ridgway managed to stabilize the military front and oust the Chinese army from the south. "It is not often in wartime that a single battlefield commander can make a decisive difference," one impressed military peer later wrote. "But in Korea, Ridgway would prove to be the exception. His brilliant, driving, uncompromising leadership would turn the tide of battle like no other general's in our history."

Having thus reacquired a position of strength on the battlefield in the early months of 1951, Truman chose to pursue a diplomatic track aggressively. He asked the State Department to prepare a statement announcing his intention to begin negotiations with the Chinese government for the purpose of ending the war. As Truman later wrote, "The reasoning was that, in the first place, since we had been able to inflict heavy casualties on the Chinese and were pushing them back to and beyond the 38th parallel, it would now be in their interest at least as much as ours to halt the fighting, and secondly, the invaders stood substantially ejected from the territory of the Republic of Korea."

MacArthur, however, became distraught upon learning of the president's plan, believing it was too accommodating to the enemy. Disregarding a cable from the Joint Chiefs of Staff that relayed to him Truman's wishes that he do nothing to jeopardize the forthcoming peace initiative, he issued a statement of his own on March 24 that effectively derailed any hopes for an early resolution to the conflict. The general claimed the Chinese had been made "painfully aware that a decision of the United Nations to depart from its tolerant effort to contain the war to the area of Korea, through an expansion of our military operations to its coastal areas and interior bases, would doom Red China to the risk of imminent military collapse." To avoid such a fate, MacArthur suggested that the "commander in chief of the enemy forces" confer with him in the field and yield to American demands. Insulted by both the threatening tone and substance of the message, the Chinese contemptuously dismissed it as the raving ministrations of "a maniac."

Truman himself stood amazed at the depth of the general's brashness and contempt for higher civilian authority. In effect MacArthur had called on the Chinese to surrender to him personally, with no prior consultation with his civilian superiors in Washington. Worse, any hope for meaningful peace negotiations with the Chinese now had to be shelved indefinitely. "This was a most extraordinary statement for a military commander . . . to issue on his own responsibility," Truman later fumed. "It was an act totally disregarding all directives to abstain from any declaration on foreign policy. It was in open defiance of my orders as President and Commander in Chief. . . . By this act MacArthur left me no choice—I could no longer tolerate his insubordination." But Truman believed the time was not yet right to cashier the general: "I wanted, if possible, an even . . . better

example of his insubordination, and I wanted it to be one . . .
that everybody would recognize for exactly what it was and I
knew that, MacArthur being the kind of man he was, I wouldn't
have long to wait, and I didn't."

The "last straw" for Truman came on April 5, when the con-
tents of a letter that MacArthur had earlier written to Joseph W.
Martin of Massachusetts, the minority leader of the House of
Representatives, were made public by the congressman. The
Republican leader had sought out the general's views on Far
Eastern policy, particularly those concerning the feasibility of
opening up "a second front" in China with Chiang Kai-shek's
Nationalist forces. Without stipulating to Martin that his response remain confidential, MacArthur took the opportunity to
lash out against what he considered the self-defeating policies of
the Truman administration. Martin was on the right track in
raising the issue of the Chinese Nationalists, MacArthur responded. He suggested that employing them in the field would
provide a "maximum counter-force" against the enemy, a view
that was "in conflict" with neither "logic" nor "tradition."

MacArthur saved his most withering criticism for last. "It
seems strangely difficult for some to realize that here in Asia is
where the Communist conspirators have elected to make their
play for global conquest, and that we have joined the issue thus
raised on the battlefield; that here we fight Europe's war with
arms while the diplomats there still fight it with words; that if
we lose to Communism in Asia the fall of Europe is inevitable;
win it and Europe most probably would avoid war and yet preserve freedom. . . . There is no substitute for victory."

Interestingly, Truman exhibited remarkable self-restraint
when first apprised of the document's release by presidential assistant press secretary Roger Tubby. "Well," the commander-
in-chief remarked blandly, "I think they are maneuvering the
general out of a job." This personal calm continued in the days

ahead when Truman made good on his observation and fired MacArthur. He formally revealed his decision to the nation on April 11.

"With deep regret," he stated, "I have concluded that General of the Army Douglas MacArthur is unable to give his wholehearted support to the policies of the United States Government and of the United Nations in matters pertaining to his official duties. In view of the specific responsibilities imposed upon me by the Constitution of the United States and the added responsibility which has been entrusted to me by the United Nations, I have decided that I must make a change of command in the Far East. I have, therefore, relieved General MacArthur of his command and have designated Lieutenant General Matthew B. Ridgway as his successor."

The news did not sit well with most Americans. A Gallup poll sampling indicated that 66 percent of the nation condemned the action while only 25 percent approved. "Quite an explosion," Truman noted coolly in his diary. According to one estimate, the White House received 78,000 letters and telegrams blasting the president over the firing. Thousands more were sent to members of Congress calling for Truman's immediate removal from office. "IMPEACH THE IMBECILE," read one of the more succinct dispatches. Sniffing blood in the political waters, a number of partisan Republicans went out of their way to capitalize on the emotionally charged atmosphere. "The son of a bitch should be impeached," exclaimed Senator Joseph McCarthy of Wisconsin, while adding darkly that Truman's decision to dismiss the general had come about after a night "of bourbon and benedictine." Indiana senator William Jenner was equally incendiary in his comments. Truman's action, he claimed, proved that the federal government was "in the hands of a secret inner coterie which is directed by agents of the Soviet Union." Former President Herbert Hoover declined

HARRY TRUMAN: *Slaying an American Caesar* 171

to take up this conspiracy charge but did characterize the decision as a "great tragedy." "It does not solve the primary question of what to do to end our war with Communist China without advantage to Soviet Russia. A strong pillar in our Asian defense has been removed." Once-avid supporters of the president also weighed in with their disapproval. "I've been a Democrat all my life," noted one disgusted resident of the nation's capital, "but darned if I'm one now. A declaration of war wouldn't have shocked me as much as the news of Gen. MacArthur's removal."

Outside Washington, critics found more creative ways to express their unhappiness. In Denver one enterprising individual created a "Punch Harry in the Nose Club" while in San Gabriel, California, enraged citizens burned the president in effigy. Flags hung at half-mast in communities from coast to coast. Biting humor also made the rounds. "This wouldn't have happened if Truman were alive," went one popular joke. "I'm going to have a Truman beer—just like any other except that it hasn't got a head," went another.

Stirring the pot further were several sensationalistic newspaper accounts that painted MacArthur as a figure of national martyrdom. The *Buffalo Evening News* said the general "sacrificed his command to make the most emphatic protest against administration and United Nations Far Eastern policies within his power." The *Daily Oklahoman* ruefully noted that the man "who bore the American flag across the Pacific island-by-island to the palaces of Tokyo is jerked out of the battle line by a former captain of the artillery." The *Chicago Tribune* attached a far more sinister meaning to the proceedings, arguing that the "hasty and vindictive removal" of MacArthur represented "the culmination of a series of acts which have shown that [Truman] is unfit, morally and mentally for his high office." The paper concluded that the nation had never been "in greater danger"

A Long Shadow: **Truman and Acheson cope with political ramifications of MacArthur's dismissal.**

and was being led "by a fool who is surrounded by knaves." The *Los Angeles Times* concurred: "A hero has been humiliated. . . . Many Americans clearly feel that their country has somehow been sold out. . . . It is a victory for Joseph Stalin."

For his part, MacArthur believed his firing was the result of a misguided personal vendetta that Truman had long harbored against him. "No office boy, no charwoman, no servant of any sort would have been dismissed with such callous disregard for the ordinary decencies," he wrote in his memoirs. Such bitterness, however, was not on public display when MacArthur made a triumphant return to the United States on April 17, 1951. The general made a point of uncharacteristically portraying himself as a humble man of the people who had simply been performing his duty to the best of his abilities. He categorically denied suggestions that his actions might in any way be interpreted as political. "The only politics I have is contained in the simple phrase known well to all of you: God Bless America," he told an enthusiastic crowd of well-wishers in San Franciso.

MacArthur continued to wear the cloak of victimhood when he dramatically addressed a televised joint session of Congress on April 19. "I address you," he began, "with neither rancor nor bitterness in the fading twilight of life, with but one purpose in mind: to serve my country." Yet his conception of serving his country did not preclude taking select potshots at his commander-in-chief for allegedly failing to give him the necessary resources to defeat the Communist enemy in Korea. "I called for reinforcements, but was informed that reinforcements were not available," he maintained. "I made clear that if not permitted to destroy the enemy built-up bases north of the Yalu, if not permitted to utilize the friendly Chinese force of some 60,000 men on Formosa, if not permitted to blockade the China coast to prevent the Chinese Reds from getting succor from without, and if there were to be no hope of major reinforcements, the position of the command from the military standpoint forbade victory." He blithely brushed aside criticisms that such actions would lead to "an all-out war with China," with probable Soviet intervention. China, he claimed, "is already engaging with the maximum power it can commit, and the Soviet will not necessarily mesh its actions with our moves. Like a cobra, any new enemy will more likely strike whenever it feels that the relativity in military or other potential is in its favor on a world-wide basis."

MacArthur's thirty-four-minute speech, interrupted several times by "fervid clapping," concluded with a memorable final flourish. "I am closing my fifty-two years of military service. When I joined the Army even before the turn of the century, it was the fulfillment of all my boyish hopes and dreams. The world has turned over many times since I took the oath on the plain at West Point, and the hopes and dreams have long since vanished. But I still remember the refrain of one of the most popular barracks ballads of that day, which proclaimed most profoundly that 'Old soldiers never die; they just fade away.' And like the old soldier of that ballad, I now close my military career and just fade away, an old soldier who tried to do his duty as God gave him the light to see that duty. Good-bye."

After this address, public opinion continued to favor MacArthur overwhelmingly. He received "a triumphal parade" through the streets of Washington that same day and basked in the encomiums of lawmakers from both parties. "It was the most masterful speech that has been delivered in the Capitol in a century," praised Senator Pat McCarran, a Democrat from Nevada. "The only answer is to undo the great mistake that has been made and send this man back to his command." One breathless congressman, Republican Dewey Short of Missouri, compared the general to the Almighty: "We heard God speak here today, God in the flesh, the voice of God."

MacArthur's status as a deity did not come up for discussion during a "gloomy" Cabinet meeting that Truman convened to discuss the ramifications of the speech to Congress. In a partially successful attempt to cheer up his colleagues, Dean Acheson related a story about an overly protective father of a beautiful girl. "He let her go out only rarely and then only with young men of whom he approved and whose backgrounds were impeccable," he said. "At last, when she was twenty, she came to her father and said that she had a terrible thing to confess. She said, 'I'm pregnant.' At that her father threw up his hands and shouted, 'Thank heaven it's over. I've been afraid of something like this all my life.'" Typically, Truman offered an earthier assessment of MacArthur's posture: "It was nothing but a bunch of damn bullshit."

Fortunately the president received the full backing of the Joint Chiefs of Staff during this troubled period. They testified before joint hearings of the Senate Armed Services and Foreign Relations committees, investigating the dismissal, that MacArthur's recommendations on Korean policy had been unwise, especially his strategy of expanding the war into Chinese territory. Such an action, Joint Chiefs Chairman Omar Bradley advised, "would involve us in the wrong war, at the wrong place, at the wrong time and with the wrong enemy." In response to having been so roundly and publicly repudiated by his military peers, MacArthur saw his public support ebb away. He eventually skulked off into an unhappy retirement where he did indeed fade away.

Still, there is no getting around the severe political damage MacArthur's firing caused Truman's presidency. For the remainder of his term, through January 1953, Truman never saw his approval ratings in the polls rise above 33 percent. Nor did he receive widespread public support for his war policies. By 1952 more than half the nation regarded the Korean engagement as a tragic blunder. It was thus a foregone conclusion that Republicans would benefit in the fall elections. Behind the successful presidential ticket of Dwight Eisenhower and Richard Nixon, the GOP scored a landslide victory, winning both houses of Congress and effectively ending two decades of Democratic rule.

Truman bore the defeat as best he could, graciously sending congratulations to Eisenhower while diligently preparing for an orderly transition of power. Yet he could not resist taking a verbal swipe at his successor. "He'll sit here and he'll say do this, do that!" Truman privately mused to staff members from his desk in the Oval Office. "And nothing will happen. Poor Ike—it won't be a bit like the Army. He'll find it very frustrating."

In his farewell address, broadcast over radio and television, Truman spoke of the great crisis he confronted during his presidency. "I suppose," he said, peering into the future, "that history will remember my term in office as the years when the Cold War began to overshadow our lives. I have hardly had a day in office that has not been dominated by this all-embracing struggle. . . . But when history says that my term of office saw the beginning of the Cold War, it will also say that in those eight years we have set the course to win it. . . ." His decision to halt the Communist advance in Korea, he maintained, would go a long way in helping achieving this end. For unlike France, Britain, and other Western democracies who cowered before the might of Nazi and Japanese armies before the outbreak of World War II, the American people demonstrated sufficient fortitude and confidence in their own free institutions to stand up to totalitarian aggression. "This time we met the test," Truman stated proudly.

Returning home to Independence, Truman filled his remaining years overseeing the construction of his presidential library, writing his memoirs, and staying active in Democratic party politics. He also made himself accessible to the media and to the general public, often reminiscing about his years in the White House with what his biographer David McCullough has called "an infectious enjoyment." One topic always guaranteed to get a rise out of the aging and increasingly frail former president was the sacking of MacArthur. To be sure, the widely discussed episode had cut a destructive political swath through the final year and a half of his administration. But given the important higher principle at stake—the centrality of civilian control over the military in a democracy—Truman never showed a doubt that he had acted properly and in the best traditions of the nation. If anything, he admonished himself for not acting earlier. "What you have to understand," Truman explained to an interviewer in the early 1960s, "is that the President of the United States has to act as Commander in Chief at all times. A civilian executive just has to run the armed forces. The men who wrote the Constitution understood that, and it's been the same all through history. . . . It just has to be that way. Other ways have been tried, but they never have worked. Somebody has to be in charge who has been freely and legally chosen by the people . . . by the majority of the people."

Just the type of thing one would expect to hear from a president unbothered by making tough decisions.

CHAPTER EIGHT

Confronting a Moral Issue

John F. Kennedy and the Integration of the University of Alabama

An air of nervous apprehension settled over the White House on the night of June 11, 1963. Three minutes before he was to go on the nation's airwaves and deliver what was destined to become the most important presidential address on civil rights in more than a century, John F. Kennedy was still without a copy of the speech in his hands. His speechwriter, trusted friend and adviser Theodore Sorensen, had yet to finish making revisions to the document he had been entrusted to write only a few hours earlier. "For the first time," Kennedy joked afterward, "I thought I was going to have to go off the cuff." Robert F. Kennedy, the president's attorney general and unofficial political alter ego, was in a decidedly less jocular mood as he waited restlessly alongside his older brother. "Even [Bobby], who's not bothered by many things, was shaken by the president not having his prepared text," recalled aide Burke Marshall.

Much was riding on what the president had to say this particular evening about events relating to the court-ordered integration of the University of Alabama at Tuscaloosa. Earlier in the day, Alabama governor George Wallace had made his famous stand "at the schoolhouse door," directly challenging the constitutional authority of the federal government to desegregate the university. "I stand here today as Governor of this sovereign state," Wallace had declared, "and refuse to willingly submit to illegal usurpation of power by the Central Government. . . . My action does not constitute disobedience to legislative and constitutional provisions. It is not defiance for defiance sake. . . . My action seeks to avoid having state sovereignty sacrificed on the altar of political expediency."

Listening to an aide describe the unfolding scene at Tuscaloosa, President Kennedy had decided on the spot to respond with a forceful statement of his own, even though several of his closest domestic advisers had cautioned against it. A speech supporting desegregation—and, by extension, civil rights for African Americans—would be too "politically disadvantageous," they argued, certainly not worth the loss of white Southern votes that was bound to occur. Yet Kennedy paid this chorus of political doomsayers little mind. He had already been cautious enough on civil rights during his presidency, he felt. It was time to forge ahead and ask every American "to stop and examine his conscience," keeping in mind "that the rights of every man are diminished when the rights of one man are threatened."

When Sorensen finally delivered the text of the speech just moments before Kennedy was to address the nation, the president appeared unruffled. "It didn't faze him a bit," confirmed Marshall. Kennedy knew what he wanted to say, even without a formal text in front of him. In many respects his entire life to this point had prepared him for this particular rendezvous with destiny.

The second oldest of nine children of Irish Catholic parents, John Fitzgerald Kennedy was born on May 29, 1917, in

Brookline, Massachusetts. His father, Joseph P. Kennedy, was a Harvard-educated business entrepreneur who later made millions on Wall Street and in Hollywood, and served as ambassador to Great Britain during Franklin Roosevelt's second term. His mother, Rose Fitzgerald Kennedy, was the daughter of former Boston mayor John "Honey Fitz" Fitzgerald, one of the most popular Irish-American political figures of the early twentieth century. Viewing his children as "extensions of himself," Joe Kennedy sought to instill in them "a burning desire" to win. "The father particularly laid it on hard trying to make the boys, and the girls, excellent in something," Supreme Court Justice William O. Douglas later remarked, "whether it was touch football. Or tennis, or boating, or something else." "For the Kennedys," Joe Kennedy said, "it is the castle or the outhouse—nothing in between."

While young Jack faithfully tried to live up to this code, he often found himself falling short. He seemed forever to reside in the shadow of his older brother Joseph Jr., who excelled both in the classroom and on the playing field. "My brother is the efficient one in the family," Kennedy once observed, "and I'm the boy who doesn't get things done." To compensate for these feelings of inferiority, Kennedy became something of an "archetypal rebel," specializing in outrageous pranks and defying authority. At one point he came precariously close to being expelled from prep school. But his father stepped in to smooth over the situation and offer a stern rebuke to his son. "Don't let me lose confidence in you again," he warned, "because it will be nearly an impossible task to restore it. I am sure it will be a loss for you and a distinct loss for me."

Properly chastened, John Kennedy spent the rest of his schoolboy career out of trouble. He moved on to Harvard, where in 1940 he graduated with cum laude honors. His senior thesis, "Appeasement at Munich," an analysis of the reasons why British Prime Minister Neville Chamberlain "appeased" Adolf Hitler at the 1938 Munich Conference, was later reworked and published as the popular and critically acclaimed book *Why England Slept*. "You would be surprised how a book that really makes the grade with high-class people stands you in good stead for years to come," his father wrote him.

With the coming of World War II, John Kennedy entered the navy as a low-level intelligence officer. Quickly bored by his duties, he arranged for his father to "pull strings" and have him transferred to sea duty as a PT-boat commander. Assigned to the Solomon Islands in the South Pacific, Kennedy found more action than he had bargained for. In the early morning hours of August 2, 1943, his boat, the PT-109, was cut in half by a Japanese destroyer, killing two crewmen and badly injuring another. "How it felt?" Kennedy later recalled. "I can best compare it to the onrushing trains in the old-time movies. They seemed to come right over you. Well, the feeling was the same, only the destroyer didn't come over us, it went right through us." Rallying the surviving members of his crew in the aftermath of the collision, Kennedy exhorted them to swim to a nearby island nearly four miles away. "I have nothing to lose," he said, "but some of you have wives and children, and I'm not going to order you to try to swim to that shore. You have to make your own decision on that." Responding to his leadership, the men safely made it to the island after being in the water for nearly fifteen hours. "During the week we spent on the island," Kennedy later recalled, "the men never beefed as they did when a request for going to town in the states was refused them. I never could praise them enough." As luck would have it, Kennedy and his crew were rescued when they stumbled across friendly islanders who agreed to relay their location to Allied authorities.

While Kennedy was universally praised by his men for his valor under fire, he was less sanguine about his own role in the affair. "None of that hero stuff for me," he sternly told a reporter afterward. "Real heroes are not the men who return but those who stay out there like plenty of them do, two of my men included." But he recognized that his wartime experience represented "the seminal, defining moment of his life." "The war made us," he later wrote. "It was and is our single greatest moment. The memory of the war is the key to our characters. It serves as a breakwall between the indolence of our youths and earnestness of our manhoods. No school or parent could have shaped us the way that fight shaped us. No other experience could have brought forth in us the same fortitude and resilience. We were much shrewder and sadder when the long battle finally finished. The war made us get serious for the first time in our lives. We've been serious ever since, and we show no sign of stopping."

Kennedy was officially mustered out of the navy on December 27, 1944, after spending several months hospitalized with malaria and the injuries incurred during the PT-boat collision. With the war safely behind him, he decided to enter politics. "I think Jack thought while he was in the hospital recovering from his war injuries that he wanted to do something for his country," said his political aide William Sutton. "Instead of just being a guy with an ailment I believe he was thinking then about what he was going to say later, about 'ask not what your country can do for you. . . .'" Another motivating factor was the death of his older brother Joe, who had been killed in action over the skies of Europe. Joe had been the family member groomed to enter politics by his father. With his passing, it was now expected that Jack would take his place. "It was like being drafted," Kennedy later told a friend. "My father wanted his eldest son in politics. 'Wanted' isn't the right word. He *demanded* it. You know my father."

But first he needed to find an office to run for. Eventually his attention fixed upon the open U.S. House seat in the Eleventh Congressional District of Massachusetts, a predominantly working-class area that embraced Cambridge and Boston. To Kennedy the situation seemed ideal as his Democratic family already had "a well-established political base" there: John "Honey Fitz" Fitzgerald had represented the district in Congress at the turn of the century. Kennedy formally announced his candidacy on April 22, 1946, and proceeded to throw his heart and soul into the race by campaigning more than fifteen hours a day. "The pros in the district thought of him as a millionaire's son," remembered his campaign adviser Dave Powers, "and they wondered how he could get longshoremen and freight handlers and truck drivers—people who worked for a living—to vote for him. He just climbed more stairs and shook more hands and worked harder than all the rest combined. He not only wanted to win, he wanted all the votes—that's what made him great."

Also helping him connect with voters was his status as a certified war hero. It was the "Year of the Veteran," and Kennedy made sure he raised issues that most concerned veterans, such as affordable housing and jobs. "You just thought this fellow would be a good representative, the kind of fellow you'd like to have in politics and you wanted to help," a veteran said later. Of course, Kennedy had the added advantage of great personal wealth, which neither he nor his family was shy about using. "You know," fellow Massachusetts lawmaker and future U.S. Speaker of the House Thomas "Tip" O'Neill later mused, "you can be a candidate, you can have the issues, you can have the organization, but money makes miracles and money did miracles in that campaign. Why they even had six different mailings. . . . Nobody had mailings in that district." Miracle or not, Kennedy easily bested the field in the Democratic primary and scored a landslide victory against his Republican opponent in the general election. No one was more delighted than Joe Kennedy. Seeing the ease with which his son had connected with voters during the campaign, he remarked, "I would have given odds of 5,000-to-1 that this could never have happened. I never thought Jack had it in him."

As a congressman, Kennedy was careful not to stray far from the issues and concerns of his blue-collar constituents. He supported expanded Social Security benefits, improved public housing, and a national health program for the underprivileged. He also opposed efforts to lower the federal subsidy for school lunches and eliminate rent control. "When I first went to Congress in 1946," he later said, "I represented a district that was very poor in Massachusetts. We had many problems, housing [for example]. Many families were in need of assistance. Therefore, my viewpoint on the necessity of social legislation came really pragmatically through just observation."

In foreign affairs Kennedy was "a committed cold warrior." He viewed the Soviet Union as "a slave state," posing a direct threat to the security of the United States and her allies throughout the world. Thus he enthusiastically supported the Truman administration's efforts to "contain" perceived Soviet expansionism through the Marshall Plan, aid to Greece and Turkey, the establishment of the North Atlantic Treaty Organization (NATO), and the commitment of U.S. ground troops to Korea in 1950. "We are faced with an enemy whose goal is to conquer the world by subversion and infiltration or, if necessary, by open war," he said.

Kennedy was reelected to Congress by overwhelming margins in 1948 and 1950. But while his political star was in the ascent, his physical health began to decline dramatically. He was diagnosed with Addison's disease, a "potentially fatal illness" characterized by a failure of the body's adrenal glands. Low blood pressure, loss of weight, discoloration of skin, and various gastrointestinal disturbances were among its more notable side effects. While Kennedy kept his ailment secret from the public for fear that questions would arise about his fitness for office, he grew privately distraught. He began to entertain fatalistic thoughts of dying young. Fortunately for him, a new "miracle drug" called cortisone was discovered in the late 1940s to effectively treat Addison's patients. Injected on the thigh, these artificially produced corticosteroids could significantly extend the life expectancies of those afflicted with the disease. Given this new lease on life, Kennedy approached his political career with a renewed sense of energy and purpose.

By 1952 he had grown increasingly dissatisfied with House life and its "stifling seniority system." He yearned for greater challenges and the chance to move ahead politically. He set his sights on the U.S. Senate seat held by Republican incumbent Henry Cabot Lodge, Jr. The scion of a wealthy and influential Boston Brahmin family, Lodge was one of the most respected figures in American politics. In 1944, he had resigned his seat in order to apply for active combat duty in World War II, the first senator to do so since the Civil War. Returning home in 1946, he ran for the Senate again and won in a landslide. "When you've beaten him," Joe Kennedy told his son, "you've beaten the best. Why try for anything less?" Waging an uphill battle, Kennedy was able to achieve an upset victory by outworking and outspending Lodge. "I felt rather like a man who has just been hit by a truck," Lodge wrote afterward. Kennedy's triumph marked a watershed moment in his career. By defeating Lodge, he instantly became "a nationally known figure and a dominant Democrat in his state," his biographer James N. Giglio notes.

He did not take his good fortune for granted. "Suddenly," Tip O'Neill said, "he became an active person. Suddenly he became a person with a future in the Democratic Party. 'Will you go to Missouri and speak for the party?' You can't go to those places unless you have a knowledge of what is taking place in the Congress of the United States. He started to do his homework." Adding to Kennedy's appeal was his beautiful young bride Jacqueline Bouvier, whom he married in 1953 in a lavish wedding ceremony in Newport, Rhode Island. Witty and accomplished, yet reserved, Jacqueline would prove to be a political asset of incalculable value in the years to come. "She had that certain something," one admirer later recalled. "I don't know precisely what word to describe this quality: beauty, charm, charisma, style, any or all of the above. Whatever it happened to be, she had it."

Not everything was smooth sailing for the new senator, however. In 1954 unsuccessful surgery on his chronically weak back nearly cost him his life. "An infection set in and, while his wife and family prayed for him, last rites were administered. But the Senator rallied and soon was well enough to be flown on a stretcher to the Kennedys' winter home in Palm Beach for Christmas," family friend and photographer Jacques Lowe remembered. While recuperating from his surgery, Kennedy wrote *Profiles in Courage*, "a group of biographical essays about a group of politicians willing to defy the clear sentiment of their constituents." The book became a national best-seller, won the Pulitzer Prize, and went far in advancing Kennedy's image as "a serious lawmaker." This visibility proved helpful two years later when he made "a surprisingly strong bid" to be the Democratic nominee for the vice presidency. Although he came up short, his campaign nevertheless convinced Kennedy that he had the "right stuff" to try for the presidency the next time around. "If I work hard for four years," he said after the loss, "I ought to be able to pick up all the marbles."

Not to be denied, Kennedy coasted through the Democratic presidential primary field in 1960, brushing aside such party no-

tables as Hubert H. Humphrey of Minnesota, Stuart Symington
of Missouri, and Lyndon B. Johnson of Texas. He went on to secure a first-ballot victory at the Democratic National Convention in Los Angeles that July. "We stand today at the edge of a
new frontier," he said in his acceptance speech, "the frontier of
the nineteen sixties. . . . A whole world looks to see what we will
do. We cannot fail their trust. We cannot fail to try. . . . Give me
your help and your hand and your voice and your vote."

In the general election Kennedy faced off against Richard
Nixon, the sitting Republican vice president who had a well-
deserved reputation for political ruthlessness. In 1950 Nixon
had defeated liberal Democrat Helen Gahagan Douglas for a
Senate seat from California when he suggested she was "pink
right down to her underwear." No stranger to hardball politics
himself, Kennedy turned the tables on Nixon during the fall
campaign by charging he was insufficiently anti-Communist.
"In the election of 1860," Kennedy said, "Abraham Lincoln said
the question is whether this nation can exist half slave or half
free. In the election of 1960, and with the world around us, the
question is whether the world can exist half slave or half free,
whether it will move in the direction we are taking, or whether
it will move in the direction of slavery." Kennedy also took
pains to point out that Nixon was not Dwight Eisenhower, the
popular president for whom Nixon had loyally served for seven
and a half years. "The choice is not President Eisenhower,"
Kennedy insisted, "the choice is whether the people in this
country want the leadership of Mr. Nixon and the Republican
party, a party that's never stood for progress. To show how desperate and despicable this campaign has become: they're hanging outside of defense plants, a poster that says: 'Jack Kennedy
is after your job.' I'm after Mr. Eisenhower's job."

The pivotal moment of the race occurred on the evening of
September 26, during the first of four televised debates before

a nationwide audience. "Nixon was best on radio," noted the journalist Earl Mazo, "simply because his deep resonant voice carried more conviction, command, and determination than Kennedy's higher-pitched voice and his Boston-Harvard accent. But on television, Kennedy looked sharper, more in control, more firm—his was the image of a man who could stand up to [the Soviets]." Television producer and debate coordinator Don Hewitt concurred. "It came down to the better performer. The matinee idol won." The standout performance gave Kennedy the momentum he needed to edge Nixon on election day. In one of the closest presidential contests of the century, Kennedy won by less than 1 percent of the popular vote. "We simply had to run and fight and scramble for 10 weeks all the way, and then we would win," assessed Robert Kennedy afterward. "We got on top with the debates, we fought to stay on top, and we did win. And if we'd done one bit less of anything, then we might have lost."

John Kennedy took the oath of office at the east front of the Capitol on January 20, 1961. "Let every nation know," he announced in his inaugural address, "whether it wishes us well or ill, that we shall pay any price, bear any burden, meet any hardship, support any friend, oppose any foe to assure the survival and success of liberty." Interestingly enough, he made scant reference to domestic affairs in his speech, and none at all to civil rights. Kennedy believed that the exigencies of fighting the cold war would leave him little time for addressing such "mundane" matters. His first months in office seemed to bear out this attitude. He and his top advisers expended most of their collective energies on meeting perceived Soviet challenges in Cuba, Berlin, and Laos. "Each day, the [foreign] crises multiply," Kennedy said. "Each day, their solution grows more difficult. Each day, we draw nearer the hour of maximum danger, as weapons spread and hostile forces grow stronger."

But civil rights would not remain an afterthought for long. Beginning with the landmark 1954 Supreme Court case of *Brown v. Board of Education of Topeka, Kansas*, which ended legalized segregation in public schools, to Rosa Parks's brave refusal to move to the back of the bus in Montgomery, Alabama, in 1955, to the Greensboro, North Carolina, lunch-counter sit-ins of 1959, African Americans had demonstrated a willingness to challenge the prevailing status quo of "Jim Crow" laws. "Separate but equal" segregation statutes made it impossible for blacks to "mingle" with whites and attend the same kinds of restaurants, stores, theaters, churches, and hotels. The laws had been established by state governments when the last federal troops left the South at the end of Reconstruction in 1877. But now blacks, emboldened by their substantial economic and social gains during World Wars I and II, were fighting back through lawsuits, economic boycotts, teach-ins, and other forms of nonviolent collective action. "We can never be satisfied as long as the Negro is the victim of the unspeakable horrors of police brutality," said Martin Luther King, Jr., who had emerged as the country's foremost black leader and spokesman for the burgeoning protest movement. "We can never be satisfied as long as our bodies, heavy with the fatigue of travel, cannot gain lodging in the motels of the highways and the hotels of the cities. We cannot be satisfied as long as the Negro's basic mobility is from a smaller ghetto to a larger one. We can never be satisfied as long as a Negro in Mississippi cannot vote and a Negro in New York believes he has nothing for which to vote. No, no we are not satisfied, and we will not be satisfied until justice rolls down like waters and righteousness like a mighty stream."

That Kennedy initially appeared tone-deaf to these demands for greater racial equality is not surprising. His privileged upbringing had afforded him little significant contact with blacks throughout most of his adult life. One longtime family friend observed that he had never seen "a Negro on level social terms with the Kennedys. And I never heard the subject mentioned." Politically Kennedy had always claimed to be an advocate of civil rights, but because there were few blacks in his constituency in Massachusetts, and because he had needed white Southern backing in his quest to win the Democratic presidential nomination, his support never went much beyond lip service. "He seemed quite oblivious to the impending social revolution," concluded his political adviser and future Supreme Court justice Abe Fortas.

With one notable exception. In the closing stages of his presidential fight against Nixon, Kennedy had been persuaded by liberal advisers Sargent Shriver and Harris Wofford to make a spur-of-the-moment phone call to Coretta Scott King and offer his sympathy when her husband was unjustly thrown into a Georgia prison cell on trumped-up charges. "I want to express to you my concern about your husband," he said. "I know it must be very hard for you . . . and I just want you to know that I was thinking about you and Dr. King." "It showed he had compassion," Shriver later said. "It showed he had feeling. It showed he had heart. Nowadays that's nothing to say, but in those days that meant a lot because for black people, if you showed you had heart, that was a huge difference."

But a similar show of "heart" was missing when Kennedy was forced to confront the first major civil rights crisis of his new administration: the "Freedom Rides." Activists from the Congress of Racial Equality (CORE) and the Student Nonviolent Coordinating Committee (SNCC) had organized these interracial bus rides into the Deep South in the spring of 1961 to protest segregated conditions at bus terminals, lunch counters, and roadside lodgings. Mob violence against the Freedom Riders quickly followed, but Kennedy was reluctant to involve the federal government. For one, he feared that federal action would upset "key Southerners" in Congress who would determine the success or failure of his domestic legislative program, which called for raising the minimum wage, enacting Medicare, and providing federal aid for education. Second, he was concerned that the unfolding "spectacle of violence" would make the country look bad in the eyes of the international community, especially when the United States was competing with the Soviet Union for the "hearts and minds" of dark-skinned people throughout the Third World. His immediate response then was one of haughty annoyance. As he told Harris Wofford, "Can't you get your goddamned friends off those buses? Stop them." As the crisis deepened, however, Kennedy sent U.S. marshals to restore order and to protect the lives of the Freedom Riders. But he wasn't happy about it, particularly with a scheduled summit meeting with Soviet leader Nikita Khrushchev in Europe on his agenda. "I wonder whether [the Freedom Riders] have the best interests of their country at heart," Robert Kennedy said.

Supporters of civil rights could have asked the same of the administration, which sought to ingratiate itself with the Southern white political establishment by appointing several segregationist judges to the federal bench. If this wasn't bad enough, John Kennedy appeared to backpedal on a highly publicized campaign promise he had made to eliminate discrimination in federally subsidized housing "with the stroke of a pen." As the first year of his administration came to a close, he had not yet signed the required executive order. In protest, civil rights advocates mailed thousands of pens to the White House, mockingly reminding the president of his pledge. Kennedy signed the order the following November, but in a watered-down form that applied only to certain areas of federal housing. "It was a weak order when he finally signed it," the activist Roy Wilkins later groused.

As 1962 gave way to 1963, many black leaders had grown disenchanted with Kennedy's inaction and had begun to criticize him openly. While conceding that the president had done "a little more" for civil rights than his predecessor in the Oval Office, Martin Luther King asserted "the plight of the vast majority of Negroes remains the same." He charged Kennedy with "a failure of leadership and with not living up to his campaign promises." This point was driven home when Robert Kennedy agreed to meet with a group of civil rights activists at his family's apartment in New York City. Initially intended as a friendly exchange of views, the meeting quickly degenerated into a shouting match as the predominantly black audience accused Kennedy of being "just another politician" and the administration itself as needlessly dragging its feet on integration efforts. "Look, man," one angry participant interjected, "I don't want to hear none of your shit."

Tempers had barely cooled when the Birmingham crisis erupted in April 1963. Local activists, in conjunction with Martin Luther King and the Southern Christian Leadership Conference, had decided to take on the Jim Crow establishment of the notoriously segregated Alabama city in a series of well-coordinated protest demonstrations. "As Birmingham goes, so goes the South," King had said. But the white establishment was in no mood to see its authority questioned, and what ensued was a violent crackdown led by the local commissioner of public safety, Theophilus Eugene "Bull" Connor. While an uneasy truce was eventually brokered between the two sides, televised images of protesters being beaten, clubbed, and set upon by vicious attack dogs left a lasting, indelible impression.

Kennedy was personally outraged when photographs of the carnage arrived at the White House. He said the images made him "sick." More important, they forced him to rethink his long-standing position on civil rights and conclude that his ad-

ministration's strategy of trying to placate white Southern opinion and to keep "one step ahead of the evolving pressures" was
no longer a workable policy. Racial warfare seemed ready to
erupt throughout the entire South. "The situation was rapidly
reaching a boil which the President felt the federal government
should not permit if it was to lead and not be swamped,"
Theodore Sorensen later wrote. Vice President Lyndon Johnson, himself a Southerner, was even more to the point. "I think
the Southern whites and the Negro share one point of view
that's identical," he told Kennedy. "They're not certain that the
government is on the side of the Negroes. The whites think
we're just playing politics to carry New York. The Negroes feel
. . . we're just doing what we got to do. Until that's laid to rest
I don't feel you're going to have much of a solution. . . . What
Negroes are really seeking is moral force." Indeed, the time appeared ripe for Kennedy to launch what the historian Carl M.
Brauer later called "the Second Reconstruction," a concerted
federal effort "to remove racial barriers and create equal opportunities for all in the political and economic life of the nation."
But before embarking on such a crusade, Kennedy had first to
deal with the developing crisis at the University of Alabama at
Tuscaloosa.

Two black students, James Hood and Vivian Malone, had
gained admission to the school, thanks to a federal court desegregation order mandating their matriculation. But Alabama governor George Wallace threatened to bar their entry physically,
claiming the students' presence on campus would violate states'
rights and undo decades of established tradition at the all-white
school. As he later put it, the "separation [of races] has been
good for the Nigra citizen and the white citizen." Kennedy took
offense at this tack, arguing that Wallace's truculent attitude
represented a "violation of accepted standards of public conduct" for an elected state official. Wallace was characteristically

unmoved by this criticism. A former circuit judge, he had spent most of his career fighting through the thickets of Alabama politics. He had lost an earlier bid for the governorship in 1958 when his opponent accused him of being too "moderate" on civil rights. He "out-nigguhed me," Wallace complained, but "I'm not goin' to be out-nigguhed again." True to his word, Wallace went on to become one of the staunchest segregationists in the South while winning the first of four gubernatorial terms in 1962. "I draw the line in the dust," he declared in his 1963 inaugural address, "and toss the gauntlet before the feet of tyranny, and I say: segregation now—segregation tomorrow—and segregation forever."

Having reached an impasse with Kennedy over the question of integrating the University of Alabama, Wallace now braced himself for an inevitable public showdown. It occurred on the morning of June 11 when Deputy Attorney General Nicholas Katzenbach arrived on the Tuscaloosa campus to confront Wallace on the front steps of Foster Auditorium, a three-story, red-brick building that housed the university's registrar's office. Katzenbach told Wallace he had come bearing an official proclamation from the president directing the governor to comply with the federal court order allowing Vivian Malone and James Hood admission to the school. "I am asking from you," Katzenbach said, "an unequivocal assurance that you will not bar entry to these students . . . and that you will step aside peacefully, do your constitutional duty as governor of this state, and as officer of the court, as you are a member of the bar, and that nobody acting under you will bar their entrance physically or by any other means. May I have [your] assurance?"

Wallace refused to concede, preferring to read from a prepared statement attacking the federal government for supposedly exceeding its constitutional authority. "The unwelcome, unwanted, unwarranted and force-induced intrusion upon the campus of the University of Alabama today of the might of the central government offers a frightful example of the suppression of the rights, privileges and sovereignty of this state by officers of the Federal Government," he contended. Unimpressed with Wallace's show of defiance, Katzenbach asked the governor twice more to step aside. "The two students who simply have been seeking an education on this campus are presently on this campus," he said. "They have a right to be here, protected by that court order. They have the right to register here. It is a simple problem, scarcely worth this kind of tension in my judgment."

When Wallace responded to Katzenbach's entreaties with stony silence, the Justice Department official turned away and personally escorted Malone and Hood to their dormitories on campus. The "next move" belonged to Kennedy back in Washington. The president acted by issuing an executive order federalizing the Alabama National Guard to carry out the court order. The troops arrived on campus late in the afternoon under the leadership of Brigadier General Harry Graham, assistant commander of the Guard's Thirty-first Infantry Division. Graham marched up to Wallace at the doorway and greeted him with a respectful salute. "Governor Wallace," Graham said to the man who had been his boss just a few hours earlier, "it is my sad duty to inform you that the National Guard has been federalized. Please stand aside so that the order of the court may be accomplished." This time Wallace did as he was told, but not before denouncing the Kennedy administration for its alleged trend toward "military dictatorship." Shortly thereafter, Malone and Hood were officially registered as University of Alabama students.

Yet the true climax to the affair took place that evening when Kennedy addressed the nation from the Oval Office during thirteen minutes of prime network broadcasting time. He

began his remarks by urging his fellow countrymen not to view
the events in Tuscaloosa as merely a sectional issue. "Difficulties over segregation and discrimination exist in every city, in
every state of the Union, producing in many cities a rising tide
of discontent that threatens the public safety," he said. Nor
could the events be defined solely as a partisan issue or as a matter of strict legality, even though, he conceded, new laws were
needed "at every level" to address the situation. "We are confronted primarily with a moral issue," he insisted. "It is as old as
the Scriptures and is as clear as the American Constitution. The
heart of the question is whether all Americans are to be afforded
equal rights and equal opportunities, whether we are going to
treat our fellow Americans as we want to be treated."

He continued: "If an American, because his skin is dark,
cannot eat lunch in a restaurant open to the public, if he cannot
send his children to the best public school available, if he cannot vote for the public officials who represent him, if, in short,
he cannot enjoy the full and free life which all of us want, then
who among us would be content to have the color of his skin
changed and stand in his place? Who among us would then be
content with the counsels of patience and delay?" Noting that a
hundred years had passed since Lincoln had freed the slaves,
Kennedy poignantly reminded his radio and television audience
that the grandsons of the slaves were still "not fully free." "They
are not yet freed from the bonds of injustice," he said. "They
are not yet freed from social and economic oppression; and this
nation, for all its hopes and all its boasts, will not be fully free
until all its citizens are free." Now, he declared, the time had
come for the country to "fulfill its promises" to the African-
American community: "The events in Birmingham and else-
where have so increased the cries for equality that no city or
state or legislative body can prudently choose to ignore them."

Indeed, the "fires of frustration and discord" were already "burning" in every major American city, North and South.

"We face, therefore, a moral crisis as a country and as a people," Kennedy concluded. "It cannot be met by repressive police action. It cannot be left to increased demonstrations in the streets. It cannot be quieted by token moves or talk. It is a time to act in the Congress, in your state and local legislative body, and, above all, in all of our daily lives." He promised that he would ask Congress to enact sweeping new civil rights legislation dedicated to the proposition that "race has no place in American life or law." Yet, he cautioned, legislation alone would not be enough to redress the age-old problem of prejudice and discrimination. "It must be solved in the homes of every American in every community across the country. . . . This is one country. It has become one country because all of us and all the people who come here had an equal chance to develop their talents. We cannot say to 10 percent of the population that you cannot have that right; that your children can't have the chance to develop whatever talents they have; that the only way that they are going to get their rights is to go into the streets and demonstrate. I think we owe them and we owe ourselves a better country than that."

The speech marked a major turning point. No president since Lincoln had taken the bold step of placing the full legal and moral authority of the executive branch behind the cause of black civil rights. Now Kennedy had done so, and the country would never be the same. Henceforward the federal government would play a proactive role in integrating American society, regardless of a person's skin color or ethnicity. "It was . . . by far the strongest speech that had ever been made in support of civil rights by any president," Nicholas Katzenbach later related. It "committed the Kennedy Administration and [other

No Flag of Surrender: JFK commits to civil rights.

administrations to follow] to that road, and I think it is a very proud moment in our history."

Not surprisingly, given their many years of sacrifice and toil for the cause, civil rights leaders were among the first to grasp the historic significance of Kennedy's remarks. "Your speech last night to the nation on the civil rights crisis was a clear, resolute exposition of basic Americanism and a call to all our citizens to rally in support of the high traditions of our nation's dedication to human rights," Roy Wilkins wrote to Kennedy on June 12. Martin Luther King was equally effusive. "I am sure," he telegrammed Kennedy, "that your encouraging words will bring a new sense of hope to the millions of disinherited people of our country. Your message will become a hallmark in the annals of history. The legislation which you will propose, if enacted and implemented, will move our nation considerably closer to the American dream." He added that it was "one of the most profound and unequivocal pleas for justice . . . made by any president."

Not everyone was sympathetic to these pleas for justice. A June 16 Gallup poll showed that 62 percent of white Southerners felt Kennedy was moving "too fast" on racial integration while only 32 percent from the same sampling approved of his performance as president. These results were particularly worrisome to Kennedy, given how vital an electoral role the "Solid South" had played in his razor-thin victory over Nixon in 1960. He had carried six Southern states in that election; now, if he ran again in 1964, it seemed quite possible he would carry none. "He always felt that maybe that was going to be his political swan song," Robert Kennedy said. George Wallace did not disagree. "The South next year will decide who the next president is," he told reporters after the Tuscaloosa showdown. "Whoever the South votes for will be the next president, because you can't win without the South. And you're going to see that the

South is going to be against some folks." If this wasn't cause
enough for concern, the very night Kennedy delivered his civil
rights address to the nation, Medgar Evers, a field secretary for
the Mississippi NAACP, was gunned down on the front doorstep
of his home in Jackson. He had been carrying an armful of
NAACP sweatshirts emblazoned with the slogan "Jim Crow Must
Go" when a sniper fatally shot him in the back. His final words
were, "Turn me loose!"

To his credit, Kennedy did not retreat from his administration's commitment to civil rights in the wake of these sobering
developments. If anything, he became even more determined to
see the issue through to its conclusion, whatever the outcome.
As he had earlier told Luther Hodges, his secretary of commerce, "There comes a time when a man has to take a stand and
history will record that he has to meet these tough situations
and ultimately make a decision." One way Kennedy demonstrated this resolve was by officially approving a planned march
on Washington by civil rights leaders on August 28. "I think
that's in the great American tradition," he told reporters at the
time. "We want citizens to come to Washington if they feel they
are not having their rights expressed." Come they did in one of
the most memorable displays of nonviolent protest in the nation's history. More than 250,000 people descended upon the
Lincoln Memorial to hear Martin Luther King deliver his stirring "I Have a Dream" speech. "I say to you today, my friends,
that in spite of the difficulties and frustrations of the moment I
still have a dream," King told the multitudes. "It is a dream
deeply rooted in the American dream. I have a dream that one
day this nation will rise up and live out the true meaning of its
creed: 'We hold these truths to be self-evident; that all men are
created equal.' . . . I have a dream that my four little children
will one day live in a nation where they will not be judged by
the color of their skin but by the content of their character. I

have a dream today." Conversing with King at a Cabinet Room reception afterward, a clearly impressed Kennedy shook his hand and said, "I have a dream."

In the early planning stages of the March on Washington, Kennedy had met with King and other prominent black leaders at the White House for a candid discussion of the stakes involved. "Okay, we're in this up to our necks," he informed them. "A good many programs I care about may go down the drain because of this. I may lose the next election because of this. We may all go down the drain as a result of this—so we are putting a lot on the line. What is important is that we preserve confidence in the good faith of each other."

As a sign of his own good faith, Kennedy formally introduced his civil rights bill to Congress on June 19. Described as "the most comprehensive piece of legislation addressing discrimination since Reconstruction," the bill outlawed "racial segregation and discrimination" in all public and privately owned facilities while strengthening voting rights protection. "The legal remedies I have proposed are the embodiment of this nation's basic posture of common sense and common justice," Kennedy said. "They involve every American's right to vote, to go to school, to get a job and to be served in a public place without arbitrary discrimination—rights which most Americans take for granted. . . . It will go far toward providing reasonable men with the reasonable means of meeting these problems, and it will thus help end the kind of racial strife which this nation can hardly afford. . . . To paraphrase Lincoln: 'In giving freedom to the Negro, we assure freedom to the free—honorable alike in what we give and what we preserve.'"

Kennedy would never learn the fate of his civil rights bill. While on a routine political visit to Dallas, Texas, on November 22, 1963, he was killed by an assassin's bullets. His death shocked the nation and the world. How was it possible, many asked, that so youthful and dynamic a leader could be taken away in such a brutal and senseless manner? The situation seemed all too unreal. It was as if, the historian Arthur Schlesinger later surmised, "Jackson had died before the nullification controversy and the Bank War, as if Lincoln had been killed six months after Gettysburg or Franklin Roosevelt at the end of 1935 or Truman before the Marshall Plan." Indeed, this sense of unfulfilled promise proved an especially bitter pill for Kennedy loyalists. As Theodore Sorensen wrote, "On November 22 his future merged with his past, and we will never know what might have been. His own inner drive, as well as the pace of our times, had enabled him to do more in the White House in three years than many had done in eight—to live a fuller life in forty-six years than most men do in eighty. But that only makes all the greater our loss of the years he was denied."

Within the African-American community, grieving was particularly intense and heartfelt. "It was the first time I cried with white people," remarked one New York cabdriver. The future author Anne Moody became so emotionally distraught upon hearing the news that she fainted in a New Orleans restaurant where she worked. Boarding a public streetcar afterward and seeing the grief-stricken black faces around her, she observed, "I knew they must feel as though they lost their best friend— one who was in a position to help determine their destiny. To most Negroes, especially to me, the President had made 'Real Freedom' a hope." The civil rights activist Andrew Young became similarly distressed when he learned of the tragedy during an educational workshop he was conducting in South Carolina. "We gathered everyone in the chapel and there we shared the sorrowful news," he remembered. "The chapel was comforting in its Quaker simplicity; the bare wooden floors and angular lines suited the somber mood that fell over the group. Somebody began to pray. This was not prayer as performance, standing regally in front of the gathered community grasping the security of a podium. This was heart-baring prayer. When it was your time to pray you got down on your knees, put your elbows on the seat of one of the cold, metal folding chairs and your head on your hands and begged for the comfort that only God can provide. The folk gathered there knew something had happened that could potentially change the course of the country and particularly their own lives."

Ironically, Kennedy's death would serve as a catalyst in moving his civil rights bill through Congress. Seeking to capitalize on the enormous outpouring of public grief and sympathy his predecessor's passing had engendered, the newly sworn-in President Lyndon Johnson made a point of portraying himself as the executor of Kennedy's political will. He pledged to enact into law every stalled piece of New Frontier legislation that was still pending before Congress. And topping the list was civil rights. "First," Johnson declared, "no memorial or oration or eulogy could more eloquently honor President Kennedy's memory than the earliest possible passage of the civil rights bill for which he fought so long. We have talked for one hundred years or more. It is time now to write the next chapter and write it in the books of law." Working closely with civil rights leaders and making full use of his talents as a backroom political operator, Johnson steered the legislation past an initially reluctant Congress.

The final product was the landmark Civil Rights Act of 1964, which for all intents and purposes marked the beginning of the end for the decades-old Jim Crow system of racial injustice in the South. "The purpose of this law is simple," Johnson announced. "It does not restrict the freedom of any American so long as he respects the rights of others. It does not give any special treatment to any citizen. It does say the only limit to a man's hope for happiness and for the future of his children shall be his own ability. It does say that those who are equal before God shall now also be equal in the polling booths, in the classrooms, in the factories, and in the hotels and restaurants, and movie theatres, and other places that provide service to the public." In making these comments, Johnson was also careful to pay special tribute to "our late and beloved president John F. Kennedy" for initially conceiving and introducing the legislation to Congress. "It has received the thoughtful support of tens of thousands of civic and religious leaders in all parts of this nation, and it is supported by the great majority of the American people," he said.

In the decades that followed, revisionist historians cast a more reproachful eye on Kennedy's involvement with the civil rights movement of the early 1960s. His actions during this crucial period were dismissed as "tepid and reluctant," not to mention "excessively political." Even sympathetic biographers like Robert Dallek expressed strong reservations. Kennedy, Dallek wrote, "was slow to recognize the extent of the social revolution fostered by Martin Luther King and African Americans, and he repeatedly deferred to southern sensibilities on racial matters, including appointments of segregationist judges in southern federal districts." While most of these criticisms are valid for the first two and a half years of his presidency, they fail to account for the dramatic transformation Kennedy underwent in the final months of his life. Deeply moved by the events of Birmingham, he concluded that drastic change was needed if the nation was ever to surmount the bitter racial divisions that had plagued it since the end of Reconstruction. His decision to confront George Wallace over the integration of the University of Alabama afforded him the opportunity to lay the moral and legal groundwork for such change. "Historians will record that he vacillated like Lincoln," Martin Luther King said later, "but he lifted the cause far above the political level."

Courage showed him the way.

CHAPTER NINE

Ending a National Nightmare

GERALD FORD AND THE
PARDONING OF RICHARD NIXON

The news arrived with all the force and suddenness of a New England Nor'easter. On the morning of September 8, 1974, Thomas P. "Tip" O'Neill had just returned from Sunday Mass to his home in Cambridge, Massachusetts, when the telephone rang. Picking up the receiver, the Democratic majority leader of the House of Representatives was startled to discover his longtime friend and current Leader of the Free World on the other end. "Hello Tip? This is Jerry," Gerald Ford cheerily announced. Taken aback by the informality of the call, O'Neill asked half-jokingly, "What gives Mr. President? You're making your own phone calls?" Without missing a beat, Ford responded, "Yes. I just got off the phone with [Speaker of the House] Carl Albert and [Senate Majority Leader] Mike Mansfield, and now I'm calling you. I just came back from church, and I've made up my mind to pardon Nixon."

Like most Americans, the ex-president's name evoked strong emotions in O'Neill. To this gregarious, backslapping

Irish politician, Nixon personified the kind of arrogance of power that undermined a people's faith in democracy. Indeed, since bringing disrepute upon the presidency as a result of his central involvement in Watergate, the tawdry political scandal that ended in the criminal conviction of several of his closest associates, Richard Nixon had become a pariah in American politics. He was "Tricky Dick," a disgraced former chief executive who had been forced to resign and whose legal fate remained under a cloud of uncertainty. Cognizant of all this, O'Neill could not resist chastising his longtime Republican colleague. "You're crazy," he told Ford. "I'm telling you right now, this [pardon] is going to cost you [reelection]. I hope it's not part of any deal."

Assuring him this wasn't the case, Ford outlined his reasons for making the controversial decision. "Some people will holler," he conceded, "but I don't think the American people are vindictive. Nixon has suffered enough. Besides, I can't run this office while this business [of Nixon's pending criminal prosecution] drags on day after day. There are a lot more important things to be spending my time on." While O'Neill remained unconvinced about the political efficacy of the pardon, he did not question the underlying sincerity of Ford's motives. "Like Jerry," he later wrote, "I believed Nixon had suffered enough. After all, it's not where a man lands that marks his punishment. It's how far he falls."

Such demonstrated compassion and decency had long been a hallmark of Ford's estimable life and political career. Born Leslie King, Jr., on July 14, 1913, the future president spent most of his childhood in Grand Rapids, Michigan, a burgeoning industrial city located thirty miles inland from Lake Michigan. He had moved there at the age of two after his mother, Dorothy Gardner, divorced his physically abusive biological father. "I heard that he hit her frequently," Ford later wrote. Still in her early twenties, Dorothy was soon courted by a young bachelor named Gerald R. Ford, who worked as a paint salesman for a local wood-finishing company. They married in 1916, and young Leslie became Gerald Ford, Jr., when his stepfather legally adopted him shortly thereafter. Although a strict disciplinarian, the senior Ford provided ample love and support to Jerry and his three half-brothers, Thomas, Richard, and James. "When Dad told us to do something, we did it," the thirty-eighth president once told an interviewer. "There was never any question about that. He was the final authority; all of us really looked up to him. But he could be your friend as well as your father. Mother was great, too, lots of fun and very soft-hearted and always doing things for us boys and Dad, the neighbors and, heck, for everybody. But I guess Dad was the strongest influence in my life. I've often thought, even nowadays: now how would he have done this?"

In school Ford received good grades, but his real passion was for sports, football especially. At six feet he was an imposing physical presence at center for his South High School football team. But it was the subtleties of the position that intrigued him most, at a time when the T-formation had not yet arrived. "The center was not just the guy who stuck the ball in the quarterback's hands," he said. "Every center snap truly had to be a pass between the legs, often leading the tailback who was in motion and in full stride when he took the ball. I don't mean to be critical, but I think that is why you see so many bad passes from center on punts and field goals nowadays—they don't have to do it enough. I must have centered the ball 500,000 times in high school and college."

His high school coach, among others, appreciated this kind of work ethic and attention to detail. "Ford was a leader—first in the huddle, first out of the huddle, knew everyone's assignment— it was like having a coach on the field," remembered Clifford

Gettings. "On defense, he was all over the field making tackles. I never saw him make a bad pass from center, and I never saw him play dirty. Yes, he could make a mistake in an easy game, but in the hardest games, Jerry Ford was at his best." Ford would go on to capture all-city and all-state honors while gaining the attention of the University of Michigan, which offered him a partial scholarship to attend the Big Ten school.

Continuing his fine play with the Wolverines, Ford achieved stardom at both center and linebacker and was named his team's most valuable player in his senior year. "Thanks to my football experience, I know the value of team play," he later said. "It is, I believe, one of the most important lessons to be learned and practiced in our lives. You learn to accept discipline. My experiences in games . . . helped me many times to face a tough situation in World War II or, in the rough and tumble of politics, to take action, and make every effort possible despite adverse odds."

Nevertheless Ford did voice regrets about devoting so much of his time and energy to the sport. "If I had to go back to college again—knowing what I know today—I'd concentrate on two areas: learning to write and to speak before an audience," he confessed years later. "Nothing in life is more important than the ability to communicate effectively. As an athlete at South High, I'd attended a number of public functions and had had some experience speaking before large groups. But I was horribly prepared for the challenge of my freshman English course. . . . Every weekend, I would labor over the one-thousand-word theme due on Monday morning. At the end of the year, I earned a C in the course—and I was glad to get it."

Following graduation in 1935, Ford received substantial salary offers from the Detroit Lions and Green Bay Packers to play football professionally. But the prospect of making the gridiron a full-time occupation did not appeal to him. "What intrigued me the most was the possibility of studying law," he re-called. "I never thought of myself as a great orator in the tradition of William Jennings Bryan or Clarence Darrow. Rather, I thought my talents would be those of the mediator and counselor. As Abraham Lincoln once wrote, 'It is as a peacemaker that the lawyer has a superior opportunity.' That appealed to me."

The only problem was that Ford didn't have the money to achieve his ambition. Enter Raymond "Ducky" Pond. The Yale University football coach was in need of an assistant line coach and came to Ann Arbor in search of a suitable candidate. On the recommendation of Michigan football coach Harry Kipke, Pond settled on Ford, who was offered a $2,400 annual salary with the stipulation he also coach the Yale freshman boxing team. Although he admitted knowing absolutely nothing about boxing, Ford eagerly accepted the position. "I saw the chance to realize two dreams at once—to stay in football and to pursue a long-nurtured aspiration for law school," Ford said. But having the financial wherewithal for law school was not the same as getting in. To accomplish this he had first to convince the Yale Law School that he was a worthy candidate for admission. As he later wrote, "They were reluctant—98 of the 125 members of the freshman class had made Phi Beta Kappa as undergraduates, they pointed out—but they finally agreed to let me take two courses that spring. I earned two . . . B's. Satisfied that I could do the work, they withdrew their objections and accepted me full-time."

Once inside Yale's hallowed halls, Ford did not disappoint, compiling a B average overall and impressing his professors with the facility of his mind. "A very solid, straight-forward, decent sort of bird," remarked one instructor. "He worked hard, did reasonably well." Finishing in the top third of his graduating class, Ford was also introduced to the revelatory concept of the law "as a paradoxical discipline—both absolute and flexible, fixed and evolving." "The law," he learned, "demands respect for institutions, yet it relies upon individuals to bring those institutions to life."

With his law studies completed in early 1941, Ford chose an unorthodox career move. On the advice of his then steady girlfriend and *Cosmopolitan* magazine cover girl Phyllis Brown, he helped launch a successful modeling agency in New York City. He quickly tired of the venture, though, and sold his share of the business. He returned to Grand Rapids to practice law, reluctantly cutting his personal ties to Brown, with whom he had once entertained the possibility of marriage. "The end of our relationship caused me real anguish and I wondered if I'd ever meet anyone like her again," he later said.

Back home in the Midwest, Ford opened a private law practice with Phil Buchen, an old college friend who had clerked for a large Wall Street firm. "From a would-be lawyer's standpoint, [Grand Rapids] was an attractive place," Buchen said. "The quality of the bar was generally good. In law school it was always talked about as a wonderful place to practice law." This is not to say, however, that newcomers Ford and Buchen caused rival legal firms to lose any sleep. "Our first 'success' was hardly auspicious: a routine title search," Ford remembered. "We billed our client fifteen dollars; when he protested that it was too much, we cut it down to ten. Phil and I were glad to have any cash in the till." Despite a modest start, the firm was gradually able to break even financially and build a sizable client list by specializing in cases involving labor law, pension trusts, wills, adoptions, and divorces.

Ford's fondness for the practice of law had to be placed on hold after the surprise Japanese attack on Pearl Harbor on December 7, 1941. "I was in the office that Sunday afternoon and didn't hear the news until I flicked on the radio while driving home that night," he later recounted. "There was no doubt in my mind that the United States would go to war, that the war would be long and that everything would change very quickly for me." Ford's life did change dramatically. He entered the navy as an ensign, serving close to half of his forty-seven-month hitch aboard the *USS Monterey*, a light aircraft carrier that saw heavy action in the South Pacific.

During the great Pacific typhoon of 1944, he came close to losing his life. "I never really had a fear of death during the war," he later revealed, "but maybe it's different when you're on a capital ship like a carrier than when you're in a tank or the infantry or flying an airplane. This typhoon was a very bad storm. During the night, three of our accompanying destroyers rolled over and sank because the waves were so violent and because they were low on fuel and thus riding high in the water. Most of the crew on the destroyers drowned." If this wasn't harrowing enough, Ford's own carrier caught fire. "I was in the sack below at the time general quarters sounded," he recalled. "I ran up to the flight deck, and the ship was rolling violently, at least twenty-five to thirty degrees. As I stepped out on the flight deck, I lost my footing and slid across the deck like a toboggan. I put my feet out and fortunately my heels hit the little rim that surrounds the flight deck—I was heading straight for the ocean. I spun over on my stomach and luckily dropped over the edge onto the catwalk just below. We lost five seamen or officers during that storm—sliding over the side and into the sea—so I guess I was one of the lucky ones."

At war's end, Ford resumed his practice of law in Grand Rapids as an associate partner at a new firm called Butterfield, Keeney & Amberg. But like many other veterans of his era, including John F. Kennedy and Richard Nixon, he soon caught the political bug and in 1948 decided to run as a candidate for Michigan's Fifth Congressional District. Enthusiastically supported by his parents, who were staunchly Republican, Ford faced off against incumbent Representative Bartel Jonkman in that September's GOP primary. In many ways his decision to challenge Jonkman had been made for him by his opponent's uncompromising isolationist views on foreign policy.

"Before the war, I'd been an isolationist," Ford later admitted. "Indeed, while at Yale, I had expressed the view that the U.S. ought to avoid 'entangling alliances' abroad. But now I had become an ardent internationalist. My wartime experiences had given me an entirely new perspective. The U.S., I was convinced, could no longer stick its head in the sand like an ostrich. Our military unpreparedness before World War II had only encouraged the Germans and Japanese. In the future, I felt, the U.S. had to be strong. Never again could we allow our military to be anything but the best. And because a strong America would need strong allies to resist the growing Communist threat, we simply had to provide the money, muscle and manpower to help the nations of Western Europe rebuild their shattered economies."

Using this broader internationalist perspective as a political cudgel against Jonkman, Ford appealed to sufficient numbers of like-minded veterans and Republican moderates to score an upset victory on primary day. He followed this with a drubbing of Democrat Fred J. Barr in the general election.

But politics was not the only thing on Ford's mind during the campaign. In October he married Elizabeth "Betty" Bloomer, an aspiring professional dancer with strong local ties. "We both had grown up in Grand Rapids, and we had known each other for years," Betty Ford later told a reporter. "But I knew him as a person, not as an admirer. Actually the first time I did go out with him was when a friend arranged it through a phone call. I didn't know he was on the other end of the line. Apparently he had asked her to call me up and see if I'd go out with him. He was rather shy. He didn't want to call me himself unless he was sure I was going to say yes."

The two immediately hit it off, though both were somewhat leery of a long-term commitment. "We were going to see each other, but we weren't going to make any future plans," the future First Lady said. "That's the way those things always happen, when they start out that way, they usually reverse themselves."

In Congress Ford developed a reputation for being a doctrinaire conservative on most domestic issues. He opposed repealing the Taft-Hartley Act, voted down efforts to raise the minimum wage, and held fast against forced busing. "We need a national government that is the servant and not the master of the people," he said. "We must strengthen our state and local units of government." In foreign affairs he was a conventional cold warrior, supporting big military spending bills and foreign aid to countries fighting Communist insurgency movements. "The way to win a peace," he maintained, "is to build up a military establishment strong enough to win a war."

Record aside, however, it was Ford's personal qualities that most impressed his fellow congressmen. "In all the years I sat in the House," recalled one former colleague, "I never knew Mr. Ford to make a dishonest statement nor a statement part-true and part-false. He never attempted to shade a statement, and I never heard him utter an unkind word." Equally appreciative of these attributes were his constituents in Michigan, who returned him to office for twelve straight terms by majorities that never dipped below 60 percent of the vote.

In 1963 President Lyndon Johnson appointed Ford to serve on the Warren Commission, the bipartisan blue-ribbon panel investigating the assassination of President Kennedy. The commission concluded that Kennedy's murder had been engineered by a lone assassin, a former U.S. Marine named Lee Harvey Oswald. Many Americans remained unconvinced by these findings, however, claiming that Oswald had not acted alone and was part of a larger conspiracy involving the CIA, the FBI, the Secret Service, and organized crime. Ford has always characterized such claims as "Nonsense!" "That was a very good commission," he maintained. "I happen to think we did a good job. And I resent and reject all these speculative stories and promotions [about a possible conspiracy]. There has been no new credible evidence."

Despite the controversy generated by the commission and its findings, Ford emerged politically unscathed. His standing within the House Republican caucus was good enough to vault him to the position of minority leader in 1965, after a number of younger party members had grown disenchanted with the staid autocratic ways of incumbent Charles Halleck of Indiana. "No man's light will be hidden under a bushel," he told his supporters after the victory. "Every Republican will have a voice in decision making and a chance to make a name for himself." True to his word, Ford effectively fulfilled the role "of opening up power and encouraging people [in his party] to exercise it."

All the while he was able to maintain good relations with members of the Democratic opposition with his disarming candor and dignified civility. "It's the damnedest thing," said Democratic congressman Joe Waggoner of Louisiana. "Jerry just puts an arm around a colleague or looks him in the eye, says, 'I don't need your vote,' and gets it." Still, not every Democrat was pleased with Ford in his new post. Lyndon Johnson became incensed when Ford took stands suggesting his administration had not prosecuted the war in Vietnam "vigorously enough" and had failed to adequately address the growing domestic crime rate. Resorting to a stinging personal attack on his intelligence, Johnson declared that Ford had played football "too long without his helmet."

Ever the gentleman, Ford did his best to shrug off such insults. "Oh, I've read all those comments," he said, "and I don't deny that I'm a hard worker, that I don't have a lot of charisma that others have, but I never had any different style, whether it was in school, or in athletics, or in politics. I've always felt that if you were in the right place at the right time you might get recognized." He achieved a measure of vindication when Johnson chose not to run again in 1968 and was succeeded by Richard Nixon. With a fellow Republican now in the White House, Ford hoped his party would secure major gains in the House by the next presidential election, perhaps even allowing him to realize a lifelong dream of becoming speaker. But even though Nixon would go on to win an historic landslide reelection in 1972, he had no political coattails. Republicans ended up gaining only thirteen seats in the House while dropping two in the Senate. Disheartened by the results, Ford began making plans for retirement in early 1973. But then "an astounding series of events" forever altered his political future.

By this time Nixon had discovered that he was unable to escape the long shadow that Watergate was casting on his presidency. What he called a "third-rate burglary" of the Democratic National Headquarters at the Watergate office complex on June 17, 1972, became synonymous with executive malfeasance. Carried out by a small but fanatical group of Nixon loyalists known as the "plumbers," who had initially been given the responsibility of plugging press leaks within the White House, the Watergate break-in was part of a larger clandestine effort to subvert Democratic opposition to the president's reelection campaign in 1972.

The dogged investigative efforts of the Senate Select Committee on Watergate, chaired by Democratic Senator Sam Ervin of North Carolina, and the intrepid reporting of *Washington Post* journalists Bob Woodward and Carl Bernstein brought to light most of the details of the illegal operation. Nixon's White House chief of staff, H. R. Haldeman, along with top domestic policy adviser John Ehrlichman and chief presidential counsel John Dean were all forced to resign from their positions and served jail terms once their complicity in the sordid affair was revealed.

Adding to Nixon's troubles was the fact that his vice president, Spiro T. Agnew, was embroiled in a messy political scandal of his own, stemming from bribe-taking while governor of Maryland in the late 1960s. Forced to enter into a plea agreement with federal prosecutors, Agnew resigned in disgrace, leaving a vacancy in the nation's second highest office. To fill this important position, Nixon came up with a short list of candidates. His first preference was former Texas governor John Connally, a onetime Democrat who had served in Nixon's cabinet as secretary of the treasury. But realizing that congressional Democrats were still smarting over Connally's defection to the GOP and were likely to block his nomination, Nixon instead chose the path of least political resistance and selected Gerald Ford. It was an astute choice, for Ford enjoyed near unanimous support among his Democratic and Republican peers. What's more, he had acquired a well-deserved reputation for honesty and integrity while serving nearly a decade as House minority leader. "Just about all of us liked Jerry and thought he'd do a good job," Tip O'Neill later recalled. Ford himself was enthusiastic about taking on the new challenge. "I believe I can be a ready conciliator and calm communicator between the White House and Capitol Hill," he said. "I believe I can do this not because I know much about the Vice Presidency but because I know both the Congress and the President as well and as intimately as anyone who has known both for a quarter-century."

His nomination won easy passage through Congress and on December 6, 1973, he was formally sworn in as vice president by Nixon in the House chamber. "I'm a Ford, not a Lincoln," he quipped to the assembled press and dignitaries. "My addresses will never be as eloquent as Mr. Lincoln's. But I will do my very best to equal his brevity and his plain speaking. . . . As I have throughout my public service under six administrations, I will try to set a high example of respect for the crushing and lonely burdens which the nation lays upon the President of the United States."

As fate would have it, Ford served only nine months in the vice presidency. On August 5, 1974, the White House made the explosive announcement that a tape recording existed revealing that Nixon had ordered a cover-up of the Watergate break-in during a conversation with Haldeman on June 23, 1972. Realizing that this "smoking gun" revelation provided incontrovertible proof that he was tied directly to the Watergate burglary and therefore guilty of an impeachable offense, Nixon decided to resign his office. On August 8 he officially informed the nation of his decision. "Throughout the long and difficult period of Watergate," he said, "I have felt it was my duty to persevere to make every possible effort to complete the term of office to which you elected me. In the past few days, however, it has become evident to me that I no longer have a strong enough political base in the Congress to justify continuing that effort. . . . Therefore, I shall resign the presidency effective at noon tomorrow. . . . In turning over the direction of the Government to Vice President Ford, I know . . . that the leadership of America will be in good hands."

Neither Nixon's resignation nor his own ascension to the Oval Office took Ford by surprise. On August 1 he was told of the damaging taped evidence against Nixon by White House Chief of Staff General Alexander Haig. Ford immediately realized that Nixon had painted himself into a political corner and would have to step down or be impeached. Haig cagily suggested to Ford that his boss might be spared the humiliation by formally resigning "in return for an agreement that the new President—Gerald Ford—would pardon him." Taken aback by this thinly veiled quid pro quo, the always careful Ford asked for time to mull over what was being asked of him. After spending the night discussing it with his wife, he gave Haig an unequivocal answer. "I want you to understand," he said, "that I have no intention of recommending what the President should do about resigning or not resigning and that nothing we talked about yesterday afternoon should be given any consideration in whatever decision the President may make."

Having thus attained the presidency without the taint of a backroom political deal, Ford went about trying to reassure his countrymen that a new day had dawned in Washington. "My fellow Americans, our long national nightmare is over," he proclaimed in his inaugural address. "Our Constitution works; our great Republic is a Government of laws and not of men. Here the people rule. . . . As we bind up the internal wounds of Watergate, more painful and more poisonous than those of foreign wars, let us restore the golden rule to our political process, and let brotherly love purge our hearts of suspicion and hate." This conciliatory tone struck a chord with the press and the general public in his first weeks on the job, as they gave Ford high marks for his frank openness and "impression of solid dependability." Even traditional political antagonists could not but be impressed. "During the first week," wrote Ford biographer John Robert Greene, "Shirley Chisholm and Charles Rangel, both New York Democrats and prominent members of the Congressional Black Caucus, had sent Ford a telegram indicating their intention to ask the black community to give the new administration a chance. Ford immediately picked up the phone and called a stunned Rangel to thank him; the president then invited the caucus to the White House, a meeting that took place almost immediately."

"Everywhere there was the feeling that the American presidency was back in the possession of the people," lauded *Time* essayist Hugh Sidey.

Ford's honeymoon in the White House was destined to be brief, however. Only a month into his presidency he had to face the harsh political reality that Nixon and his misdeeds still occupied center stage in the nation's psyche. As one jaded reporter observed, "Watergate is harder to wash away than the spray of a skunk." At his initial press conference as president on August 28, the very first question Ford received had to do with the legal fortunes of his predecessor. "Mr. President," asked Helen Thomas of United Press International, "aside from the special prosecutor's role, do you agree with the bar association that the law applies equally to all men, or do you agree . . . that former President Nixon should have immunity from prosecution? And specifically, would you use your pardon authority, if necessary?"

Expecting to be asked about the poor state of the economy or about the prospects of another war in the Middle East, a clearly frustrated Ford tried valiantly if unsuccessfully to steer the conversation in other directions. He bluntly told Thomas it would be "unwise and untimely" for him to make any commitments about Nixon's status "until the legal process had been undertaken." Unimpressed by this answer, other reporters in attendance continued to badger Ford for details, to his ever-growing consternation. "At the conclusion of the press conference," he later recalled, "I walked back to the Oval Office and asked my advisers how long they thought this would go on. Was I going to be asked about Nixon's fate every time I met with the press? Each of them said it would continue as long as Nixon's legal status . . . remained unclarified. Their scenario was discouraging. I'd been hoping to have press conferences every two or three weeks. I realized now that I'd be repeatedly questioned about him and his many legal problems."

To get the proverbial monkey off his and the country's back, Ford concluded there was only one thing to do. He would grant Nixon "a full, free, and absolute pardon" for the disgraced president's crimes. When an adviser protested that Ford's popularity in the polls would suffer greatly as a result of such a move, the president responded with indifference. "I'm aware of that," he said. "It could easily cost me the next election if I run again. But damn it, I don't need the polls to tell me whether I'm right or wrong." His political instincts on the subject had earlier been confirmed in a conversation with one of his military aides. "We're all Watergate junkies," army Major Bob Barrett informed him. "Some of us are mainlining, some are sniffing, some are lacing it with something else, but all of us are addicted. This will go on and on unless someone steps in and says that we, as a nation, must go cold turkey. Otherwise, we'll die of an overdose." Put another way, Ford needed to rescue the country from the deadening malaise of Watergate.

His mind made up, Ford solemnly announced the pardon in a nationally televised address from the Oval Office on September 8. "Ladies and gentlemen," he began, "I have come to a decision which I felt I should tell you and all of my fellow American citizens as soon as I was certain in my own mind and in my own conscience that it is the right thing to do. . . . After years of bitter controversy and divisive national debate, I have been advised and am compelled to conclude that many months and perhaps more years will have to pass before Richard Nixon could hope to obtain a fair trial by jury in any jurisdiction of the United States under governing decisions of the Supreme Court." He then proceeded to describe just what such a postponement of justice would mean to the country and its overall standing in the world. "During this long period of delay and potential litigation, ugly passions would again be aroused, our people would again be polarized in their opinions, and the cred-

GERALD FORD: *Ending a National Nightmare*

ibility of our free institutions of government would again be challenged at home and abroad. In the end, the courts might well hold that Richard Nixon had been denied due process and the verdict of history would be even more inconclusive with respect to those charges arising out of the period of his Presidency of which I am presently aware."

Nonetheless Nixon's ultimate fate was not what troubled Ford most, despite his personal belief that the former chief executive and his loved ones had "suffered enough." "As President," Ford insisted, "my primary concern must always be the greatest good of all the people of the United States, whose servant I am. . . . My conscience tells me clearly and certainly that I cannot prolong the bad dreams that continue to reopen a chapter that is closed. My conscience tells me that only I, as President, have the constitutional power to firmly shut and seal this book. My conscience says it is my duty, not merely to proclaim domestic tranquility, but to use every means I have to ensure it. . . . Now, therefore, I Gerald R. Ford, President of the United States, pursuant to the pardon power conferred upon me by Article III, Section 2, of the Constitution, have granted and by these presents do grant a full, free, and absolute pardon unto Richard Nixon for all offenses against the United States which he, Richard Nixon, has committed or taken part in during the period from January 20, 1969, through August 9, 1974."

Word of the pardon generated "deep dismay and high outrage" across the land, according to the media. Findings from a Gallup poll indicated that Ford's overall approval rating as president plummeted from 71 percent to 49 percent in a month, "the biggest single drop" in the survey's history. "I feel betrayed," bemoaned Lorice Bartos, a twenty-seven-year-old legislative aide on Capitol Hill. "Ford was making great advances, but now the honeymoon's over with me. . . . [Ford absolved] a man who tried to steal my country, and I don't take kindly to

'Now to shut the book on Watergate . . .

A Crash Course: **The impact of Watergate
on Ford's presidency.**

that." A young African-American man in Cambridge, Massachusetts, angrily told a reporter that "democracy took it on the
chin yesterday when President Ford pardoned Nixon." "It's not
fair," Clarence Ricker said. "They would jump on me fast if I
did something wrong." A county judge in Grand Forks, North
Dakota, registered his contempt by freeing two people he had
sentenced to jail earlier in the day. "In response to the pardon
given Richard Nixon by Gerald Ford," Judge Kirk Smith formally declared, "this court is determined to present an act of
clemency to any and all prisoners serving jail sentences for convictions in this court for the commission of any criminal offenses."

Politicians from both sides of the aisle were also quick to express their displeasure. "While I have boundless compassion
and sympathy [for Nixon]," Republican leader Howard Baker
said, "I am apprehensive that President Ford's action today may
ignite a new round of controversy and conflict the country can

ill afford." Congressman John Moss of California was likewise put off. "This is an outrageous act, rewarding Nixon for his crimes and proving that our country maintains a double standard of justice," he said. "At least the nation should know what crimes Nixon committed, and Nixon should admit to them before receiving any pardon." Fellow Democrat and national party chairman Robert Strauss agreed: "What President Ford has done is a travesty of justice to the judicial process. It unhappily raises the question of a calculated move by President Ford to accomplish, during his honeymoon period, an action that he knows would be considered an absolute outrage during other times."

Former Watergate special prosecutor and Harvard law professor Archibald Cox argued that a deeper set of principles were at stake, claiming that "an advance pardon" undermined the fundamental integrity of "a free society." "The guilt or innocence of a high official charged with crime, especially a president, should be determined once and for all by the established processes of justice in order to lay to rest claims of political vendetta. To short-circuit the process invites endless uncertainty." Nationally syndicated columnist Mike Royko of Chicago was less politic in his analysis, preferring instead to impugn the underlying motives of Ford's action. "With a stroke of his pen, President Ford has brought a new dignity, solemnity, and historic perspective to the old business of putting in the fix," he wrote. "Until Sunday's pardoning-in-advance of Richard Nixon, the fix had always been treated as something politically shady, so a certain degree of stealth was the tradition. No lawyer would dream of standing in court and pleading 'Motion to fix your honor, motion to fix.' This motion is as old as Chicago's court, but the canons of this city's legal ethics require that it be presented in a whisper, and usually in a parked car. . . . This is the first time I ever heard of a man

going straight from church to a press conference to announce
a fix on network TV."

Royko's cynicism was further amplified by conservative
commentator Marquis Childs, who took particular exception to
Ford's sense of political timing. "It would be hard to imagine
any better way to give new life to the whole Watergate horror
than for President Ford to grant a precipitous blanket pardon to
former President Nixon," Childs maintained. "Until he did so,
Mr. Ford had seemed to be ushering in a new era of reconciliation. Then contrary to previous statements—he jumped in before even the first steps in the judicial process had been taken."
Childs concluded his jeremiad by voicing doubts about Ford's
overall capacity to lead the nation. "The new President must
prove he is his own man. But if the precipitous pardon is an example of that new man then we are in for trouble."

Convicted Watergate defendants and their spouses also got
in their rhetorical licks. Calling the pardon "a corruption and
perversion of the criminal justice system," the burglar James
McCord accused Ford and his advisers of continuing "a
coverup" that had begun under Nixon. "Ford bypassed the
whole system by taking the law in his own hands," he charged.
Maureen Dean, wife of former White House counsel John
Dean, chose to focus on "the limitations" of Ford's expressed
compassion for his predecessor. "Mr. Nixon and his family are
not the only ones who have suffered enough because of Watergate," she said in a prepared statement released to the press.
"Since the President has adopted this posture, I pray he will not
overlook those who have fully cooperated with the government
in getting out the truth of Watergate to the American people.
These individuals are also suffering because they told the
truth—which is something we have yet to hear from Mr. Nixon.
Why didn't Mr. Nixon have to pay at least the price of truth for
his pardon?" Martha Mitchell, wife of former Attorney General

John Mitchell, concurred. "I don't believe in pardoning one person and not pardoning everybody else—especially when they're the ones who did the dirty work [for Nixon]," she said. "And that goes for even old Haldeman and old Ehrlichman, whom I hate."

Hitting even closer to home, Ford had to endure the indignity of being publicly upbraided by his own White House press secretary, Jerald F. terHorst. A longtime Washington correspondent for the *Detroit News* who went on to become the first appointee of the new administration, terHorst had done an effective job in securing favorable press coverage for Ford in his first month in office. But he bristled at being peremptorily informed of the pardon the night before Ford addressed the nation. He personally handed in his resignation at a closed-door Oval Office meeting the next day. "When the President made his decision in good conscience I felt it was my duty to advise him also in good conscience that I could not defend his position as a spokesman in a credible manner," terHorst told reporters afterward. "I felt that mercy, like justice, should be even-handed." Taken aback by the move, Ford expressed no hard feelings. "Jerry," he told terHorst, "I regret this. I think you've made a mistake. But I respect your views, and I'm sorry if there was any misunderstanding. As to the pardon, it was a decision I felt I had to make. I've made it and I'm going to stick with it."

True to his word, Ford did stick by his controversial decision, but in doing so he inflicted irreparable damage on his administration and his own political standing. For he was no longer seen by most Americans as a decent, salt-of-the-earth kind of guy striving to do his best for the country, but as just another politician. In his memoirs Ford intimated that this characterization and all it implied hurt him most. "I knew when I became President that hard decisions would produce some bitter reactions," he wrote. "Still, I wasn't prepared for the allegations that the

Nixon pardon prompted. What I had intended to convince my fellow citizens was necessary surgery—essential if we were to heal our wounded nation—was being attacked as a 'secret deal' that I had worked out with Nixon before he had resigned."

In an attempt to clear the air and win back the confidence of the nation, Ford took the unprecedented step of appearing before the House Judiciary Committee on October 17. Sitting alone at a large wooden witness table, he spent close to two hours testifying about his reasons for pardoning Nixon. "The purpose [of the pardon] was to change our national focus," he said. "I wanted to do all I could to shift our attention from the pursuit [of] a fallen President to the pursuit of the urgent needs of a rising nation. Our nation is under the severest of challenges now to employ its full energy and effort in the pursuit of a sound and growing economy at home and a stable and peaceful world around us. We would needlessly be diverted from meeting those challenges if we, as a people, were to remain sharply divided over whether to indict, bring to trial and punish a former President who is already condemned to suffer long and deeply in the shame and disgrace brought upon the office that he held."

Unfortunately for Ford, his congressional testimony did little to dispel the popular notion of "a fix." The *New York Times*, which had initially lauded Ford's elevation to the presidency, could not resist sounding a note of extreme skepticism. Ford was either "not persuasive or was inadequately interrogated" in describing the "major aspects" of his decision, the paper editorialized. "The hearing skipped blithely past the fundamental question whether the pardon itself was valid. Despite the certitude expressed by the President . . . there is a respected body of scholarly legal opinion that this pre-emptive use of the pardoning power covering all crimes known and unknown over a five-year period was unwarranted and unjustified."

Inevitably, Ford and the Republican party were made to pay a price politically. In the midterm elections in November, Democrats gained forty-three seats in the House and another four in the Senate. Overall the results represented an unmitigated disaster for Ford, who now "faced a Democratic majority in the House that could override his vetoes and a Democratic Senate where Republican filibusters were less of a threat with only 30 GOP members."

Aside from Democratic gains that fall, Ford also had to contend with discord inside his own party. Judging the new president to be "a lightweight" because of his pardon-related travails, California governor and former Hollywood movie actor Ronald Reagan now gave serious thought to challenging him for the GOP presidential nomination in 1976.

A hard-core conservative, Reagan believed that Ford had frittered away the mandate that the electorate had given Republicans during Nixon's landslide reelection in 1972. "The tragedy of Watergate and the traumatic experience since then has obscured the meaning of that '72 election," he said. The meaning, as Reagan saw it, revolved around popular support for lower taxes, less federal regulation, and a stronger national defense. Unfazed, Ford dismissed Reagan's budding candidacy as so much hot air, coming as it did from someone he regarded as a phony. Still, the hope remained among party loyalists that the two would be able to work out their differences before the start of the 1976 campaign, despite the obvious bad blood that existed between them.

Reagan chose instead to break what he described as the Eleventh Commandment—"Thou shalt not speak ill of another Republican"—and run openly against Ford for the Republican presidential nomination. He informed the president of his intentions in a short telephone conversation on November 19, 1975. "Well, Governor, I'm very disappointed," Ford said. "I'm sorry you're getting into this. I believe I've done a good job and I can be elected. Regardless of your good intentions, your bid is bound to be divisive. It will take a lot of money, a lot of effort, and it will leave a lot of scars. It won't be helpful, no matter which of us wins the nomination." When Reagan replied that he didn't think his challenge would be divisive, Ford fumed, "How can you challenge an incumbent President of your own party and *not* be divisive?" As it turned out, Ford was right. He and Reagan engaged in a bruising primary fight that was not settled until the Republican National Convention the following summer. But in successfully fending off Reagan's challenge, Ford expended enormous amounts of time, energy, money, and political capital that could have been used against his Democratic challenger in the general election.

In former Georgia governor Jimmy Carter, Ford faced a surprisingly formidable foe. A U.S. Naval Academy graduate and wealthy peanut farmer, Carter affected an earnest, down-home manner that sat well with disillusioned voters, who were then just getting over the Sturm und Drang of the Watergate years. More important, as a Washington outsider Carter promised to bring a welcome change to the status quo politics of the nation's capital, adding solemnly that he would never tell a lie to the American people. Taking this to be a thinly disguised attack on his own leadership and personal integrity, Ford did his best to fight back, claiming that Carter lacked the proper gravitas to assume the presidency. "It just doesn't seem to me that he's ready for this big league," Ford declared. "I don't think he's dangerous. I don't think he is focused on the complexities of the problems we have, or ready to face up to the hard decisions that have to be made." While this line of attack appeared to make some headway with voters, it was not enough to topple Carter from his perch as the front-runner in the campaign. On election day, Ford lost by 297 to 240 electoral votes.

In most postelection analyses, Ford's pardoning of Nixon received most of the blame for his defeat. But Ford chose not to get caught up in Monday-morning quarterbacking as he prepared to transfer power to the new president. "As one who has been honored to serve the people of this great land both in Congress and as President," he wrote Carter, "I believe we must now put the division of the campaign behind us and unite the country once again in the common pursuit of peace and prosperity. I want to assure you that you will have my complete and wholehearted support as you take the oath of office this January. I also pledge to you that I and all members of my Administration will do all that we can to ensure that you begin your term as smoothly and effectively as possible."

With his presidency over, Ford settled into a comfortable retirement, delivering an occasional lecture, sitting on several corporate boards, and playing in charity golf events. As the years passed, his decision to pardon Nixon came to be seen in an entirely new light. Most historians and pundits now regard it as a brave and necessary measure to move the country beyond the scandal-plagued years of Watergate. As Bob Woodward wrote, "Nixon had already paid the political death penalty of resignation, and for Ford the pardon was the only way of ending the public and media obsession with his predecessor's future." A still greater accolade arrived in 1999 when President Bill Clinton presented Ford with the Presidential Medal of Freedom during a special ceremony in the East Room of the White House. Recounting how he had initially opposed Ford's action as a young Democratic operative, Clinton dramatically turned to him and exclaimed, "You were right, and the country thanks you for it."

It was a long overdue gesture of appreciation for the humble Michigander who helped heal a nation.

A Note on Sources

The following books and materials provided major sources of information for *A Higher Purpose*.

CHAPTER ONE: SLAYING A HYDRA OF CORRUPTION

Claude Bowers, *The Party Battles of the Jackson Period*. Boston, 1922.
H. W. Brands, *Andrew Jackson: His Life and Times*. New York, 2005.
Andrew Burstein, *The Passions of Andrew Jackson*. New York, 2003.
Richard N. Current, *Daniel Webster and the Rise of National Conservatism*. Boston, 1955.
James C. Curtis, *Andrew Jackson and the Search for Vindication*. Boston, 1976.
Marquis James, *The Life of Andrew Jackson*. New York, 1938.
Alan Nevins, ed., *The Diary of John Quincy Adams, 1794–1845*. New York, 1945.
James Parton, *Life of Andrew Jackson*, Vol. III. New York, 1860.
Edward Pessen, *Jacksonian America: Society, Personality, and Politics*. Chicago, 1978.
Robert V. Remini, *Andrew Jackson*. New York, 1999.
——, *Andrew Jackson and the Bank War*. New York, 1967.
Arthur M. Schlesinger, Jr., *The Age of Jackson*. New York, 1971.
Carl Schurz, *Henry Clay*. New York, 1980.
Harold C. Syrett, *Andrew Jackson: His Contribution to American Tradition*. New York, 1953.

Martin Van Buren, *The Autobiography of Martin Van Buren*. Washington, D.C., 1920.

Jules Witcover, *Party of the People: A History of the Democrats*. New York, 2003.

Sean Wilentz, *Andrew Jackson*. New York, 2005.

CHAPTER TWO: ENDING A MONSTROUS INJUSTICE

Charles Francis Adams, Jr., *Charles Francis Adams*. New York, 1980.

Paul M. Angle, ed., *The Lincoln Reader*. New Brunswick, N.J., 1947.

Eleanor Atkinson, *The Boyhood of Lincoln*. New York, 1908.

Henry Steele Commager, ed., *Living History: The Civil War*. New York, 2000.

David H. Donald, *Lincoln*. London, 1995.

J. Matthew Gallman, *The North Fights the Civil War: The Home Front*. Chicago, 1994.

Allen C. Guelzo, *Lincoln's Emancipation Proclamation: The End of Slavery in America*. New York, 2004.

Emanuel Hertz, *The Hidden Lincoln: From the Letters and Papers of William H. Herndon*. New York, 1938.

Stefan Lorant, *Lincoln: A Picture History of His Life*. New York, 1969.

Reinhardt H. Luthin, *The Real Abraham Lincoln*. Englewood Cliffs, N.J., 1960.

James M. McPherson, *Abraham Lincoln and the Second American Revolution*. New York, 1991.

———, *Battle Cry of Freedom: The Civil War Era*. New York, 1988.

Walter M. Merrill, ed., *The Letters of William Lloyd Garrison*. Cambridge, Mass., 1981.

Stephen B. Oates, *With Malice Toward None: The Life of Abraham Lincoln*. New York, 1977.

Geoffrey Perret, *Lincoln's War: The Untold Story of America's Greatest President as Commander in Chief*. New York, 2004.

Benjamin Quarles, *Lincoln and the Negro*. New York, 1962.

Benjamin P. Thomas, *Abraham Lincoln: A Biography*. New York, 1994.

Geoffrey C. Ward, with Ric Burns and Ken Burns, *The Civil War: An Illustrated History*. New York, 1990.

John C. Waugh, *Reelecting Lincoln: The Battle for the 1864 Presidency*. New York, 1997.

CHAPTER THREE: FROM GENTLEMAN BOSS TO REFORMER

Kenneth D. Ackerman, *Dark Horse: The Surprise Election and Political Murder of President James A. Garfield*. New York, 2003.

George S. Boutwell, *Reminiscences of Sixty Years in Public Affairs*. New York, 1902.

Sean Dennis Cashman, *America in the Gilded Age: From the Death of Lincoln to the Rise of Theodore Roosevelt*. New York, 1993.

Justus D. Doenecke, *The Presidencies of James A. Garfield and Chester A. Arthur*. Lawrence, Kans., 1981.

John A. Garrity, *The New Commonwealth, 1877–1890*. New York, 1968.

George Frederick Howe, *Chester A. Arthur: A Quarter Century of Machine Politics*. New York, 1957.

William C. Hudson, *Random Recollections of an Old Political Reporter*. New York, 1911.

David M. Jordan, *Roscoe Conkling of New York*. Ithaca, N.Y., 1971.

Zachary Karabell, *Chester Alan Arthur*. New York, 2004.

Philip B. Kunhardt, Jr., Philip B. Kunhardt III, and Peter W. Kunhardt, *The American President*. New York, 1999.

Thomas C. Platt, *The Autobiography of Thomas Collier Platt*. New York, 1910.

Thomas C. Reeves, "Chester A. Arthur: War Claims Lawyer," in Norman Gross, ed., *America's Lawyer-Presidents: From Law Office to Oval Office*. Evanston, Ill., 2004.

———, *Gentleman Boss: The Life of Chester Alan Arthur*. New York, 1975.

James D. Richardson, *A Compilation of the Messages and Papers of the Presidents 1789–1897*, Vol. VIII. Washington, D.C., 1898.

Ira Rutkow, *James A. Garfield*. New York, 2006.

CHAPTER FOUR: A MATTER OF HONOR

H. W. Brands, *The Reckless Decade: America in the 1890s*. Chicago, 1999.

Alyn Brodsky, *Grover Cleveland: A Study in Character*. New York, 2000.

J. A. Gillis, *The Hawaiian Incident: An Examination of Mr. Cleveland's Attitude Toward the Revolution of 1893*. Freeport, N.Y., 1970.

Henry F. Graff, *Grover Cleveland*. New York, 2002.

H. Paul Jeffers, *An Honest President: The Life and Presidencies of Grover Cleveland*. New York, 2000.

Albertine Loomis, *For Whom Are the Stars*. Honolulu, Hawaii, 1976.

Alfred Thayer Mahan, *The Influence of Sea Power upon History, 1660–1783*. Boston, 1918.

Robert McElroy, *Grover Cleveland: The Man and the Statesman; An Authorized Biography*. New York, 1923.

Alan Nevins, *Grover Cleveland: A Study in Courage*. New York, 1933.

Thomas J. Osborne, *Empire Can Wait: American Opposition to Hawaiian Annexation, 1893–1898*. Kent, Ohio, 1981.

William Adam Russ, Jr., *The Hawaiian Revolution (1893–94)*. Selinsgrove, Pa., 1959.

Anders Stephanson, *Manifest Destiny: American Expansion and the Empire of Right*. New York, 1995.

Richard E. Welch, *The Presidencies of Grover Cleveland*. Lawrence, Kans., 1988.

Warren Zimmerman, *First Great Triumph: How Five Americans Made Their Country a World Power*. New York, 2002.

CHAPTER FIVE: TAKING ON THE TRUSTS

Louis Auchincloss, ed., *Theodore Roosevelt: Letters and Speeches*. New York, 2004.

H. W. Brands, *T.R.: The Last Romantic*. New York, 1997.

Anthony Brandt, ed., *The Adventures of Theodore Roosevelt*. Washington, D.C., 2005.

James Chace, *1912: Wilson, Roosevelt, Taft, and Debs—The Election That Changed the Country*. New York, 2004.

Ron Chernow, *The House of Morgan: An American Banking Dynasty and the Rise of Modern Finance*. New York, 2001.

John Milton Cooper, Jr., *The Warrior and the Priest: Woodrow Wilson and Theodore Roosevelt*. Cambridge, Mass., 1983.

Steven J. Diner, *A Very Different Age: Americans of the Progressive Era*. New York, 1998.

Lewis L. Gould, *The Presidency of Theodore Roosevelt*. Lawrence, Kans., 1991.

Nathan Miller, *Theodore Roosevelt: A Life*. New York, 1992.

Edmund Morris, *Theodore Rex*. New York, 2002.

Henry F. Pringle, *Theodore Roosevelt*. New York, 1956.

Eric Rauchway, *Murdering McKinley: The Making of Theodore Roosevelt's America*. New York, 2003.

Edward J. Renehan, Jr. *The Lion's Pride: Theodore Roosevelt and His Family in Peace and War*. Oxford, 1988.

Theodore Roosevelt, *Theodore Roosevelt: An Autobiography*. New York, 1985.

Jean Strouse, *Morgan: American Financier*. New York, 1999.

CHAPTER SIX: SAVING DEMOCRACY

Conrad Black, *Franklin Delano Roosevelt: Champion of Freedom*. New York, 2003.

James MacGregor Burns, *Roosevelt: The Soldier of Freedom*. New York, 1970.

Peter Collier, with David Horowitz, *The Roosevelts*. New York, 1994.

Frank Freidel, *Franklin D. Roosevelt: A Rendezvous with Destiny*. Boston, 1990.

Albert Fried, *FDR and His Enemies*. New York, 1999.

Doris Kearns Goodwin, *No Ordinary Time: Franklin and Eleanor Roosevelt: The Home Front in World War II*. New York, 1995.

Richard Hority and Ralph Martin, *Man of the Century: Churchill*. New York, 1962.

John Gabriel Hunt, ed., *The Essential Franklin Delano Roosevelt*. New York, 1995.

Warren F. Kimball, *Forged in War: Roosevelt, Churchill, and the Second World War*. Chicago, 1997.

Joseph P. Lash, *Eleanor and Franklin*. New York, 1971.

Francis L. Loewenheim, Harold D. Langley, and Manfred Jonas, eds., *Roosevelt and Churchill: Their Secret Wartime Correspondence*. New York, 1973.

Patrick J. Maney, *The Roosevelt Presence: A Biography of Franklin Delano Roosevelt*. New York, 1992.

Jon Meacham, *Franklin and Winston: An Intimate Portrait of an Epic Friendship*. New York, 2003.

Norman Moss, *Nineteen Weeks: America, Britain, and the Fateful Summer of 1940*. Boston, 2003.

David Reynolds, *From Munich to Pearl Harbor: Roosevelt's America and the Origins of the Second World War*. Chicago, 2003.

Eleanor Roosevelt, *The Autobiography of Eleanor Roosevelt*. New York, 1989.

CHAPTER SEVEN: SLAYING AN AMERICAN CAESAR

Dean Acheson, *Present at the Creation: My Years in the State Department*. New York, 1987.

Omar N. Bradley, with Clay Blair, *A General's Life: An Autobiography*. New York, 1983.

Robert J. Donovan, *Tumultuous Years: The Presidency of Harry S. Truman, 1949–1953*. New York, 1982.

Robert H. Ferrell, ed., *The Autobiography of Harry S. Truman*. Columbia, Mo., 2002.

Alonzo L. Hamby, *Man of the People: A Life of Harry S. Truman*. New York, 1995.

Walter Isaacson and Evan Thomas, *The Wise Men: Six Friends and the World They Made*. New York, 1986.

Roy Jenkins, *Truman*. New York, 1986.

Douglas MacArthur, *Reminiscences*. New York, 1964.

William Manchester, *American Caesar: Douglas MacArthur, 1880–1964*. Boston, 1978.

David McCullough, *Truman*, New York, 1992.

Merle Miller, *Plain Speaking: An Oral Biography of Harry S. Truman*. New York, 1974.

Steve Neal, *Harry and Ike: The Partnership That Remade the Postwar World*. New York, 2002.

Laurence Stallings, *The Doughboys*. New York, 1963.

Harry S. Truman, *Memoirs of Harry S. Truman: Year of Decisions*. Garden City, N.Y., 1955.

Margaret Truman, *Harry S. Truman*. New York, 1972.

Ralph E. Weber, ed., *Talking with Harry: Candid Conversations with President Harry S. Truman*. Wilmington, Del., 2001.

CHAPTER EIGHT: CONFRONTING A MORAL ISSUE

John Brauer, *John F. Kennedy and the Second Reconstruction*. New York, 1977.

Dan T. Carter, *The Politics of Rage: George Wallace, the Origins of the New Conservatism, and the Transformation of American Politics*. New York, 1995.

Robert Dallek, *An Unfinished Life: John F. Kennedy, 1917–1963*. Boston, 2003.

Drew Associates, *Crisis: Behind a Presidential Commitment*. DVD, directed by Robert Drew. New York, 2003.

James N. Giglio, *The Presidency of John F. Kennedy*. Lawrence, Kans., 1991.

Nigel Hamilton, *Reckless Youth*. New York, 1992.

Charles Kenney, *John F. Kennedy: The Presidential Portfolio*. New York, 2000.

Ralph G. Martin, *A Hero for Our Time: An Intimate Story of the Kennedy Years*. New York, 1983.

Christopher Matthews, *Kennedy and Nixon: The Rivalry That Shaped Postwar America*. New York, 1996.

Anne Moody, *Coming of Age in Mississippi*. New York, 1968.

Richard Reeves, *President Kennedy: Profile in Power*. New York, 1993.

Theodore C. Sorensen, *Kennedy*. New York, 1965.

Evan Thomas, *Robert Kennedy: His Life*. New York, 2000.

Thomas J. Whalen, *Kennedy versus Lodge: The 1952 Massachusetts Senate Race*. Boston, 2000.

Juan Williams, *Eyes on the Prize: America's Civil Rights Years, 1954–1965*. New York, 1988.

Harris Wofford, *Of Kennedy and Kings: Making Sense of the Sixties*. New York, 1980.

Andrew Young, *An Easy Burden: The Civil Rights Movement and the Transformation of America*. New York, 1996.

CHAPTER NINE: ENDING A NATIONAL NIGHTMARE

Stephen Ambrose, *Nixon: Ruin and Recovery, 1973–1990*. New York, 1991.

James Cannon, "Gerald R. Ford, 1974–1977," in Robert Wilson, ed., *Character Above All: Ten Presidents from FDR to George Bush*. New York, 1995.

Lou Cannon, *Reagan*. New York, 1982.

Editors of *Time*, *Hugh Sidey's Portraits of the Presidents: Power and Personality in the Oval Office*. New York, 2004.

James A. Farrell, *Tip O'Neill and the Democratic Century*. Boston, 2001.

Betty Ford, with Chris Chase, *The Times of My Life*. New York, 1978.

Gerald R. Ford, *A Time to Heal: The Autobiography of Gerald R. Ford*. New York, 1979.

Lewis L. Gould, *Grand Old Party: A History of the Republicans*. New York, 2003.

John Robert Greene, *The Presidency of Gerald R. Ford*. Lawrence, Kans., 1995.

David Horricks, "Gerald R. Ford: All-American Counsel," in Norman Gross, ed., *America's Lawyer-Presidents: From Law Office to Oval Office*. Evanston, Ill., 2004.

Ron Nessen, *It Sure Looks Different from the Inside*. New York, 1978.

Tip O'Neill, with William Novak, *Man of the House: The Life and Political Memoirs of Speaker Tip O'Neill*. New York, 1987.

Bruce J. Schulman, *The Seventies: The Great Shift in American Culture, Society, and Politics*. New York, 2001.

Jerald F. terHorst, *Gerald Ford and the Future of the Presidency*. New York, 1974.

Bud Vestal, *Jerry Ford: Up Close*. New York, 1974.

Jules Witcover, *Marathon: The Pursuit of the Presidency, 1972–1976*. New York, 1976.

Bob Woodward, *Shadow: Five Presidents and the Legacy of Watergate*. New York, 1999.

Index

A NOTE ON THE AUTHOR

Thomas J. Whalen was born in Salem, Massachusetts, and studied at Bates College and at Boston College, where he received a Ph.D. in history. His writings have appeared in a number of publications, including the *Boston Globe*, and he is also the author of *Kennedy versus Lodge: The 1952 Massachusetts Senate Race* and *Dynasty's End: Bill Russell and the 1968–69 World Champion Boston Celtics*. Mr. Whalen now teaches social science at Boston University and lives in Peabody, Massachusetts.